The Sword and Shield

The Sword and Shield

Today's Christian Crusader

JOHN W. EDWARDS III

Edited by Jessie S. Edwards and Pamela A. Edwards

iUniverse, Inc.
Bloomington

The Sword and Shield
Today's Christian Crusader

iUniverse books may be ordered through booksellers or by contacting:

"Scripture taken from the New American Standard Bible, Copyright 1960, 1962, 1963, 1968, 1971, 1972, 1973, 1975, 1977, 1995 by The Lockman Foundation. Used by permission. All scripture quotes are out of this translation.

Notes and quotes from authors are illustrated with the examples used. Many thanks to them for their inspiration and information they provide to all. The images used for Nimrod were taken in 1978 by John. John also provided the image used of the Mother Mary statue prayer center which is actively used outside a Florida Catholic Church.

iUniverse
1663 Liberty Drive
Bloomington, IN 47403
www.iuniverse.com
1-800-Authors (1-800-288-4677)

ISBN: 978-1-4620-4465-8 (sc)
ISBN: 978-1-4620-4467-2 (hc)
ISBN: 978-1-4620-4466-5 (ebk)

Printed in the United States of America

iUniverse rev. date: 08/19/2011

Contents

"Dear gracious and most heavenly Father. We meet today to worship your name, in a world where your name has become forbidden, in a world that does not know it is lost and in a world that has lost its narrow way to the cross. Your faithful servant is humbled before you, unworthy of your mercy and grace, but seeking your power and authority to bring a lost or drifting soul to you. Bless the one who holds this book in their hands, that they might receive your blessings, and listen to your call for their sanctification, salvation and inspiration. We ask your Holy Spirit to be among us, in this hour of need for you, oh Lord, that in your mercy and grace we would find eternal peace, through Your Son, Jesus Christ. Thank you Father for your generosity, your sacrifice and for all you do in providing all we have; for all I have is yours. Now Father let your will be done and move me into holy service, in your name, for your glory and your kingdom.

I pray this in Jesus, holy and precious name, Amen."

Now we may begin . . .

Christian Crusader

Prepare to

Draw your Sword

Ephesians 6:10-20

The Sword and Shield
Today's Christian Crusader

So why write another book about the Bible? As times change, so do generations, lifestyles and the obstacles we face. Many people are still wandering-wondering and have not experienced REAL sanctification of the Holy Spirit. Many people still struggle with demons and burdens that weigh them down to earthly desires. And there are also many atheists who have not answered simple basic questions that I have to ask. Ravi Zacharias once said, "If you are not in a regular battle with Satan, then maybe he doesn't see you as a worthy opponent!" Wow, what a profound statement! I thought to myself, "Have I truly stepped out for my Lord and spoken His truth or am I one of those "secret agent" Christians that claim it but seldom ever reveal it?" I know that I know and need to know that you know. Then we will both know that we know. You know?

> "For the grace of God has appeared, bringing salvation to all men,
> instructing us to deny ungodliness and worldly desires and to live
> sensibly, righteously and godly in the present age, looking for the blessed
> hope and the appearing of the glory of our great God and Savior, Christ
> Jesus."
>
> Titus 2:11-13

Here is the bottom line; if there is one person that is in doubt, I want to live my life to help them remove that doubt. If there is one person that needs assurance; I want to be that one who leads them to the Light. If there is one person who needs hope; I want to be there for them pointing the right way. If there is one person needing clarity in understanding how to receive righteousness, I want to be there for them. You will come to know that I am very humble about the skill that God has blessed me with. I am very thankful and owe all I do and all I am to Christ. To flaunt my credentials to a crowd is not my style. To go on and on about my education is less productive than it is to put it to use. I write like I talk, so what you read is the same as if we were sitting on the front porch chatting about life. I am a research analyst, investigative reporter with a sincere desire to please God. That is simply who I am.

So why write another book about the God? The main reason is because He hasn't returned yet and too many people wonder why. Too many people are overly concerned with this side of death and less concerned with the other side of it. I meet people every day who are worried about death and some are truly consumed with it. Many wonder;

- o   What happens the moment that you die?
- o   Is there a bright light when you pass?
- o   Is there an angel that meets you on the other side?
- o   Do we have guardian angels that are assigned to us?
- o   Do they give you a "new spirit" orientation guidebook when you cross over?
- o   What are they doing right now in heaven?

Those who worry may not have their Sword securely in their hand or their shield firmly in place. So, let us explore those questions and see if we can see a sign that will secure some worthy confidence in our faith.

You see signs at ballgames, rallies and events that shout:

$$\boxed{\ldots \textbf{John 3:16} \ldots}$$

But does the world truly embrace the significance of: *"For God so loved the world, that He gave His only begotten Son, that whoever believes in Him shall not perish, but have eternal life."* I struggle with the numbers of people who claim the name of Christ yet do not live in His word. Are the people around you truly saved or do they walk through the motions of life comfortable as they compare themselves to others OR does their confidence come from walking in obedience of Christ? Do you know the difference? Are you saved? Have you truly received the Holy Spirit in a fulfillment of sanctification? Should we concern ourselves with the many who do not believe? What does the Bible say about our role as Christians? How do I know Jesus is speaking to me? These are typical questions of those who straddle the fence, unsure of their salvation or waiver in complete surrender. It is comfortable for some to say they are not as religious as they should be, then continue in a worldly walk. As we move forward, let us answer life's questions with God's word rather than mans opinion.

The Sword is a Christian's history, ancestry, glory, story, and God's Holy word. The Creator and the authorized writers scribed our past, present and future in the Holy Bible. It is **the** answer for every question of this world as well as a promise of a new eternal bliss. God in His eternal wisdom is always right and has provided a narrow path for eternal bliss. It is the difference between going to church and being the church. The Bible is the most read library of books that has ever been written. Yes, it is a library of books between two bookends of time. It is the beginning, an explanation of the end and an insight of new beginnings. Those who study and understand God's word are called to salvation by a single moment of sanctification that moves you into a life of Christianity. It is an acknowledgement, then belief, and then a movement to receive. This is a process that takes you into a daily devotional fellowship with Christ. There are so many people that walk in His creation, and as they breathe His air, they mock His name and His Word. Those who mock and refuse His direction have fallen into damnation. This is not a movie, a cartoon or a made for TV show! To avoid demons and damnation we must become skilled Swordsman and this skill is a learned process. We will walk from an acceptance of belief through the learning of our history through the development of knowledge and into a confirmation of discipleship. It is a daily plan against legendary temptation!

When our faith becomes firmly centered in Christ,
Satan will move on those close to us. He works every angle and he's good at it!

There are many who have paved the road for us to follow and there are many who will steer you off into the ditch, down the dirt road and into darkness. Some teach the Bible truth while some practice deception and are self-serving. The only way to know the difference is to read the word of

God, study His word and know the difference between a lamb and a wolf. Wolves' will devourer this world in packs. A lamb is a humble servant of this world that desires greener pastures into the Holy Land. Wolves seem to consume it all right now while the lamb drinks from an eternal cup where he or she will never thirst again. There is only one place that maintains this promise and it is the word of God. His holy word is your Sword and your solemn faith in His word is your eternal shield.

The Bible speaks of many miracles witnessed and people wonder where all the miracles of today are. The disciples and followers of Christ write about them every day. The problem is that most news broadcasts announce the sin, not the loving kindness shown by God every day. People lost in sin worry most about what they are going through. Christian's who are truly saved are concerned with where they are going, not where they have been. And there is a major difference! It is a conscious choice and there are only two roads to travel. One is wrong and the other is right. Christ is on the right . . .

This composition contains historical evidence that I believe offers vision, provides clear guidance and documents prophesy of new beginnings. Each chapter of this book contains Bible teachings and the fight of a history of patience in God's will. Histories of many events are listed though this book that parallel today's real life breaking news. A good example is of myths and debates about global warming. This was discussed many times over in my book titled **2012 Global Warning**. The earth will be destroyed by fire. But God doesn't have a clock on us and time is not a factor in His warnings. He has a path that has not yet been fulfilled. When you walk a path, you do not arrive at the end until you reach your <u>predetermined</u> destination. God has predetermined our end, it is described in several books of the Bible but we have not yet arrived at our research destination. But we will.

Our responsibility is to read, listen, learn, grow, give, teach, tell, help, forgive, love, and care today. We live by faith and trust. It is a divine faith in God and trust in our deliverance from evil. Our gift is prayer and salvation by grace. We have the distinct gift of being able to speak directly to God, our Father, Lord and personal Savior as we ask Him directly for the gift of salvation that Jesus shed over 10 pints of blood for in less than

12 hours. When the Roman soldiers came by to break his legs before removing Jesus from the cross, they noticed He was already dead so one of the soldiers pierced the side of Jesus with a spear and immediately blood and water came out. Ten to twelve pints of blood fill the average body, but medical journals say that plasmas surround the heart and when spilled it has the look of water. Jesus died of a heart attack and He was dead before the two thieves who were crucified next to Him had died. His heart literally stopped because of the weight of the worlds sin He had taken from the past, present and future. Draw your Sword and verify these facts for yourself in John 19:31-37. Be always on-guard with Bible ready because we will do this a lot! When you are ever in doubt, draw your Sword. God's word is our final authority!

This was the physical destination of Jesus and out of an empty tomb was the Christ who ascended into Heaven to prepare a place for all those who believe, accept and follow. See, Jesus is His earthly name and Christ is His spiritual name that confirms His deity. This is a Christian's foundational belief. Jesus Christ is the Son of God. And, He is part of the Trinity of the Father, The Son and The Holy Spirit who is One. God dwells in the Promised Land and a true born again person in Christ does not wait for the promise to be fulfilled. He is One God who is Spirit and became man to provide a sacrifice for our sin. We go to Him to fulfill the promise <u>WE</u> make to Him. That promise is simple yet many find too difficult to see:

John 20:29 where Jesus said, "**Because you have seen Me, have you believed? Blessed are they who did not see, and yet believe**."

John 20:30-31 where John informed all that man other signs were performed that were not recorded in the Bible but that these things that have been written so you may believe that Jesus is the Christ, the Son of God and that believing you may have life in His name.

John 21:17 where Jesus asked Peter if he loved Him and Peter replied, "Lord, You know all things; You know I love You." And Jesus said, "Tend My sheep."

Revelation 21:27 where John wrote that nothing unclean will enter Heaven but only those whose names have been written in the Lambs Book of Life.

But don't take my word, you decide for yourself! This is your foundation and supports a lifestyle of obedience to His every word. This is where we will begin; on this day, in this culture and in this century as the same as it was in the first century. Let us begin our walk through His word, His way and in His will . . .

"For this you know with certainty, that no immoral or impure person or covetous man, who is an idolater, has an inheritance in the Kingdom of Christ and God. Let no one deceive you with empty words, for because of these things the wrath of God come upon the sons of disobedience. Therefore do not be partakers with them for you were formerly darkness, but now you are light in the Lord; walk as children of Light."

Ephesians 5:5-8

About the Sword

"Take the helmet of salvation and the sword of the Spirit, which is the word of God. With all prayer and petition pray at all times in the Spirit, and with this in view, be on alert with all perseverance and petition for all the saints, and pray on behalf, that utterance may be given to me in the opening of my mouth, to make known with boldness the mystery of the gospel for which I am an ambassador in chains that in proclaiming it I may speak boldly, as I ought to speak."

Ephesians 6:17-20

The Bible; God's Holy Word, Testaments of His chosen Prophets, the Apostles of Jesus Christ, the Epistles, the Canon and my Sword. They include a collection of letters that are assembled to organize, inform, educate, govern, provide comfort, provide accountability, instill discipline, and honor the Lord our God. **The Holy Bible** provides a collection of evidence for all to follow the instructions of God to the people of the Old Testament and introduces His Son as the New Testament from His birth through forever where His Grace covers The Law . . . It is an unquestionable gift of God loves desire for His people to love Him as their Father and know Him through His word and His Son's saving grace. **GOD!**

The first thing man must do is decide what god they intend to worship and where they will place their complete faith, trust and love. It means everything to do this first and understand who is the creator of all things as well as who is in control of the universe. There are many gods to choose from and man creates more and more idols each and every day. If anything is placed between you and God, it then becomes your idol . . .

Today's Christian Crusader must know how to define the differences in worship. Worship must have a figure of divine trust and hope. Let's walk through a few of the better-known gods of today's religions or "polytheism", which is the belief in multiple deities.

- Allah: The god of Islam as written in the Qur'an (kor-an) and is the fundamental pillar of faith for Muslims. Allah never took human form and Muslims refuse the thought of Jesus as the Christ as well as deny the Trinity as holy. Muhammad ibn Abdullah founded Islam and Allah in 632AD, wrote the Qur'an and he died then stayed dead. This religion does not recognize heaven as an eternal destination because they do not recognize the path through Jesus Christ as THE Way to get there. It is written in the Qur'an to anyone who leaves Allah and worships the Almighty Living God through Jesus Christ must die a physical death. Christians recognize that if you ignore Christ you will die a spiritual death, forever.

- Baha'i: The Bahaullah was originally a follower of the babi religion founded by the Babi and he is dead. Shoi Effendi Rabbani was the leader in succession to Abdul Baha and he is now dead as well. They both have remained among the dead. Those who died believing in bahai are spiritually dead forever.

- Brahma: In Hindu Brahma is the creator and senior member of the triad of Hinud gods. Braham is their creator of the universe. He was man made and has never shown visible signs of true life. So, it is difficult for something to die that has never lived. This "man-made" thing is part of this world and has no value into the next.

- Buddha: Its founder Siddhartha Gautama, prince in northern India around 483BC, created the statue that has covered the globe in popularity. He created Buddhism as a form of atheism, which found it difficult to entrust anyone with his or her eternal soul. He is dead now and the statue has taken on many forms and many different materials used since this era. Most people of today think that Buddha is a god but he was mortal man and never wandered more than 200 miles from his home therefore he never knew of Jewish worship or world creation. His sole being was to become one as the earth. Buddha is looked up to and thought well of as a teacher, much like a prophet and he found his own perfection in nirvana. This meant he found himself to be perfectly moral, perfectly ethical, and found to be perfect. A sort of legend in his own mind but he is now perfectly dead. I also find it interesting that the lead rocker of the band Nirvana, earlier named "fecal matter", with years of a drug and drunken life, committed suicide in 1994 with a shotgun to his chin and a departure note. So, the meaning of nirvana is one who has attained ultimate wisdom? Both were famous in their own right, in their own world and both remain dead in this world. But he was right about one thing; he became part of this earth when they buried his earthly physical body but his spirit is very much alive. The difference is in his eternal destination. Like the Buddha symbols, a rabbit's foot is about as lucky.

- Vishnu: In Hindu Vishnu is the preserver of the universe and there are ten avatars of Vishnu: Matsya the fish, Kurma the turtle, Varaha the boar, Narasimha the man-lion, Vamana the dwarf, Parashurama a sage with an axe, Rama the king of ayodhya, Krishna, brother to Balarama, Buddha the thinker, and Kalki the destroyer. George Lucas could not have asked for a better star line-up of aliens or new world orders. All of these characters were man made, man created, therefore one who never lived cannot create. They are simply dead creations. I thought these guys were at the bar in the first Stars Wars movie but I could be mistaken.

- Cheng-huang: These are Chinese protective gods who provide them with rain, harvests and are guides to souls into the heavens. The communistic People's Republic of China needs this with there 70 million plus people. Men imagined these gods, created by man and are as dead as the men who created them. China is ghastly again becoming a world dominating power. I wonder who is behind communist power . . .

- Sky gods or deities include: ouranos, shu, indra, tyr ullr, cabaguil, torngasoak, anu, nyame, denka, altjira, shanga, gamab, tengri, ukka and a several Lithuanian sky deities like; dievas, ausrine, dalia, gabija, laima, menuo, perkunas, saule, zemyna, asvieniai, and zvaigzdes. All of these gods have no appearance of life and were created by man therefore they died when man's imagination died.

- There are many mother figures that are worshiped and prayed to for blessings, safe keeping and nurturing love: potnia theron, Aphrodite, Mary, brigid, cybele, Demeter, devi, durga, freyja, frigg, gaia, hathor, hecate, ishtar, isis, jord, kamakhya, kali, laxmi, mut, nerthus, ops, pachamama, rhea, tawaret, triple goddess and yashoda. None of these gods represent an appearance of life today. The Mother Mary, mother of Jesus is a figure of respect but she is not a god to be worshiped or prayed through or to. Many Catholics will cringe at this statement but if you kneel before Mary then you are kneeling before the wrong one. If this statement offends you then you are really going to be livid later on! Refer to Matthew 2:11 where they came to worship HIM . . .

- Christadephians: This was a religious sect founded by Dr. John Thomas in 1832 as his ship encountered many storms and he swore oath to God if He would spare his life he would honor Him forever. God did His part and Thomas studied with the Cambellites for some time until he decided to split the group and start the "Brethren of Christ". Then in the 1800s church leaders split off from this group to form Mormonism, Jehovah's Witness, Christian Science, Seventh Day Adventism and Spiritualism. These groups began calling out the end of time beginning with the Civil War. As with most groups they concentrate and dwell on the end of time. Many of these groups wrote different books of doctrine claiming the sole right to biblical occurrences and beings. All the creators of these different religions are dead. The spirit of Christ is in everlasting life, not death. Don't preach or teach the end, focus on NEWness of life in Christ.

- Scientology: Scientologists look at god as being "infinity" and the "allness of all" where god is simply a vague concept. They believe that man is of three dimensions: soul, mind and body. This cult was the revolutionary invention of L. Ron Hubbard in 1954 based on his own theories. (Remember, the Holy Bible is not theory.) Ron later wrote science fiction books and claimed to be an art of the world he wrote about. Ron then crawled in a cave somewhere and died in 1986. His legacy lives on through famous folks like; Kirstie Alley, Tom Cruise, Priscilla Presley, Lisa Marie Presley, Kelly Preston, John Travolta, Greta Van Susteren, Edgar Winter and many more. Scientologists who are now dead are now in infinity and in their all-ness of Hades. Ron Hubbard never survived his experience with death but has most definitely experienced the full measure of his religious practice. He is dead in body and in spirit. This practice of faith will grow into the new age religion and has already found a good foothold in America as well as Great Britain. I believe this new age thinking will be the path of the anti-Christ and move to one world church religion.

- New god: Yes, you can invent your own god because all the others have and the men who created these gods feel it served them well on this earth. There is a great story in the Old Testament about a golden calf that was "man made" and many people donated their gold to the creation of this idol. You should read it sometime. The problem is that you are only here for a little while then your god dies with you. And nowhere has any other god ever promised eternal life in paradise with him or she except God, Yahweh, Jehovah King of Kings, Lord of Lords and the only way to heavenly paradise is through Jesus Christ who died as sacrifice for our sin. The only God, undisputed in any language, rose from death and lives today. The only God ever to have defeated death. Exodus 20

- Almighty God: God the Father, God the Son and God the Holy Spirit is the Trinity being of one God as written in Isaiah. The living God and Creator of heaven and earth as well as the first man and his wife, Adam and Eve in Genesis. The God of the living Bible and the Word of God spoken through Moses, Joshua, Samuel, Abraham, David, Daniel, Solomon, Job, Isaiah, and Amos. The God who came to us as Jesus, God in flesh, to offer Himself as a living sacrifice for our sin and provide the gift of eternal life through Him and fill our lives with the Holy Spirit as He did Matthew, Mark, Luke, John, Paul, Peter, James and Jude. He is the All Mighty, glorious, in majesty, with dominion and authority for now and forever. The New Testament created by God through Jesus: Also known as Christ, born of the Virgin Mary. His genealogy is recorded in Matthew 1:1-17 through Joseph and Luke 3:23-28 through Mary. Born as a Nazarene then moved to Egypt for His protection from king Herod who feared the newborn King. Jesus was baptized by John the Baptist, tempted by Satan, performed many healings, brought Lazarus out of his tomb after fours days of death, and fed five-thousand plus people from a child's lunch basket. He was seen transfigured with Moses and Elijah, prophesized His own death, was arrested, held in trial, crucified and died with no legal statement made of any crime. **Then He arose** . . . The Alpha and Omega, the beginning and the end, He is the just and deserving King of Kings. These are the Gospels of Jesus Christ in Matthew, Mark, Luke and John. I began this composition with Him and I will close with Him, just as I have done here above all man made idols of past, present and future. To live forever in His Kingdom, these things must fill your heart and your mind. If He lives within you then He will live in you beyond today into His eternal way!

No other god has ever raised himself or herself from death except Jesus Christ. So why would anyone serve a dead god or a spiritualistic being with no past experience or future existence? If you are worshiping any other variation than the Almighty God Jehovah according to His world scribed in His Holy Bible then you are worshiping an idealistic view of our Creator and outside His knowing you. Any variation to His Holy Bible, additions or deletions of God's word is against God's word (Revelation 22:18-19). The Holy Bible is The Living Word of God and by faith alone will you receive the gifts His word has in store for you but it begins with a complete unconditional trust in Him. You will see this again and again through this literature as a validation of His greatness. Understand today that no matter what scientific statement is made, someone had faith in his or her belief that it is truth. Every word that an atheist or agnostic speaks is based on their faith in what they believe to be truth. Even though they cannot answer one question: how do you get something from nothing? At some point in history, there was nothing then something was formed. It is the difference between Creator and evolution. But how could we evolve from nothing?

Understand also that someone, because of his or her faith, believes every word of the Qur'an. Every person that believes they are one with the earth has faith that this is true. Every person that asks Buddha for help is asking it based on faith that he will deliver. Everyone who rubs a rabbit's foot, or knocks on wood, or saves a lucky charm; must have faith that this belief is truth. If a person says they do not believe in any spiritual being and when you die, you die, that person has faith that their belief is true. Every person in this globe has faith in something. The difference is that no other belief system in the universe has a living Father that has documented His creation, has documented the birth and life of His Son, has absolutely no argument of the death of His Son Jesus Christ, hundreds of witnesses of His resurrection and inspired the most read and longest living literature ever recorded in the history of the universe. **Ever!** It is trust in this evidence and it is faith that will comfort you in every word and every step you take in this life. Faith through Jesus Christ is the only thing that gets you into an eternal life with Him. Read, learn, listen, know, understand, ask questions, work at it, research it, pray about it, and He will speak to you as well as deliver you from any doubt. Place your faith in the word that is God and know you will be saved by His grace through Jesus Christ. This will become evident through your studies. Your study and understanding will help you when you are face to face with a demon. Know now that you will face many demonic deceptions! Being skeptic is understandable but being unprepared is foolish. Wisdom comes from being prepared. Proverbs 1:7

The Old Testament is our life's ancestry, the paths that they carved, the mistakes they made, the battles, the wars, the sacrifices, the pain, the rejoicing, and the following of God's plan. The Old Testament is filled with marvelous love stories, stories of greed, stories of kingship, battle strategies, war, and descriptions of incredible journeys, magical mysteries, biographies of great men and women, and life before the birth of Jesus. This time was filled with sacrifice, burnt offerings to God, elaborate temples, blood offerings of honor and men who spoke with God. Like today, they experienced the temptations of demons that worked on every fiber of their being. The same demons that haunted their lives are alive today. There are many people who are still living their lives today out of the Old Testament ways. Many denominations still practice celebrations and traditions of old and do not recognize the New Testament of Christ. Many religions base their history from the Old Testament and ignore the New Testament as if Jesus Christ did not exist. The Moslem religion is one that does not recognize the New Testament and they created their own. The Latter Days Saints still recognize the old Passover and never moved forward with the resurrection of Christ being the new salvation and New Testament of blood passage into heaven. These many people will have some explaining to do upon their name being called on judgment day. God's chosen the Jewish people and their traditional beliefs, is an entirely different topic of research. Maybe my next book idea . . .

The New Testament began with the birth of Jesus, Son of God. Many knew of His coming and knew of His birth yet did not seek Him. In His youth He sat and amazed Priests with His wisdom and knowledge of the Old Testament and ancient documents. He asked questions seeming to test the priests' knowledge rather than His own. When it was His time, He then returned to teach as an adult. Great men, who walked with Jesus during those few years that He graced us with His physical presence, wrote letters of testimony. He laid out very clear instructions for a successful life on earth and a successful path to heaven. He healed, showed compassion to the weak, validated His authority to all, chose 12 men who would record the walk to eternal life and then made the ultimate sacrifice of His blood so there would be no need to shed ours. He left us a pattern for life in His death. He is the vineyard of the earth and we are His branches. Branches of any tree are expected to be fruitful and any branch that does not produce fruit is a dead branch. Dead branches are pruned then burned. Faith without works is a branch that is dead. To believe in God's word and follow His will means to have faith in His promise and tell others of His works in you. Faith and belief without works is useless to a Christian's commitment. His second coming has been announced and I wonder if you will have the faith that it takes to want to seek a place in His grace. As each day passes of your indecision the temperature rises. Bless those that know.

Your Sword has two edges and the Old Testament is one edge while the other edge is the New Testament. The handle is your hold on His divine word and the point leads to salvation only obtained through Jesus Christ. Jesus is the divine Light and the only way to heavenly paradise. While you have your Sword firmly in your hand there is nothing in this world that can take you from His hands. How do I know this? It is the promise directly from His lips. Get ready to draw your Sword! John 10:10

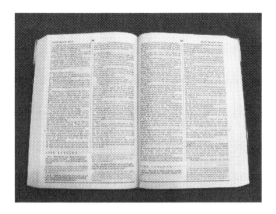

But, before we travel further, let's choose our Sword carefully. As many Crusaders of the Faith, choosing the right Sword is important so you will have something comfortable to wield. There are several translations to select from and I would recommend a Study Bible. A Study Bible helps with translation, time, who, why, reason, reference, etc. Here are a few translation options, in no particular order:

The New American Standard Version (NASV)

The American Standard Version (ASV)

The New King James Version (NKJV)

The New International Version (NIV)

The King James Version (KJV)

The New World Version (NWV)

I have several translations that I use to research but the Bible I carry with me everywhere I go is the NASV, The Charles F. Stanley Life Principles Bible. I have great respect for Dr. Charles F. Stanley and find his life's learning lessons to be relevant and easy to understand in applications for anyone's every day life. His style of ministry is smooth, basic, and thorough. He has the ability to speak on all topics with scriptural truths. He takes no credit for the success of his ministry, www.intouch.org and gives all the glory to God. I concur with the good doctor from Atlanta Georgia and when I have a question, he has a scriptural answer. He is my Bible study hero. Much of this work is because I listen to wise Christian Crusaders.

The Sword is a library of books and contains some of the most famous writers who have ever lived. These books are a must read in order to understand prophecy, promises and principles for living. To know the end, you must know how we began. Here is a "very brief" letter-by-letter review of the only book you will ever need for every situation you will ever face in this lifetime that prepares you for your eternal journey. Draw your Sword, review the books in the front of your Bible and turn the pages of life as we go forward. Write notes in your Bible and in this workbook so you may refer to it always. Write the page number of each books beginning beside the titles listed below as it coincides with your Bible and follow along as we open God's word.

The Old Testament

The Old Testament is the time where God was directly involved in the people and Prophets as they battled temptation and evil. He spoke to them, gave them visions and dreams of right and wrong as well as eternal perspectives in life. There were many, many times where God was very frustrated in man's inability to halt His urge to the temptation of the flesh. However, in the midst of battle, pain, sorrow and immorality many great men and women pleased Him and stood for His word faithfully. They walked upright with God.

    Genesis—Is believed to have been written by Moses around 1400BC and this 1st book provides the very beginning of time, identifies our Creator, our ancestral parents, the story of Noah, the creation of nations, the authority of Abraham, the life of Isaac, Esau and Jacob, and the introduction of Israel as well as the Jewish people as a tribe or nation. Genesis 1:1, in the beginning was God. This is the very foundation of God's people and His divine creation. You!

_____**Exodus**—Is the 2nd book of Moses. It is the powerful deliverance of Israel, the walk through the wilderness, the covenant of God to Israel, the establishment of the tabernacle, the trials of Israel, and the authority of God confirmed.

_____**Leviticus**—Moses 3rd book as it offers the alter sacrifice descriptions, the acknowledgement of Aaron and his sons and the complete law.

_____**Numbers**—Moses 4th book is filled with military strategies, the march to the land promised by God to Israel, rebellions, prophecies, Moses humanized, the birth of the census and rules for a people to live by. Chapter 6 verses 22-27 are God's blessing upon His people. Are you securely named and known in His flock?

_____**Deuteronomy**—Moses 5th book established his work with God in the writing of the 10 Commandments, twice . . . Rules of law were established for all nations. We'll discuss Moses and his impact as an important Prophet for God in greater detail later. Moses was by all rights the greatest leader ever that moved a mass of unruly people across land. There were many great Bible leaders but it was Moses faith in God that walked them out of bondage to the edge of the Promised Land.

_____**Joshua**—Was written in part by those close to Joshua's life around 1350BC and records the times of the Promised Land, the unity of Israel, the fall of Jericho, battles for real estate and confirmation of religious rights. This begins the separation of tribes and establishment of nations.

_____**Judges**—The writer is believed to be a follower of David's life path, possibly Samuel, and knew the life cycle of Saul. It contains the disobedience of Israel, the price they paid for disobedience, the story of Samson & Delilah, and stories of tribal lawlessness.

_____**Ruth**—Possibly written by Samuel around 950BC is a short love story about a young woman who trusted Naomi and was guided by God to establish a foundation of faith and path to the parental ancestry to Jesus. She is a very important piece to the artwork of God's loving hands to the arrival of His birth in the flesh.

___**1st Samuel**—Was likely written by Joshua, Samuel and assistance from Nathan and Gad. These are likely writers. This book is about Saul's path to king, the story of David and Goliath, Saul's many attempts to kill David, Samuel's death, David's many battle successes, and Saul's death.

___**2nd Samuel**—The continuance after Samuel's death, David named King of Israel, David's mistakes, his victories, the death of his son, adultery, and the famous affair with Bathsheba. Murder, conspiracy, and David's struggle with his faith is a very important study as he regains God's confidence through a moment of sanctification. David's prayer for forgiveness, David's plea with God's Angel, the great alter is built and God saw peace across Israel. No soap opera in the world could measure the drama in the stories in 1st and 2nd Samuel! We will discuss David again.

___**1st Kings**—Jeremiah is the likely writer around 600BC and he records David's command to Solomon, his relationship with Nathan, David's death and burial in the City of David. This book also begins the reign of King Solomon, his prayer for wisdom, his twelve officers, (including the famous Hollywood portrayal of Ben-hur), Solomon's wisdom, his proverbs, the construction of Solomon's temple, his palace, and many of God's blessings on Israel because of Solomon's faith as well as his relationship with God.

___**2nd Kings**—This book was part of the first book but was separated for translation and convenience. Elijah was a great man of God and this documents the witnesses to his path to Heaven on a chariot of fire. It documents the prophet Elijah's path, his healings and his prophecy. 2nd Kings also records the mass murders of God's prophets by Jehu. His intimidation practices of piling heads at the gates of the cities, slaughtering seventy sons of Ahab that were beheaded and thus continued the trials of leadership of Israel. This is a historical reign of terror that would compare to Nguema, Hitler, Al-Qaddafi, Castro, Ze-Dong, Stalin, Tojo, Enver, Konoe, Gowon,

Sung, Amin, Mussolini, Pot, Menghistu and Hussein. Yesterday's evil repeated today and will be worst as we move forward.

1st Chronicles—Ezra and Nehemiah are likely writers of 1st and 2nd Chronicles around 450BC. 1st records the genealogy from Adam to Israel and lists the tribes of Israel through Saul and David. It was important to keep the ancestry and genealogy from the beginning through the decades so all would know that the prophesies of the Prince of Peace would have the birthright of the earthly throne of David as well as the heavenly throne of God.

2nd Chronicles—Some believe this book was written by Ezra and it documents the life of Solomon into how important his life was to the rebirth of Israel. It includes the story of King Solomon and the Queen of Sheba. Solomon's wisdom created a foundation of historical construction techniques, respected leadership, respect of all people, and a treasured relationship with God, steadfast prayer for blessings and how the people of Israel fell apart after his death under poor leadership. It was a glorious time of peace.

Ezra—Also written by Ezra around 450BC and he was a Prophet of God and teacher from Babylon. Ezra preached in Jerusalem during and around the time of Israel's captivity as he was well versed by Moses. The pulpits today don't speak much of Ezra but God's Holy Spirit but it certainly reflects the authority of God's word.

Nehemiah—Most likely written by prophet Ezra around 430BC follows the life of Nehemiah, a Hebrew leader that lead his people by the word of God and this story provides the history of events from the Babylon days to Jerusalem. Nehemiah constructed a wall to protect Israel and was very convincing in his methods of bringing people to God. His methods would place this modern world in shock today but then again, there are many that need a good shock from Nehemiah best practices! People seem to move when authority is reflected with results . . .

Esther—Believed to be written by Mordecai around 400BC and specifically documents the tradition or institution of the Feasts of Purim. Esther did a very brave and dangerous deed of facing her husband Haman's kingdom while being respectful of her husband's position. There are many festival celebrations in this book as well as choices made. This book illustrates the difference between God's plan and what moves the believer beyond mere coincidence.

_____**Job**—Believed to be written by Moses or Solomon around 1400BC and is an awesome story of Job's love for God, the tests and trials that Satan placed him in and the faith Job maintained during these trials. In Job's pain and loss he became the strength of God's will and was rewarded beyond compare. The first chapter of Job gives us insight to Satan, how he moves and the ways of his deception.

_____**Psalms**—Was written by more than one writer but was mostly recorded by David between 1000-400BC. This book is a collection of 150 psalms by several writers and spans over many different topics. These psalms or prayers or poems were obviously written and inspired by wars, sin, regret, sorrow, worship, celebration, announcements of the Messiah, guilt and a deep love for God. Psalms is the largest book in the Bible and the collector of this book was surely instructed by God in his placement as well as selection. Psalms Chapter 118 means to be centered on God rather than man and Psalm Chapter 118 Verse 8 is the very center of the Bible and says, Trust in the lord.

_____**Proverbs**—Written and collected in Solomon's wisdom around 900BC. Chapter 1 verse 5 says; "let the wise listen and add to their learning, and let the discerning get guidance". And the 7th verse separates the wise from the foolish: **"the fear of the Lord is the beginning of knowledge, but fools despise wisdom and discipline".** To me, this book writes a pattern for life's walk with God.

_____**Ecclesiastes**—Written by Solomon toward the end of his reign as king around 930BC in all his wisdom understood that everything he physically built in this world was meaningless. Chapter 12 verse 1: "remember your Creator in the days of your youth, before the days of trouble come and the years approach when you will say, "I find no pleasure in them." Verse 13: **"now all has been heard, here is the**

conclusion of the matter: fear God and keep his commandments, for
this is the whole duty of man." Wow, what a powerful statement!

    Song of Solomon—Written by Solomon and could be dated
around 965BC. These songs number over 1,000 written by Solomon
and paint a picture of love, care, delight in poetic pleasures, and
honesty in marital commitment. Solomon clears the confusion of
relationship and marriage while illustrating the need for praise, not
criticism, giving rather than getting and reassuring your love of your
commitment to each other. There is also the essence of forgiveness in
his words. Read and see.

    Isaiah—Written by Isaiah around **700BC** and a wonderful
prophet of God who prophesied the coming of Jesus in Chapter 9
verse 6: "**for to us a child is born, to us a son is given, and the
government will be on his shoulders. And He will be called
Wonderful Counselor, Mighty God, Everlasting Father, Prince of
Peace.**" Wow, one of my favorite prophecies written 700 years before
Jesus was born.

    Jeremiah—Written by prophet Jeremiah around 600BC and is
the confirmation of reprimand for Judah's idolatry and slide to evil.
Chapter 23 verses 5 & 6 represent a prophecy of the coming of a King
who will reign wisely and be called The Lord of righteousness. This
was rock solid!

    Lamentations—This was written by prophet Jeremiah around
600BC and laid witness to the destruction of Jerusalem by Babylon.
This book is God's voice of wrath when we do not listen and follow
His word. Many civilizations have fallen because of this and we will
look at a few fallen civilizations later in this book.

    Ezekiel—Written by prophet Ezekiel around 570BC during the
time of captivity in Babylon. Ezekiel was not your typical Prophet but
then again he was not in typical times. The evil that he faced called
for different strategies to obtain the attention of Israel. Read this book
with both eyes open.

_____**Daniel**—This was written by the prophet Daniel around 530BC and confirmed by Jesus as the writer. This book scribes the life of Daniel during his captivity in Babylon to his assignment to the royal court of King Nebuchadnezzar. An example is in the trials of Shadrach, Meshach and Abed-nego in the blazing fire furnace. Daniel is recorded as to have solved the troubling visions of Nebuchadnezzar that landed him great favor in the king's eyes. It describes the famous story of Daniel as the first Lion tamer and with God's help; any beast is but a gentle kitten. Daniel also prophesied of the coming of the Messiah, His righteousness, His message and His purpose. Study this book twice.

_____**Hosea**—Written by prophet Hosea around 750BC and he was God's Prophet of Israel to steadily remind everyone that God is loyal to His people. Even though we have recorded a history of unfaithfulness to God, He still loves us and is forgiving. All we have to do is call His name.

_____**Joel**—Written by prophet Joel around 835BC and describes the destruction of Judah by swarms of locusts that consumed everything. When I say everything, I mean nothing was left! Years of famine followed the damage done by the swarm. Was this early signs of global warming or climate change? Read and see for yourself.

_____**Amos**—Written by the prophet Amos around 750BC. Amos was not an educated man, nor was he a trained preacher but God chose him to minister to Israel because of their deep slide into evil, idolatry, greed, pagan worship, poor leadership and a people who ignored God. This story is for all those who believe they are unworthy of stardom. God has a place for every star and Amos is a star example.

_____**Obadiah**—Written by the prophet Obadiah around 845BC contains only 21 verses that call the people of Edom out on their evil state. He states the problem with the Edomites not allowing Israel to cross their land. Verse 4 says it all: **"though you soar like the eagle, and make your nest among the stars, from there I will bring you down, declares the Lord."** And he did! Our U.S. administration should read this book. They should read all of them but this book is a great place to dig in.

     Jonah—Written by the prophet Jonah around 700BC and is the well-known story of Jonah and the great fish. But the story in the story is not as well known and it is Jonah's ability to preach when highly motivated in the face of divine acknowledgement of exactly who is in charge of things. God does extraordinary things with ordinary people.

     Micah—Written by the prophet Micah around 700BC begins with verse 2: **"hear, O peoples, all of you listen, O earth and all who are in it, that the Sovereign Lord may witness against you, the Lord from His holy temple."** Israel did not listen. There are many who still do not listen.

     Nahum—Written by Nahum around 650BC and out of the city of Nineveh by the Sea of Galilee. The people of Nineveh had returned to their evil lifestyle as they had before the prophet Jonah witnessed to them. The Assyrians were a brutal people who hung their enemies from poles and skinned them to get other enemies attention. Nahum had called for the destruction of the Assyrians while comforting the people of Judah. It worked! Hollywood, lend Nahum your ear!

     Habakkuk—Written by Habakkuk around 605BC and is the example of how important prayer is and how powerful God can be when asked with humility. Paul makes mention of Habakkuk in the New Testament and his reference is how faith sustains us through life. Not to mention that it is never permissible to challenge God but He is open to questions and His request line is always open . . .

     Zephaniah—Written by the prophet Zephaniah around 730BC who could only see Judah and the nations that surrounded him but was very clear in announcing judgment on the world for its sinful nature. Chapter 1 verse 18 is a powerful statement and worthy of today's headline news.

_____**Haggai**—Written by the prophet Haggai around 520BC and bases his writings on life's perspectives and how we place what is important in our life. The faith of a few, guided them to rebuild the temple of Jerusalem while they faced many who opposed their work. A few today could make the same impact.

_____**Zechariah**—Written by Zechariah, a prophet of God, around 500BC. Chapter 7 verse 13: **"When I called, they did not listen; so when they called, I would not listen, 'says the Lord Almighty."** How many people and communities does this apply to today? Many today wonder why God doesn't answer their prayers. Read Zechariah and find out what this means.

_____**Malachi**—Written by the prophet Malachi around 430BC and closes the Old Testament with a final warning to all people. Chapter 1 verse 6 is God's challenge to mankind and those who lead the church. In Chapter 3 verse 1 God announces his messenger who will come before Him. I believe He speaks of John and Himself as the Son. How does God speak through you in this passage?

The New Testament

The New Testament is the epistles of new beginnings and separates the old way into *The Way*. Many religions still live and operate according to the Old Testament. It is God's word and it is good. To understand God's goodness into God's greatness then you must support your traditional structure from the old way with the new way. This "new way" is in the birth of our Savior, Jesus Christ, as He offers this opportunity for all to believe as well as know He is the newborn King. Jesus taught so that all would understand God's will, God's word and God's way. Jesus died and arose so that all would live through One eternal King. No words are better or sweeter than His words. Read, understand and obey His word and the word of God through His disciples. I call it; "Clarity in Sanctification." Through Jesus Christ: He is the only way.

John 12: 26

"If anyone serves Me, he must also follow Me; and where I am, there My servant will be also; if anyone serves Me, the Father will honor him."

John 12: 46

"I have come as light into the world, so that everyone who believes in Me will not remain in darkness."

John 14: 1-3

"Do not let your heart be troubled; believe in God, believe also in Me. In My Fathers house are many dwelling places; if it were not so I would have told you; for I go to prepare a place for you. If I go and prepare a place for you, I will come again and receive you Myself, that where I am, there you may be also."

Matthew, Mark, Luke & John, known as the Four Gospels, were all written on the actual factual life of Jesus but each had his own reason and unique writing style for recording historical facts with eternal foundations.

    Matthew—Written by the Apostle Matthew about 55AD speaks directly to the Hebrews and walks the reader from the Old Testament prophecy to the fulfillment of the promise of The King, "Son of David", and established Jesus on the throne of Israel. Witness the birth of God into flesh and His walk with/on His creation. Matthew writes the facts of Jesus' teachings, His Way, His prophecy in His life, in His death and in His resurrection then into the promise of His return. Matthew begins the testimony of a faith and trust in the only path to salvation.

    Mark—Written by the Apostle Mark about 50AD gave eyewitness testimony to the life of Jesus and wrote of Jesus as a servant and His suffering for the world's sin. Mark was a close friend of Peter and wrote for the Gentiles. He records the Gospel and the life we are to live.

    Luke—Written by the Apostle Luke, also known as the Physician, wrote his book around 60AD. His writings are substantiated by eyewitness accounts of the events surrounding Jesus as he respectfully calls the "Son of Man". This term is used very honorably and signifies God born into this world so He could teach His word, invite His will upon us and sacrifice His body so His deity would give us the gift of grace eternally. Luke was the voice of logic and reason. Luke understood one God, one Savior and one Holy One as One. There is but One.

__**John**__—Written by the Apostle John about 90AD affirms Jesus as the "Son of God', the "Savior of the world", and the "word was God". John records the early and later life of Jesus. He also made it clear that Jesus performed many other miracles and acts of kindness not recorded in any book. I would imagine they were too numerous to write. Many were healed by simply touching the garment of Jesus so who in this world could keep such an accurate record. The Book of John is in part, a basis for my ministry, which is named: "John21Ministry", because of the twenty-one chapters within John's gospel. It also happens to be a common multiple of the Hebrew magical seven not to mention the honorable formula for a patriotic gun salute to a fallen soldier. We will discuss this topic in more detail later.

The sinner's prayer is not biblical but is foundationally based on the four gospels, the repentance of sin, the declaration of faith in Jesus Christ and a dedication into your covenant with God. The example God gave us was at the river with His Son as Jesus rose up out of the water baptism, God's Holy Spirit came upon Him. This was God's example to His Son and this is His Son's example to His people. If you are among His people, you will follow His example. Not because it is a church practice or ceremony, but because it represents becoming one with Christ. The prayer is symbolic as baptism where we receive then we begin our ministry. Matthew 3

A Sinner's Prayer
"Father, I know that I have broken your laws and my sins have separated me from you. I am truly sorry, and now I want to turn away from my past sinful life toward you. Please forgive me, and help me avoid sinning again. I believe that your son, Jesus Christ died for my sins, was resurrected from the dead, is alive, and hears my prayer. I invite Jesus to become the Lord of my life, to rule and reign in my

heart from this day forward. Please send your Holy Spirit to help me obey You, and to do Your will for the rest of my life. In Jesus' name I pray, Amen."

The sinner's prayer opens the door to a path that is difficult to walk and all those who have walked it before you and all those who walk it with you, walk it humbly in the shadow of our King, Lord and Savior, Jesus Christ. He is the gospel of good news and this is how His message was started in the 1st century.

_____**Acts**—Written by the Apostle Luke, the only Greek Disciple, about 60AD records the witnesses of Jesus in Judea, Samaria, and Jerusalem. Luke's records indicate the gifts of the Holy Spirit as our powerful guide as well as our counselor. He records the many healings performed by the disciples as well as the power of evil but if you believe on the Lord Jesus Christ you will be saved. Acts 14:19-20 speaks of the stoning of Paul as he spoke the gospel. In those days when a person was stoned they were stoned to death. Paul popped up after they had walked away, went back into town and continued his message. How many preachers of today would commit to this earnest preaching of the gospel? If God is for you then no man could take a stand against you!

_____**Romans**—Written by the Apostle Paul about 50AD served as an introduction of Paul to the church in Rome, and he defines the trinity. Chapter 3 Verse 23: **"For all have sinned and come short of the glory of God"**. Chapter 6 Verse 23: **"For the wages of sin is death, but the gift of God is eternal life in Jesus Christ our Lord"**. Keep these two verses close to your heart. These are powerful statements that separate the saved from the unsaved. The Letter to the Romans should be read every month in its entirety. It is the foundational Christian life.

_____**1st Corinthians**—Written by the Apostle Paul about 55AD and to the church he had founded concerning false teachings, improper use of church funds, boastful pride and misrepresentation of the scriptures. This church saw denominational division just as we still see today and it is obvious again that we have not learned lessons from those who have walked before us. I would be willing to bet that you will see 20th century practices in many of these 1st century writings.

_____ **2nd Corinthians**—Written by the Apostle Paul and no doubt the prophet Timothy was influential in these writings around 60AD. Paul had seen improvement on his second visit to Corinth and shown great appreciation for those who had repented their ways. This book reveals clear direction for us to use our talents for work offerings as well as money. Learning quality stewardship is the message of Paul.

_____ **Galatians**—Written by the Apostle Paul soon after the death and resurrection of Jesus. Paul warns the Galatians that they will not receive grace in works without the Holy Spirit of God and following the doctrine of Jesus. Jesus must live in us and through what we do.

_____ **Ephesians**—Written by the Apostle Paul just a few years after the death and resurrection of Jesus around 60AD as it reaches out to our submission to Christ and scribing the one faith philosophy (4:4-6). Chapter 6 is written to help us with today's struggles.

_____ **Philippians**—This was written by the Apostle Paul soon after the death and resurrection of Jesus around the following year, 61AD. Paul scribed this book, probably with the assistance of Timothy, while in prison and begins his letter with a gentle passage of faith. Chapter 1 verse 21 simply reads, **"For to me, to live is Christ, and to die is gain."** Then labeling Christians strength in chapter 4 verse 13: **"I can do everything through Him who gives me strength."** If your body is in bondage, never allow your heart to be bound as well. God is always in control and you have a conscious choice. Like Paul, a true Christian's life begins when the old life is replaced in "newness of life".

_____ **Colossians**—Written by the Apostle Paul around 62AD and provides every Christian with a script for life in this world. He recaps our creation in the first chapter, understanding confidence in the scriptures in chapter 2, living in forgiveness of others in chapter 3 then understanding wisdom in chapter 4. Stay clear of false visions by a scientist, scientologist, astronomer, or whoever. They attempt to explain life from a lab, a test-tube or a telescope, which are all man-made instruments to see His creation. Christ's' word is secured as evidence and has been witnessed as well as firmly documented. Not a theory but evidence beyond any reasonable doubt!

    1st Thessalonians—Written by the Apostle Paul around 51-52AD to the church of Thessalonica. He sought ground in finding comfort for the questions and challenges from the unrighteous. Paul writes in chapter 5 verse 16: **"be joyful always; pray continually; give thanks in all circumstances, for this is God's will for you in Jesus Christ."** God said it and that settles it!

    2nd Thessalonians—Written by the Apostle Paul about 51-52AD to the church comprised of Jew and Gentile, so to assure the people that the 2nd coming had not yet occurred. Some thought that Jesus had come and gone and they missed it therefore they stopped working. Paul explains the end of times and assured the church that it has not happened yet. I've said before, many knew He was coming and when He came they did not go to Him. Now many still do not go to Him and when He returns, at the very moment the trumpet sounds, all will be done and again they will have missed Him.

    1st Timothy—Written by the Apostle Paul around 65AD to Timothy who was working in Asia. Paul wrote this letter to give confidence, encourage, inspiration while laying out some rules and mentor the young pastor in his preaching.

    2nd Timothy—Written by the Apostle Paul around between 67AD as he was sitting in a Roman prison and felt he would not survive his term incarcerated. Chapter 4 verses 7 through 8 resonate with me, as I believe Paul was finding peace in the face of death.

    Titus—Written by the Apostle Paul around 66AD to Titus who was leading the church in Crete. This letter was probably a welcomed sight since Titus was probably struggling in how to preach to a disobedient people. Paul offers life lessons to those things we should embrace as well as those we need to avoid.

    Philemon—Written by the Apostle Paul around 60AD and is a brief letter concerning slavery. Paul wrote from prison to Philemon because he was a slave owner and his slave, Onesimus was stolen from Philemon. Both Philemon and Onesimus had accepted Christ as their savior therefore Paul's letter was to smooth the path of Onesimus back to Philemon. Before Christ came in his life, Philemon would have certainly killed Onesimus for his actions.

     Hebrews—The writer of Hebrews is unknown but many scholars believe a combination of writers scribed the material and were no doubt lead by God's Holy Spirit. The book writers relied on information and first hand knowledge from individuals who knew Jesus, walked with Him and provided eyewitness accounts of His life. The letter was recorded around 65AD and provides three separate groups of thought: 1) It speaks to the believers in Jesus Christ who faithfully follow Him. 2) It speaks to those who have heard but deny following. 3) It speaks to those who reject Him. Number 1 thought is the proper choice and the smartest. Two and three get you a free trip to warmer climates in eternity. Real warm . . .

     James—Written by the Apostle James, the half-brother of Jesus. This book compliments Paul's teachings in prayer, faith, Godly wisdom and the constant practice to turn from evil temptations. James parallels the sermon that Jesus made on Mount so stated in Matthew, Chapter 5. James speaks very clearly and God's Holy Spirit leaves no questions unanswered.

     1st Peter—Written by the Apostle Peter written around 60AD and is to the followers of Jesus Christ who were receiving a lot of resistance. Peter was arrested for preaching the gospel but not before they beat him. After this, the very first thing Peter does is praised God and Father of our Lord Jesus Christ in His great mercy.

     2nd Peter—Written by the Apostle Peter before his death, which was before 68AD. This small book lists the ingredients of discipleship. We will speak often of these characteristics or ingredients and it would behoove you to study Chapter 1 until you can see it in your sleep. Peter was upset concerning false preachers who had become increasing in number. Peter's message is one of confidence in the Christian faithful and integrity of those who personally witnessed the life of Jesus Christ. Our focus today is the same as yesterdays and it is the foundational faith in the return of Christ and our confirmation in the eternal kingdom of our Lord and Savior Jesus Christ.

___**1st John**—Written by the Apostle John around 85AD and it is apparent that false teachers are rich in the 1st Century and have continued through the centuries to the 20th. Chapter 3 verse 6 says: **"No one who lives in Him keeps on sinning, No one who continues to sin has either seen Him or known Him."** Attention all church members! It is the "A.B.C." philosophy of Christianity. A-accept, B-believe, C-commit! Bet you will see this again as well . . .

___**2nd John**—Written by the Apostle John between 85 to 90AD and the verse to follow is in Chapter 2 verse 6: **"And this is love: that we walk in obedience to His commands. As you have heard from the beginning, His command is that you walk in love."** Attention church!

___**3rd John**—Continuous writings by the Apostle John around the same time as the first and second books. This book compliments Gaius for his work in the mission; he condemns the work of Diotrephes and commends the work of Demetrius. We have many who act like Diotrephes today.

___**Jude**—Written by the Apostle Jude, Jesus' half-brother, around 60AD and is spoken about very little but has heavy meaning to us today as it did when Jude wrote it. Beware of false teachers, use caution when listening to disobedient men of the church and take serious the word of God as the only authority. Period! Woe to those who do not listen to Jude! I used this little book firmly in my first book, "2012 Global Warning".

___**Revelation**—Written by the Apostle John around 90AD and is highly believed to be written either with Jesus by his side or Jesus came to John in a vision. Revelation is the most talked about book in the globe simply because it discloses visions of the end of mankind. But those of us who are recorded in the Lambs Book of Life know it as our homecoming. Many researchers, historians, philosophers and comedians made visions and predictions after this book was written. And in the end, there was God and all heads will bow, all knees will kneel before the King of Kings.

Attention: Revelation specifically states that no other scriptures shall be added to or taken from the word of God. All those churches that have adopted other books and/or altered doctrine to worship from are in direct violation of God's word. Do not take His word and make it fit the life you would like to live. You take the words as they are written, fit your life into His word and be obedient to His word! No Christian should be concerned of the apocalypse as long as you are obedient. Know this without exception cause in Revelation: In the end, we win . . .

"So that whoever believes will in Him have eternal life."

John 3:15

The Skilled and Unskilled Swordsman

Jesus said: "Do you now believe? Behold, an hour is coming, and has already come, for you to be scattered, each to his own home, and to leave Me alone; and yet I am not alone, because the Father is with Me. These things I have spoken to you, so that in Me you may have peace. In the world you have tribulation, but take courage; I have overcome the world."

John 16:31-33

While God inspired each book, He used different writers with different bios to record His messages to describe each purpose separate from the other. The men He selected were not scholars. With exception of Matthew, they were noble and men of honor. Matthew was a tax collector and you could find few that liked a tax collector, then or today. The brilliance in His selections was in the diversity of the group. Each apostle had his own writing style, each book represents its own meaning and each message is a guide for us to apply solutions from our ancestors into today. When you hear it said, "Preach and teach the Gospel", then this is it. **His name is Jesus . . .**

To know is to study, to tell is to teach, to preach is to shepherd. God has different callings for different people and He gives each of us a talent. An example of one simple man with talent was Amos. The Prophet Amos was a simple shepherd tending his flock and picked fruit when it was in season. He lived in a small Judean village called Tekoa, which was about ten or eleven miles south of Jerusalem. Amos was not formally educated, did not attend seminary school, was not formally ordained by the church, had no media experience and was not flashy in style or dress. However, he was specifically hand selected by God to fulfill a task. He received his calling and God in turn gave him inspiration, wisdom and a guided path. With God as the wind behind his words, he could not and did not fail. Without God we are simple people but with God we become moved with **His** authority. Amos was chosen to scribe God's word and what an honor it must be to be a simple shepherd and have your name on a book in God's Holy Bible. I am humbled and honored just to write this word about Amos must less have the honor to write about my Advocate, Jesus Christ . . .

Jesus loved Peter and in Matthew 26:34 told him that he would deny Him three times. This took Peter off guard and Peter said; "Even if I have to die with you, I will not deny you." Jesus never lied and His prediction became true in Matthew 26:69-75. In Matthew 26:21 Jesus spoke of one of the Disciples would truly betray Him. In Matthew 26:25 Judas came close to Jesus and said; "Surely it is not I, Rabbi?" In Matthew 26:49 Judas walked up to Jesus and identified Him to the priest and men who came to arrest Him in the Garden of Gethsemane. Draw your Sword and learn of the obstacles these men placed in between them and God.

We all have one of two choices to make in our lives; to follow Jesus or to deny Him and betray the sacrifice He endured for our salvation. Most everyone, except Bill Maher, knows the story of Peter and the three denials of Jesus until the rooster crowed. Upon the resurrection, Peter came to Jesus remorseful and Jesus asked Peter three times, "Peter, do you love me?" And Peter each time became more remorseful and sought forgiveness from his Savior. He chose wisely. Judas on the other hand walked up and kissed Jesus on the cheek to identify Him to the mob that would walk Him to His death. In Matthew 27, Judas tried to return the money he was paid to pick Jesus out of the crowd and the priests would not accept it. In shame, he exited the city and hung himself. Judas chose poorly. Bill Maher made a film called "Religulios" that used today's technology to do the same to Jesus as Judas did over 2,000 years ago. Bill chose poorly as well. Just not sure if he will find as good a tree as Judas did but we have solid Oaks in the south that would serve him well. However, he still has time to settle his sin as long as God gives his lungs operation.

On January 28, 1986 seven people placed their complete faith in a man made vessel that is used to press the envelope from the blue sky into the outer atmospheres. The spacecraft Challenger carried Michael Smith, Dick

Scobee, Ronald McNair, Judith Resnik, Christa McAuliffe and Gregory Jarvis into the afterlife. At about 11:38am est. instantly they were absent their bodies and immediately launched into the afterlife. Now, I have no way of knowing what the spiritual beliefs of these seven people were but I wondered if anyone in their right mind would sit on a rocket and not know Jesus Christ personally? Could you buckle yourself in the seat on a rocket and not ask the Creator for safe travel? Everyone who knows anything about auto racing knows of the speed these folks travel and the dangers involved in this sport. The Daytona Speedway is probably the most famous super-speedway known to mankind and on February 18, 2001 it felt the crash of one of the sports most famous racecar drivers, none other than Dale Earnhardt, Sr. The very moment that Dale's head snapped his spirit left his body and was driven to a road with two very different directions. One way was the path of Jesus Christ and the other was the path to Hades. The road he traveled would have been predetermined before he ever hit the wall. None of these individuals planned to die on the day that they were taken. Very few people have planned their death. Many speak of death as untimely. The certainty is that each one of us will die; it is simply a matter of time. Some may have more of it than others.

As some leave unexpectedly, some choose a path that leads to their own destruction. As God spoke to Apostle Paul he wrote the book of Galatians. In Chapter six verse seven he wrote: **"Do not be deceived, God is not mocked; for whatever a man sows, this he will also reap."** This was not a threat from God. It was a natural fact of life. If you choose the rocky road then expect to have a rough ride. If you choose to laugh at danger expect to have your bumps and bruises. If you always play and swim with creatures of the wild then you have increased your odds of deadly proportions. And the old saying is true; if you play with matches then you are destined to play with fire. If you play with fire then your destiny may be burned. It's just a matter of time.

Here are a few individuals that someone thought to bring into the limelight because of their life; character and the unrighteous walk through it. They are noted on snopes.com and included several email chains that I found interesting.

- Tancredo Neves, President of Brazil, ran for the presidential campaign and said that if he got 500,000 votes not even God would be able to remove him from office. It was said that he made the 500,000 plus votes to elect him into the presidency but oddly became ill and died the day before he was to take office. Neves actually became ill on March 14, 1985 and died on April 21st in the same year. He was Governor at that time and part of the DSP (Democratic Socialist Party). His alleged comment would have been a natural comment since he was socialist. But, whether this "God" comment was said or was not said is not the real point. Death is the forbidden subject of our generation and we speak of it as if it only exists in the movies and as we do of all bad news, we avoid the reality of it. People have a tendency to defend the ones they love more in death than in life. And you will hear me say this several times; being religious does not necessarily mean that you are a Christian. Being religious just means that you do have faith in something.

- Billy Graham was said to have visited Marilyn Monroe during a show and he allegedly told her the spirit of God had called him to her and Marilyn simply said that she didn't need his Jesus. It was further said that one week after this show she was found dead in her apartment from a drug overdose. True enough that she was found dead in her apartment of an alleged "pill overdose". I am truly not sure who started this babble but I heard Rev. Billy Graham speak in July 2008 on technology and faith and he told a story of a plane trip he took where a drunken man was causing a disturbance while on the flight, pinching the Flight Attendant and acting a fool. A man leaned over to the drunk and said, "Do you know who is sitting adjacent to you sir?" And the drunk said, "no who?" The man said, "Billy Graham, the Preacher." The drunken man looked at Rev Graham and said, "Well I'll be, I have heard your sermons many times and they have really helped me a lot." Billy found much humor in the drunken state of one of his devout fans because the message the drunk heard obviously didn't stick with him for very long. Whether Marilyn heard Billy or not, she made a choice when she mixed with the company she kept and Marilyn had the conscious ability to drink and not keep her thoughts silent. If you always walk a dangerous line then you are bound to find dangerous results from the life you have chosen to live. Both Marilyn and the drunken airline passenger should have listened to Billy then obeyed God.

- Christine Hewitt was a Jamaican Journalist and was noted as saying that the Bible was the worst book ever written. In June 2006 she was found burned and charred in the back seat of her car. Her body was burned so badly that the only recognizable item on her was her wedding band. Police believed that she was shot and placed in the back seat before the car was set ablaze. When you display radical behavior about radical people then people see you as radical. Some may see you as a dead radical. Some one did exactly that and every moment of every day prior to that, God had His hand out trying to save her.

- John Lennon was documented on TV and radio saying that the Beatles had become more popular than Jesus and he didn't know which would go first, rock n roll or Christianity. This comment caused uproar and albums were broken and burned. In 1966 Lennon's comment was that it didn't really matter because people had already bought the records they were destroying. John was shot six times and died. A stupid comment in 1966 and being shot 6 times seems worthy of coincidental note but know this, John Lennon said this from the heart and later was instructed to recant this statement for the betterment of the groups future. Understand this as well: there are thousands who could tell you the names of every Beatle in the band before they could tell you the names of the twelve disciples. This is the seed that Jesus finds shame in mankind. Paul, John, George and Ringo or Simon (Peter), Andrew, James, John, Phillip, Bartholomew, Thomas, Matthew, James, Thaddaeus, Simon and Judas. And David played a harp but was not part of this band. Just in case you were wondering . . .

- The designer/builder of the Titanic made a comment that even God could not sink the ship. Well, everyone knows what happened when a chunk of ice pierced the ships hull. I find this an interesting comment and one that probably had little foundation but it has certain curiosity because so many died in a massive vessel that seemed so indestructible. But the lesson learned in this thought is that there is nothing of this world that cannot be taken down and destroyed. It is simply man made therefore unable to survive a world bigger than it is. And in case you were wondering, Thomas Andrews designed the Titanic and he worked for Harland & Wolff designs. There were 1,517 people who died out of a 2,223-passenger list. I believe the appropriate comment that was made from the ships many who assisted with the design and creation of the ship that it was virtually indestructible and described as unsinkable. The view from the bottom is another story.

- Cazuza, a singer from Brazil performed in Rio de Janeiro and was heard making a joke as he smoked a cigarette he blew smoke in the air and said, God that's for you. Cazuza (born Agenor Miranda Araugo) died on July 7, 1990 at the young age of 32 of aids and his death was not a pretty sight. Does it really matter what he said? But the real question should be why did he die? Was his lifestyle inevitably leading to his death? Unprotected sex is deadly and he can now vouch for his mistakes.

- Bon Scott was a singer for the rock group AC/DC, in one of his songs he sang, don't stop me, I'm going down all the way, down the highway to hell. On February 19, 1980 Bon was found alone and dead. He had choked on his own vomit after a long night of drinking and partying like there was no tomorrow. As a matter of fact, there wasn't. Like many rockers before him they do not learn from the tragedies of their lifestyles. So many musicians are killed inside and out by the drug of Satan's choice. If it were Satan's choice why would it be yours unless you are destined on that highway headed for hell?

- Campinas, Brazil a group of teens had been drinking and they all jumped in a car to go pick up a friend. One of the girls mother went to the car and pleaded for her not to go but of course the girl argued and said they would be right back. The mother was unable to talk her drunken daughter out of the trip so she told her daughter, "Go with God and may he help protect you". Her daughter laughed and said, "Only if He rides in the truck cause inside here is already full". Some time later news traveled back that they were involved in a traffic accident and all who were in the car were dead. Police responded to the scene and the car was totaled with one exception. The trunk was completely intact and to their surprise a crate of eggs was in the trunk and not a shell had been cracked in the impact. This all makes for good drama but God didn't put these teens in the car drunk, Satan's influence did. Remember, Satan doesn't temp based on statistic he does it based on "it feels good." The truth is 5myteen.com reports that 25% of the teenage accidents reported teens with a blood alcohol content of .08 or higher. $40.8 BILLION dollars in the economic impact of car crashes involving young drivers between the ages of 15-20 years. Cell phones caused another 25% of their accidents and this figure was before texting became popular. God created none of this so if He is not the cause then He certainly cannot be held to blame. These are man made theories, man made problems and man made mistakes that lead to man's demise.

These claims and allegations took on quite a group of debates on snopes. com as well as wordpress blogs. They were about equal on both sides of the argument as to opinion. From myth busters to slanderers to unknown comics to sincere Christian concerns, they all got their opinions made. Understand this and know it well; God does not tempt nor does He kill those who mock Him. He offers His love with an open invitation for salvation so every day you breathe in confidence of knowing your destination is secured. He is divine and His love is offered to all who will accept and believe. God knows your heart the moment you pass. So do you . . .

In much of Paul's writings, he threw caution to those who mocked Christ's' name, made jokes of His divine Spirit and admonished those who would rather get a foolish laugh than realize truth. Also understand that there is a difference between death and judgment. These people as well as many others simply experienced physical death. Their eternal judgment will be at a later time. God didn't take these people out for the things they said or had or had not done. I am quite sure He has better things to do than make examples out of these few who scoffed His Holy name. Their paths left them little option but tragedy and death. If you travel a road of many hazards your odds are in hazards favor. Swim with sharks and the odds are in your favor that one will bite you! Read your Bible, draw the Sword of God's word and make sure you choose wisely in this life because it is the only opportunity you have for salvation. Choose whom you hang with but make sure that Jesus is the only one you follow.

My specific leadership experience and education span over thirty-three years. My investigation experience and education is over twenty-one years. I write what I believe God moves me to write and I use the talents He has given me to express them. It doesn't take a theology major to understand a decision of faith and God has offered you an ear to hear, a conscience that receives, and a mind for understanding. Your desire comes from *wanting* to please Him. In all my knowing, I know I must walk as a humble servant who serves Him faithfully in order to know His will upon my life. I applaud those who seek an education in theology and have years of experience on researching God's word. This may not be your calling, but reading and studying His word is! Like those mentioned in the previous scenarios; we have a choice and in every turn there is a decision to be made. With a pure heart comes a right decision . . .

Ask God to grant you peace in your choices thru turbulent times . . .

The ACLU and some in the governmental agencies have remained consistent in their mission to remove the Pledge of Allegiance and prayer from our schools. The same schools that we pay our taxes to support. But I find it interesting to know that one of our most popular politicians read the Bible in school. All the students took turns reading scriptures from the Bible. An interesting read on President Abraham Lincoln is on the website of Abrahamlincolnsclassroom.org. His biography reflects a lifetime of education in the Bible and tells stories of how he used the Bible prophets as a comfort in the decisions he made during wartime. His stability was confirmed from his youth in the early 1800's until he placed his hand on the Bible to be sworn in as President of the United States. On January 20, 2009 Barack Obama used the same Bible as in Lincoln's inauguration on March 4, 1861 and 1865. The only difference is that Lincoln's Bible was opened during both his ceremonies and Obama chose to have his closed. I'm not sure if a closed Bible has any subliminal meanings or not but you can't see God's word unless you open it! This was just an observation that I thought was odd but then again, he is a confessed Muslim (in his own admission given in a September 7, 2008 recorded interview with George

Stephanopoulos) and as a Muslim this would be an act of Christianity. You'll learn later that this act in today's nation of Islam would mean certain immediate death. So far he has played the fence well enough to not be in fear from Islam. Yet . . .

Now, don't be ignorant to God's word and do not take the opinion of anyone. Look it up, study it, pray about the message and find quiet moments to listen to God's answers. Understand, not always does He say what we want to hear. So don't start separating the "I want" with the "His need" . . . You will lose every time.

If you are not seeking God then don't look for Him to seek you . . .

Use this motto as well as Bible or scripture resources as you ask or are asked questions. Have your Bible next to the resource be it a magazine, a book, a newsletter, a TV program, a radio program or whatever the source. It is good to validate the message as well as learn the value of research and obtaining confirmation. Always be a student of God and His Holy word.

As a follower of Christ everyone has an old and a new testament. It is a testimony of where you have come from to where you are now. At this time I thought I would share my old and new testimony with you. It is my witness of Christ and His ability to be your all. I would like to title it; "It was not my time."

* In January 1957 my mother chose to keep me and I am here because of her strength and faith in Christ. She did not abort and decide to kill my little heartbeat because it was not my time. I am very thankful for her decision!

* At 2yrs of age I slipped out of the house, down the street and sat on a tree stump watching the construction equipment dig and build a new housing complex. I had laid my ball cap on the ground beside me and when I picked it up and placed it on my head it was full of fire ants. It motivated me to get home where I belonged because it wasn't my time.

❋ At 6yrs old I was playing in the forest, down by the creek and had lain down in the bushy grass as Secret Agent 007. When I stood up I became covered with wasps that evidently didn't appreciate where I had decided to hide and suddenly I was no longer a secret. I ran home safely to my mom where I belonged because it wasn't my time.

❋ At 11yrs of age at Calvary Baptist Church Thomasville GA I walked to the front of the church and said a prayer with Pastor Earl Justice. Saved by the blood of the lamb and forever recorded in the book of life. Then I met Sidney, Satan's little helper and demon terror of the neighborhood. He was a smoking, drinking, cussing, and motorcycle riding 12yr old. I thought that dude was the coolest so we became best buds and I followed his lead. Satan relished at taking a newly born again Christian and showing him the pleasantries of this world. Even with all the hellish ways of those days, it was not my time.

❋ At 17yrs old I worked at Sing Service Station and was promoted to night manager. The franchise owners were very proud of me so we celebrated at Alligator Point Florida, which was a little over an hour away from my home. This celebration included all of the alcohol located in Franklin County Florida and I believe I had measured it all. My managers were so proud of me that they put me in my car and wished me well in my drive home. I drove from Alligator Point to the north side of Tallahassee Florida near Lake Jackson where I pulled in my driveway. My father safely took me inside because it was not yet my time.

❋ At 18yrs of age I finished boot camp at San Antonio Texas where I made friends with my first bottle of Tequila. Yes, on Friday afternoon my boot camp buddies and me left the security of Lackland AFB and went down town because we had deserved a celebration of our successful completion of basic training. I was introduced to Tequila, the River Walk and stayed introduced until sometime that Sunday where I woke in my room on the floor with a bandage over my arm. I lifted up the corner of the bandage and noticed that I had also earned and deserved a tattoo for my weekend celebration with tequila. A snake and a rose were inked in my forearm and remind me today that that weekend was not my time.

❋ I served faithfully in the United Stated Air Force and was honorably discharged at the end of my tour. I spent time on foreign soil and returned home safely because it was not my time.

❋ I served with three different Law Enforcement agencies as a law enforcement officer in the great state of Florida for a little over nine years. During this time I pulled and fired my weapon in the line of duty. During this time I saw many injured, a fallen fellow comrade and danger was always a dispatch call away. During this time I witnessed many broken families, loss of life and people all alone. I learned many lessons with many close calls but all in all, it was not my time.

❋ For over twenty years I have traveled coast to coast across America with Wal-Mart Stores Inc and Sam's Club. As a retail leader I have had success, felt failure, overcome stressful moments, made many friends and acquired many life lessons. We experienced major hurricane, tornadoes, earthquakes and fires over these years. Through the dangers of road travel, severe weather experiences, the few rowdy criminal customers and a horrible fast food diet; I have survived because it was not my time.

❋ At any age you are an easy target for Satan and he embellishes the celebration of winning at temptation. He places the bait and you swim over and take it. Then you come to like it because it is earthly pleasure and worldly happiness. At any age if Satan sees you step toward Christ he places a little suggestion in front of you that will make you trip. Some obstacles are small like a little lie to keep you out of trouble. Some temptations grow like having a beer because it is really not like drinking alcohol. Then having alcohol because it is really not like taking drugs. Then taking prescriptions drugs because it is not really like an illegal drug. Then voting to legalize an illegal drug because it really is good for some people. Then you are pressing a needle in your arm because that voice inside your head says you need just one more, just one more high. Many people cave into this roll of temptation because the next best thing is just a temptation away from hell. I was able to stop in the middle before it became worse because it was not yet my time. (1 Corinthians 6:10) You are reading this today because today, it is not your time.

✳ At any age when Satan sees you step out of church pew and make a walk of faithful commitment toward the front before God and you say a little prayer then step away alone, unaware of the power of influence that Satan truly has over God's people. What has your temptation been and did you fall? Some call these chains that bind you to this world. Some call them an anchor that weighs you down to this world. In any form of calling it, it is not your call. Your calling is at the cross; it is a faithful walk in the light of Christ. It is on the path of righteousness and a daily partnership with the Holy Spirit because Jesus Christ left Him here as our Helper. This knowing was my moment in time because it was past my time.

✳ In 2008 I had a moment of sanctification that will not fade, it will not fall, and it will not fold, because it was pre-paid. It will not stop, it was freely given, it comes with unconditional love and I was pre-approved. At one moment, one single second, my life stopped in a hesitation of understanding where I was and where I was not. I had placed my job before Christ. I had placed my job before my family. I had placed distance between both. In one single moment while on my knees I gave it all to Christ and placed my life in correct order. God, family then everything else fell into its rightful place. This was my time.

✳ I gave up my position; a chunk of salary and location then moved it all to the cross. Less than a year later God gave it all back, with a better home, a stronger family, more time with my family, an inspiration of writing, an inspiration of worship, an everlasting peace and an eternal life in His footprints. Amen!

What is your greatest possession? I made a profound discovery that my most valuable possession was my affirmation of acceptance into a covenant with God. I realized that at any moment my physical life could end and not only was I lost, but I had not developed my life into a walking talking witness for the very one who died so that I might live. My number one moment was in my repentance for my sin and surrender to my Lord and King, Jesus Christ. I learned quickly that I needed His word in my hands often and His word became my Sword. With His word in my hands, He became my confidence against deception, misunderstanding, the unknown and the abyss. A Christian with a firm grip on His Sword becomes a light in any dark situation. I am never without Christ. **Never** . . .

Christian is not something you do. It is who you are . . .

The History of the Sword

"Nevertheless, the firm foundation of God stands, having this seal, "**The Lord knows those who are His**," and, "**Everyone who names the name of the Lord is to abstain from wickedness**."

2nd Timothy 2:19

God is the foundation of The Word. Jesus is the head of the church and people make up the body of His church. Through the death and resurrection of Jesus lies the path to eternal salvation. And it has and will come with a great price. There have been many prophets since the beginning and I will review some of the most influential. These men were truly loved by God and have a special purpose that is revealed in each book as well as mentioned in the New Testament. You have a purpose in God's work as well and it is in these passages that you will find your true north and the skill that God has blessed you with.

The Sword of Moses

Moses: his birth, his youth, his awakening, his leadership and his relationship with God are like none other in the Bible. Moses was Hebrew born into Egyptian royalty while Israel was in slavery, extreme bondage and was under regular physical abuse from Pharaoh, King of Egypt. Draw your Sword and find Exodus 2:1 and you will begin with his birth and why this time was so important to the beginning of his life.

Exodus 2:12 was pivotal in his youth as he took the life of an Egyptian who was beating a Hebrew man. This caused Moses to flee from his home.

Exodus 2:16 provided a safe haven for him after he protected the priests' daughters against shepherds at the well.

Exodus 3:1 and the next verses will provide you with vision of Moses' first visit with God.

Exodus 4 was the heated conversation with God and Moses as he learned a valuable lesson in delegation . . .

"When you take your vision off God and place it on yourself, He will humble you."

Exodus 5 is the first encounter of Moses and Aaron with Pharaoh the Egyptian King.

Exodus 6 is the meeting of Moses and Aaron with "the sons of Israel".

Exodus 7, 8, 9, 10, and 11 are the plagues of Egypt and the challenge of Pharaoh.

Exodus 11 explains the Passover, a key moment in the history of God's power and His love.

Exodus 13 God leads Moses and Israel out of Egypt.

Exodus 14 Pharaoh and his military might are in hot pursuit and the parting of the Red Sea is in front of them. God's breath parted the sea and offered dry soil for the Israelites to cross and it collapsed on the Egyptian mighty army.

Exodus 15 Moses and Israel celebrate their freedom.

Exodus 16 Moses leads Israel through the wilderness of sin and on to Mount Sinai.

Exodus 17 God brings water from the rock but not like He had commanded Moses. Moses struck the rock in anger instead of commanding it as God had directed. When have you struck in anger? When was the last time that anger came from your mouth, a sharp comment or spiteful remark? It is easy to be deceived and if Moses can sin I am sure you are not above it either. Moses was strong enough in faith to ask God to forgive him. How's your faith been doing lately?

Exodus 18 Moses wife's family joins the journey. Yep, the in-laws have arrived!

Exodus 19 Moses meets with God on Mount Sinai and scribes the 10 Commandments in Chapter 20.

Exodus 21, 22, 23, 24 Moses delivers the law and rules to live by to Israel.

Exodus 25 is the detailed instruction or blueprints for the Ark of the Covenant.

Exodus 26, 27, 28, 29, 30, 31, Moses receives detailed instructions or blue prints to build God's temple. This is a measurement of discipline.

Exodus 32 the ignorance of a free people and their construction of the Golden Calf. It illustrates Moses anger upon his return from being in the presence of God.

Exodus 33 Moses returns in God's presence to receive a new set of new tablets and gain journey instructions from God.

Exodus 34 Moses restored the tablets of the Ten Commandments and the covenant is renewed.

Exodus 35 Moses established the Sabbath and the importance of offering, both in wealth and in skills.

Exodus 36, 37 and 38 Moses begins construction on the temple. This is an important piece of scripture because it describes how each individual brought skill to construct God's house. An example of this today is our churches of today. Every person in the church brings a different skill level to the body of the church. To build and grow the church every individual should offer their skill and this places all the church body parts in unison as well as in motion. In faith comes action . . .

Exodus 39, 40 Moses and Aaron establish the church on God's word.

Moses was a pillar of strength and even though he doubted his own ability God used his leadership skills to lead an entire nation to safety. He was a humble man that gained his confidence through God. I cannot find one instance where Moses asked or did anything that was for his own gain. He was committed as he learned God's will and also as he grew in faith, belief and trust in God's plan. Moses learned of his protection and power that God flowed through him. Moses also learned of God's promise and how he came through on every one. Moses traded the treasures of Egypt, gold, jewels, luxury items, servants to serve his every need, solid shelter to live in, power, authority and all the glamour of an Egyptian prince for a walk with God. And as a follower of God he suffered at times, celebrated at times, stood in awe of the Lord our God and was gifted with high honors in eternal life. God truly loved Moses and He had the Angel Michael protecting him in his final days. This is a hero's reward.

Worshiping God is not a religion it is a covenant.

It's not about denomination or tradition it is about salvation.

It's not about a revelation it is a relationship with a daily fellowship.

It's not about this feel good physical happiness in this life it is His grace that fulfills us into eternal life by our walk in holiness.

It's not about when you die but did you try.

It's not about what you achieve it's what you believe.

It's not about you it is about Him and He believes in you . . .

Just some insight to the future; Moses isn't done with this world yet . . . I believe he will return in Revelation's as a world witness. Stay tuned, we will dig deeper into this later.

The Sword of Elijah

Draw your Sword and open to 1st Kings 17.

Elijah, or Elias in the KJV, God's prophet was a Tishbite and truly appears from out of nowhere to announce to King Ahab that it will not rain in Israel until Elijah speaks the word. Elijah declares this in the name of Yahweh, the God of Israel, 1st Kings 17:1. This name did not just roll off the tongue of the people in this era either. To speak God's name standing on your feet was just not done. The reverence before God today is nothing compared to this day!

God then instructs Elijah to hide himself by the brook Cherith, where he could drink from its waters and be fed bread and meat morning and evening by the ravens, 1st Kings 17:2-6. When the drought became extreme and the brook dried up, God instructed Elijah to go to Zarephath, a city in Sidon, not far from where Jezebel used to live. In other words, God had Elijah hide out in the heart of Baal country, where no one would have been more eager to capture and to kill Elijah than Jezebel's father, the King of the Sidonians, 1st Kings 16:31.

In Sidon, God cares for Elijah through a Gentile widow. They are saved from certain death by starvation, and the boy is raised from the dead, all by the word of God through Elijah, 1st Kings 17:24. Then God tells Elijah to go to Ahab, and the famine in Samaria was severe. It was long before Al Gore and Michael Moore predicted global warming . . . . It was hot, it was dry and people were dying from what? The carbon emissions from an automobile? The billions of people in the world breathing? The millions of industrial plants cranking carbon monoxide into the air, cutting the life out of our ozone? No! Kings, presidents and people sometimes need to understand just who is in charge and in control of this world . . .

Elijah knew God; he trusted God and followed God's direction to the letter. And Elijah, like Moses, will be back . . .

Moses and Elijah knew God from a faith that is not common among common man. It is a special relationship that is established and never tarnished by doubt. There is a story of this category of faith that is worthy of mention right here with these two men. Most folks know that China is an almost completely communist country and Christians are considered trash and the scum of the earth to China's leadership. China has become a powerful nation again and it has regained this power from the backs of the lower class citizens in that country. But there was a light that shined brightly in that land and his name was Watchman Nee. Born in 1903 he was a Christian, followed his faith is Christ, was a published author of his faith and lead many to Christ in the 20th Century. Watchman Nee was not an educated man, he did not attend seminary, he was not a theologian and never attended a Bible institute for advanced learning but he traveled the country of China opening churches on his solid faith in God.

Watchman ministered the gospel to China for thirty years and in March 1952 he was tried, judged and convicted of crimes against the communist party. The crime ruled upon was his faith in God. He was placed in prison because he refused to deny his faith in Jesus Christ. Does this sound a little too familiar? Jesus was persecuted for His divine authority. His disciples were each persecuted for their faith and their work. Watchman was another who established over 700 churches and lead more than 70,000 Chinese to Christ then spent twenty years in a Chinese prison for his faithful work. Before he died on May 30, 1972 he no doubt witnessed to every prisoner that he came in contact with. When his niece came by the prison to claim what little belongings he had, the guard handed her a small piece of paper that Watchman had kept by his bed that said:

> "Christ is the Son of God who died for the redemption
> of sinners and was resurrected after three days. This is the
> greatest truth in the universe. I die because of my belief in
> Christ. Watchman Nee."

In America our western culture has us so spoiled to the point that faith in God is no longer tested, it is being pushed out the back door. How's your faith doing so far? If you completely accept Christ in your life today you will meet this great prophet of God one day and you will recognize Watchman Nee for he will hold many crowns.

The Sword of Solomon

Solomon, the son of King David and Bathsheba, was the third king of Israel. Solomon was renown for his wisdom, wealth and for his construction projects. Israel enjoyed an era of peace, security, prosperity, and international political and economic importance under Solomon. With God's hands, he made Israel what it is today.

Solomon was anointed king when his older brother, Adonijah, rashly tried to proclaim himself as ruler when their father, King David, became old. But Bathsheba and the prophet Nathan, with the support of others, crowned Solomon as King. Bathsheba knew she could speak openly to David and Nathan was a powerful messenger from God. He did not waste his words nor did he hesitate to tell it like it was. Where are all the Nathan's today?

Solomon began his 40-year reign in 967 BC while David was still alive. Thanks to the conquests of David, Solomon's domain stretched from Tipshah on the Euphrates to Gaza on the border of Egypt. The Lord appeared to Solomon in a dream and told him to ask for anything he wanted. Solomon asked for wisdom to lead the Israelites. God was so pleased with Solomon's reply, He not only gave him wisdom, but riches and honor as well.

It was in the fourth year of Solomon's reign, that he began the construction of the Temple. Seven years later it was completed, and the Ark of the Covenant was moved from the Tabernacle in Zion, the City of David, to the Temple. He also built a large palace for himself, Fort Millo, the wall of Jerusalem, and the cities of Hazor, Megiddo and Gezer.

Solomon was the writer of 3,000 proverbs and wrote 1,005 songs. The Books of Ecclesiastes, The Song of Solomon, and parts of the Book of Proverbs are ascribed to him. The story of Solomon is found in 1 Kings, chapters 1-11, and in 2 Chronicles, chapters 1-9. The name Solomon means "peace/welfare."

Solomon took many foreign wives—700 wives and 300 concubines, and they turned his heart away from the Lord, and they encouraged him to worship their gods. He even built temples for these foreign wives to use for burning incense and for offering sacrifices to their gods. No doubt God was disappointed in His chosen one and He told Solomon that after his death He would take the Kingdom away from Solomon's son, except for one tribe. Never ever place any worldly object between you and God.

The Sword of David

I placed this section out of order for a reason. 1st and 2nd Samuel records the life of David. While Solomon was wise, his father, David was king of kings in this land. A monument in Jerusalem stands in honor of a young shepherd boy who became king and united the Nation of Israel. His unusual appointment to this honor began just outside of Bethlehem about 1,000 years before the birth of Jesus. This monument represents a man of God, a man of great authority, a man who won favor of the people but found hate from the very king who took him under his wing. David was a man once forgiven for bad behavior, made human by poor choices of the flesh, then found the courage to return to God for guidance and passed as a man truly blessed by God. His life represents failure and forgiveness from a forgiving Father, Lord of Lord's and <u>THE King</u> of all kings.

Before David's appearance, God rejected King Saul for his greed and unwillingness to seek Him for leadership, glory and blessings. David was a simple boy, tending to sheep when his journey to the throne began with playing a tune for King Saul on his harp. This pleased King Saul and David became a member of Saul's court. David also wrote many poems and psalms in his youth. These writings follow his life, his journey and his relationship with his environment. If you only knew this much of David's life you would think he was a sissy boy. But David also was a student of battle, strategies of war, weaponry and close observation of military progression not to mention the original true grit. This would prove to be useful in the famous meeting with Goliath. David had placed five smooth river stones in his pouch and carried this on the battlefield. As David decided to meet the giant, Saul tried to put his armor on David but it was too bulky and restricted David's movement. Walking across that open field with no armor must have been a sight to behold. David used a slingshot and a river stone to bring down the giant and this began his leadership and fame in Israel. The people of Israel lost their minds over David's quick kill of the big man. David immediately became champion of the guard and the crowd shouted his name in victory.

But let us take a deeper look on the chance meeting of the sheepherder and the giant that has not yet been considered. Goliath was not just a big man that led thousands of troops and taunted his enemy with his size. Oh no, he had a way about him that is familiar to us today. Now those of you who are familiar with southern folks could just imagine Goliath being a big loud obnoxious redneck that steps out and challenges anyone to anything. If Goliath had been from Alabama he probably would have stumbled out into the field with a wad of tobacco in his cheek, a skoal ring in his back right pocket, his name on the back of his sword belt, his big belly hanging over his belt, nappy hair from just getting off the couch, a big BBQ stain on the front of his shirt, a skin of Budweiser in his hand, a black cap turned around backwards with the number 3 on it, a loud gravel voice and a slight turn to the crowd just before entering the field saying something like; "Hey, yaw watch this!" David would have walked on the field and met this loud obnoxious giant and Goliath would have no doubt begun to laugh and making rude short remarks like; "boy, you still got goat milk on your lip." Or, "you're going to break out a can of what?" Or, "I hope that set of balls you got are bigger than that little rock in your hand!" Then, "What's that? Oh a little toy sling shot?" And the last thing he would have said was, "Hey boys, pop me another beer, I'll be right back." And the lights went out of Goliath . . . BAM, he was on the ground! The rest of the giant's rednecks would have silenced immediately when the giant fell. They had to have been in utter shock.

Thousands of the king's armies went nuts and the news shot back to the city of David's kill and this made King Saul extremely jealous and angry. The good king desired victory but didn't need his following to be more excited over David than himself. This amount of pride, greed and jealousy could have brought this nation to its knees. Saul was so angry that he sought after David's life. David continued to lead battles and Saul made many attempts to kill him. But David had the perfect opportunity to take King Saul's life but spared his life by only cutting a piece of Saul's garment off while Saul lay asleep. Later David showed Saul the piece of material he had removed in Saul's sleep. David told him that he could have taken his life in a mere moment but he did not because of his love and respect for his king. Saul was thankful for his life and overwhelmed with gratitude. Saul welcomed David back into his arms.

Then David received word that King Saul and his son Jonathon had been killed in battle. David was immediately named king of the south and Abner was king of the north. Then Joab, David's right hand guy, kills Abner whereby vacating the northern kingship of Israel. David rose to power from murder and Israel felt the wrath of the House of David. He was very aggressive for the period of time that he was out of touch with God. David left no breath in his enemy's life, not a living soul remained when he left the battleground and no stone was left unturned for the presence of life. When you are out of the will of God your life has zero spiritual meaning and you live for today.

David named Jerusalem as the capital of Israel but had to deceive the people with their need for clean drinking water. The cities underworld was carved pipelines that channeled water to the city. These pipelines also offered easy access to those who wanted inside the city but didn't want to use the front door. David's wise battle strategies and ability to gain their trust won favor among the Israelites. He was able to unite Israel as one nation. Then David was almost killed in battle and his commanders encouraged him to stay home for his own protection. Against his want and his will, David managed the battles from his palace. David became bored and when you are bored you become idle and prone to temptation. Satan never tires, is never bored and never sleeps.

The story of David and Bathsheba is rarely spoken of because it was this part of David's life that took the strength out of his knees and from beneath him . . . There are two separate stories here: David's lustful desires and Bathsheba's desire to bed with power. David made a habit of getting up in the morning, stepping out of the palace doors and walking around on the upper level of his estate. Bathsheba was a lower level residence within close naked eye range of the castle rooftop. Bathsheba's upper level bedroom and bath opened onto her naked roof where she bathed in all her nakedness while her husband was away. No doubt she had seen the king take his stroll each morning and she made a nude appearance with her doors open wide so the king could see her bathe nude. She must have been quite a babe, with incredible beauty, incredible desires, incredibly naked but incredibly married. Without thought or care David summoned for her and in a few moments they were in his palace engaged in lust and adultery. The Bible is not specific on the time but some time later Bathsheba sent word to David that she was pregnant. Now they didn't have pregnancy test strips back then and they were probably not real sure of conception times but you know she was curious after a month with no period. This was her first experience with pregnancy so she was probably a little unsure of her symptoms. Then she probably waited a few more weeks waiting to see if her period would come and it didn't. Then she had taken some time to figure out how to tell the king of Israel that she was pregnant with his child. She could have been several months into her pregnancy by the time she worked up the nerve to give the king the news. David, now around 80 years of age, knew the child was his because her husband had not returned from the battlefields. Her husband Uriah, was a dedicated soldier and military leader in the army led by Joab, commander and chief. David sent word to Joab to return Uriah on leave with intension that he would return to Bathsheba, sleep with her and would believe the child was his. From the battle post back to the palace was not a jeep ride back. The travel would have taken a few weeks to get the message there and get Uriah back. So, now how far along is this pregnant young beauty? Now they had two problems; Uriah was a dedicated soldier who had honor for his men and when he returned and looked upon his young beauty with the smooth round belly . . . I would imagine that he could not think of being at home, sleeping with his beautiful wife while his men fought and he wondered who knocked up his babe? Now his wife was probably about six months pregnant so they tried getting Uriah drunk and forcing him to go home and lay with Bathsheba and this didn't work either. David, set a plan that would make two wrongs another wrong. David sent word to Joab to place Uriah on the front lines of the fiercest battle then back his troops away so Uriah would meet with certain death in battle. Joab followed his king's instructions without question. Lust, greed, adultery and murder surrounded the decisions of one broken man.

Just how far away from God is David now? How far have you drifted? So, you are looking at David's life and thinking, wow, mine isn't as bad as I thought it was . . . Remember, a weak moment is a weak moment and Satan is at his best when we are at our weakest.

Satan will never warn you of the consequences of your actions. He will only inform you of the pleasures then he will find pleasure in watching you fall then fail.

After her husband's death there was little time for mourning since Bathsheba was close to giving birth. David then took Bathsheba into his palace and made her wife number three hundred something. Nathan, a prophet of God confronted David with the acts of a greedy king and a fallen chosen one. This was a very gutsy move on Nathan's part to stand before a proven warrior, pointing his finger at him and telling him that it was you, King David, who has sinned before God. David fell to his knees and sought God's forgiveness for his sins. Then David and Bathsheba had a son, which became ill and died within seven days of his illness. This almost crushed David as you can well imagine. The loss of a child is one of the most difficult pains to overcome.

David's other son, Absalom, was very aggressive in nature and was obviously after the throne of David. Absalom slept with David's concubines and claimed rights to the throne. David, being a pretty aggressive guy as well, read Absalom moves to take over. Battles arose as Absalom rose in revolution. Absalom met a brutal death for his conspiracy as his head or hair was caught in a tree branch while riding underneath and his mule continued while he was left dangling from the tree. Joab took three javelins and thrust them into Absalom's heart as ten of his men made sure he was dead, dead, dead. David still mourned the death of his son.

David returned to Jerusalem, fought many battles until he became weak in the face of the Philistines and faced near death against Ishbi-benob, with a seven-pound spear. Abishai came to David's side and killed the Philistine and David's men swore they could not risk their king's life in battle again. 2 Samuel chapter 22 documents David's song to God in his appreciation for deliverance and being thankful for all God's blessings. 1st Kings Chapter 2 documents David's death. This was Israel's greatest loss of these times.

There are several differences in opinion in where David was truly buried and many people get caught up in his final resting place when the story is not in his death, but in his life. The Sword documents that David slept with his fathers and was buried in the city of David. But learn this; the decisions you make in this world go forward in the Day of Judgment and you will be held to God's standards. It doesn't matter where your final resting place is, it only matters what your life was about.

David's struggles are similar to our struggles of today when life and lust interfere with our faith and obedience to God's will. When this lure of temptation knocks on your door, step away, turn and find comfort in God's word. He will offer you comfort and joy beyond the flesh.

The Sword of Daniel

Daniel's name alone means, "God is my judge." His testimony and eyewitness accounts in the book he scribed were a fulfillment of God's work through him as a prophet and servant. Daniel's story includes several visions, moments of inspiration, obedience to God, and prophesies of the end of this world including the rise and fall of Satan's boy, the antichrist. Let us walk in Daniel's footprints and look at what God can do when we listen and follow Him.

While Chapter 1 validates Daniel and who he is, in Chapter 2, Daniel describes the reigning king of the land, Nebuchadnezzar. The dream of the king's four world empires was challenged upon the magicians and sorcerers to interpretation and not a one could do so. Nebuchadnezzar became furious of his servants inability to explain his dream and he used his great power to command destruction of all the wise men of Babylon. Guess he figured if they were unworthy of their talent then why keep them on the payroll.

God spoke to Daniel and provided him with clarity of the king's dream and told Daniel to go and confirm the vision to the angry king in His name. Daniel did so in Chapter 2 verse 28. Daniel began to describe the king's dream in Chapter 2 verse 31 and you may draw your Sword and read the results of this dream.

In Chapter 3 Nebuchadnezzar built a golden god and commanded all to come see and kneel before this new god. This is one of the most famous stories of the Old Testament and reminds us of the sovereignty of God. The king commanded that whenever anyone heard the sound of his horns, flutes, lyre, trigon, psaltery, bagpipe and all other music, you were to drop to your knees and worship the golden image. Anyone who refused would be surely tossed into the fiery furnace. The king hit the music and everyone in the kingdom dropped to worship the golden image, all but three Jews and they were called out (or tattled on) for not obeying the king's command. Shadrach, Meshach and Abed-nego were brought before the king and given another chance to follow his command. They refused and the king having the extreme temper that he had commanded that the furnace be cranked up seven times the normal temperature and get ready to cook the three who would not obey him. Once the furnace had reached the appropriate cooking temperature he had the three tied with ropes, as they remained fully clothed. The three men were tossed into the blazing fire and the good king sat back to watch the show but he suddenly jumped to his feet and challenged the ones who tossed the three in the furnace because there were now four figures walking around in the fiery furnace. Nebuchadnezzar shouted for Shadrach, Meshach and Abed-nego to come out of the fire and all three men walked out. The king was in awe of the sight they had seen and called out to God and praised His name. The now humbled king knew this was not magical but truly majestic. Only the three men in the furnace knew who walked them thru the furnace without harm and anyone else would be guessing. My guess was an early visit by Gabriel . . .

Daniel is called to the king again in Chapter four. He is called to explain the king's dream of a great tree and the vision was prophesied and the prophecy came to truth. Then the king had a great party and this party would have been worthy of attendance by the Rolling Stones, The Grateful Dead, Ozzy Osborn and a host of other rockers. The party went so well that just after they praised the gods of gold and silver, a man's hand was revealed and the hand began writing on the wall. The king became immediately afraid and it doesn't say so but I am willing to bet that he wet his "pants". Daniel was called immediately to interpret the message and he did in Chapter five. What a sight this must have been!

Chapter six the new king Darius lays out his laws and commandments for all to follow and that no one in the kingdom shall write or speak an oath to any other gods other than his gods. Daniel obviously did not follow this command from the new king and the neighborhood tattletales turned Daniel in. The king gave orders to have Daniel tossed in the Lion's den. The king had a stone rolled to cover the door and placed his seal on the door that it was not to be opened. The next day the king went to the den and called out to Daniel and Daniel answered his call. The king was elated and found Daniel with no harm, no scratch and comforted through the night. The king commanded that the neighborhood tattletales be brought before him as he had them tossed into the Lion's den. They did not fair very well and I am sure the lions appreciated the snack.

Chapter seven is the prophecy of the four beasts or four world empires. Chapter seven also identifies the "Son of Man" as Jesus was seen through the clouds of heaven. Chapter seven then into Chapter eight reflects the apocalypse and the introduction of "Antiochus" or the antichrist. Daniel describes the end of times and the prayer for all people as these visions, I am sure, took a toll on Daniel. I encourage you to stop and read Chapter nine verses 3 through 10 as these very well apply to today.

> **"As it is written in the law of Moses, all this calamity has come on us; yet we have not sought the favor of the Lord our God by turning from our iniquity and giving attention to Your truth."**
>
> Daniel 9:13

2,600 years later and we are still in denial of the Lord our God and through all the visions, prophesy and reality this world has seen, many still cannot see the truth in God's word. Chapters 10, 11 and 12 will walk you through Daniel's visions of what we are living today and what we are about to face. Draw your Sword and turn on the news then dare to compare His word to the breaking news of today.

The Sword of Paul

Paul was a main Apostle in the New Testament and his Sword was well respected. I could have included other Apostles as Sword carriers and writers as well but I chose to review Paul. I can relate with Paul's transformation from his old life into his new life. Paul was Saul before Jesus gave him a wake-up call . . . Saul had great people skills, very respected among his peers and was tough as nails. God chose Saul to use those specials skills to do His work as Paul. Known as "Paul of Tarsus", he was born Hebrew in what is now known as south central Turkey. Born from the tribe of Benjamin and raised a man with vast education.

Prior to Saul's conversion he was very hard on Christians and persecuted them and arrested anyone who followed Jesus. He was witness to the stoning death of Steven and I believe it was this moment that provided a question in his heart of his life's work so far. Around 35AD, not long after the resurrection of Jesus, Saul rode to Damascus to capture those who followed Jesus teachings and while on the way Saul was stricken with blindness. A bright light-struck Saul and his men were startled by voices but could not understand them or explain the light. This blindness also included a personal visit from Jesus. Saul was blinded until Ananias laid his hands on Saul and healed his eyes. Saul's vision was cleared both physically and spiritually. His new life became as Paul where he sought the souls of men for Jesus instead of their lives for Caesar.

After his sight was restored, he preached, was a teacher of teachers and he must have been very affective because those who opposed Christ really wanted him silenced or dead. When priests and government leaders want to kill you, you know that you have become very effective in your ministry . . . With Jesus for you, who cares who is against you! Paul was relentless and I lean on his relationship with God, his faith in Jesus Christ and his writings every day for wisdom. Follow Jesus and listen to His chosen ones for higher learning.

Asia Minor was captured completely by the Roman Empire after the 2nd century BC or around 190BC. The Romans defeated King Antiochus for this land and its people.
Roman rule was the largest empire of governorship from about 27BC until 1453AD. Their reign covered about 2.3 million square miles of country and they were a powerful force to be reckoned with.

The Romans established Ephesus as their Capital City, which was about 44 miles from Izmir as well as Lydia. These two cities were important to that part of the world because of their strategic trade location. Izmir is now about the 3rd largest city in Turkey and this region was known as Asia Minor. Now why is this important? Because this was where Saul's ancestry is and where he returned in his new life as Paul, an apostle carrying the word of Christ.

Paul, born as Sergius Paulus in Tarsus of Cilicia, located in the southern part of Turkey. He was born a Roman citizen, as were his parents. He was said to have been a short stocky man, going or gone bald with a thick gray beard. He studied Jewish Law from Rabbi Gamaliel as in Acts 22:3. He had taken many prisoners and was on the road to Damascus so he could take more prisoners as in Acts 22:5. Then in Acts 22:6, Jesus Christ called to Saul and he fell to the ground. Blind for 3 days, Saul laid in Damascus blind until he was visited by Ananias and in Acts 22:12-16 Saul was given his sight, forgiven of his sin and baptized as obedience to Jesus. Born, a new child in Christ, Paul began his journey ministering to all that would hear. Paul was one of the most instrumental Apostles of the first century as well as today.

Paul studied in Arabia the returned to Damascus as in Galatians 1:17 then over three years traveled to Jerusalem. This is where he was supposed to have returned with Jewish prisoners but instead he came to witness for Jesus Christ, Son of God. Paul then traveled to his hometown Tarsus then to Judea with Barnabas where they returned with John Mark as in Acts 12:25. When you get a chance look at a map of Paul's travels to minister the gospel and remember that the majority of this travel was done on foot. Paul was the writer of 14 epistles; Romans, 1st-2nd Corinthians, Galatians, Ephesians, Philippians, Colossians, 1st-2nd Thessalonians, 1st-2nd Timothy, Titus, Philemon and Hebrews. Do you know who the author was? Yes, it was Jesus! Or you could say that Jesus was Paul's inspiration but the way Paul scribed these letters, I would lean more toward Jesus as the main author of all the letters written whereby Paul was an awesome instrument for the work of Christ.

Asia Minor was constantly under attack and battle strategies created constant fear in these people. I can't imagine why . . . From the Trojan wars, to Alexander the Great, Hittites in and out of the territory then Roman rule and Byzantine battles back and forth. Finally the Seljuk Turks but then Europe invaded by the Crusades and then Turkish reign with financial support from surrounding countries especially the United States. There have been centuries of issues, suffering and assorted beliefs. I traveled the roads of Turkey in 1979 and walked the Euphrates and Tigris rivers. Visited Malatya, Diyarbakir, Batman, Adana, walked along the shores of the Mediterranean Sea at Mersin, dipped my feet in the Black Sea at Samsun and walked the mountain of Nemrud Dag. The waters of Van Golu are at the mountain base and have the depth in color of pure aqua blue. These lands are unspoiled from the western world and are so humbling in spirit. The skies are not cluttered with the noises of jet engines and the smaller villages still feel as if they were centuries of old. The people are rich in culture and know a strangers face in town immediately. But know this today that Christianity is no longer the dominant faith of these Turks. The majorities are now Muslim and have replaced Christ with Mohammed. If you travel this country, never travel alone and be cautious of the cross you bear in open. Insure you don't lose your head over it before your time.

In this area of God's world, Christianity was fought for, died for and taught for centuries. Paul brought the gospel along with many others and was beheaded for his faith, belief and relentless work for Christ. As we move forward in time others followed to continue the efforts. Both John, son of Zebedee and Mary, mother of Jesus were there. Peter built the first Christian church along with the teachings of Philip. But today their memory is fading away.

There is a bit of Paul in us all. For the most part everyone can think of a troubled past, a time you drifted astray or at some time in your life you were afflicted with chains. Not always are these chains physical chains that others can see. They are the spiritual chains preventing you from being free. Chains can be a shaded past or a deed so heavy on your heart that you feel the weight is sometimes overwhelming.

The European Crusaders spilled blood all over this land all the way to Jerusalem and freed the people of Turkey of tyranny. The Sword of Paul was and is divine as well as instructional but yet his homeland is today about 95-97% Muslim. Out of the total estimated population of 73,000,000 only about 120,000 are Christian and about 27,000 are Jewish. Keep these numbers in mind because they are important to the global percent of "God's people". "God's people" are those who are <u>saved</u>, born again in Christ, according to John 6:69 and John 11:25-26.

To understand the Sword of today you need to understand the price paid for the Sword of yesterday.

"You were bought with a price; do not become slaves of men."
1 Corinthians 7:23

Divine Swordsmanship

Jesus said "For judgment I came into this world, so those who do not see may see, and that those who see may become blind."

John 9:39

Where does our divine inspiration come from? Where does our desire to be better come from? Why do the majority of the people in this world not commit murder? Is it because the large majority of the population understands right from wrong and generally would like to be right more than they are wrong? Who should we place our spiritual trust in? What church do I go to or activity should I do to become closer to being a bondservant?

These are all great and common questions. Our understanding of law comes from our parents, our friends, our mentors, our teachers and our developing character from the Word of God. All these ingredients make up who we are. If you include the church and a steady learning of His word, then you have a very good understanding of right, wrong, up and down. This includes a basic understanding of who you are and who took a stand before you in their beliefs. I have said in many of my bold statements that I am not religious. I am Christian and being religious places me in a category that Jesus did not teach. He never taught alternative religious lifestyles. He taught love and obedience to abide by His word. There are no other paths to heaven. All paths lead to the cross and where Jesus gave His life for my sin. And it was finished . . .

Here are my five ingredients to being a faithful Christian, follower of Christ:

1. I am in daily devotion and fellowship with Christ.

2. Nothing is mine, it is all His.
3. I find peace in obedience to His word.
4. He is my absolute truth.
5. My life in Him reflects in my character and discipleship.

Then there are the **ABC**s of Christianity; maybe you have heard it before:

A = **A**ccept Him
B = **B**elieve in Him
C = **C**ommit to His word

Some people just can't see the **C**. Most people believe if they have **A** and **B** then they are saved and safe from an eternal life in hell. Commit is a problem in the spiritual and in the physical world. This is the main part that I needed to completely understand and that was I physically and spiritually cannot do it alone. I had not completely given everything to God and had that complete understanding that everything I had was already His. Worship is our greatest asset to our belief. We need others around us for support and angels among us comfort us. God sends His angels to do many things in this world that need His directional control and need to guide our needs. I believe, along with many others that there are Angels around us that wait for our call as well as God's instructions. There are a few well-known Angels that have been around since the beginning of time and God created each one as helpers to our walk in life. Here is a look at who they are and what little information is provided about them.

Some people know God like they know their neighbor down the street. Think about this for a moment . . .

Gabriel

When Gabriel is close to you there is peace, love and understanding. He is the angel of reasoning and God's first angel of negotiation. He may also come to you making a very important announcement.

To Daniel, explaining the vision of the ram and the goat—

"When I, Daniel, had seen the vision, I sought to understand it; and behold, there stood before me one having the appearance of a man. And I heard a man's voice between the banks of the Ulai, and it called, "Gabriel, make this man understand the vision." So he came near where I stood; and when he came, I was frightened and fell upon my face. But he said to me, "Understand, O son of man, that the vision is for the time of the end." (Daniel 8:15-17)

To Daniel, explaining the 70 weeks prophecy—
"While I was speaking in prayer, the man Gabriel, whom I had seen in the vision at the first, came to me in swift flight at the time of the evening sacrifice. He came and he said to me, "O Daniel, I have now come out to give you wisdom and understanding. At the beginning of your supplications a word went forth, and I have come to tell it to you, for you are greatly beloved; therefore consider the word and understand the vision. "Seventy weeks of years are decreed concerning your people and your holy city, to finish the transgression, to put an end to sin, and to atone for iniquity, to bring in everlasting righteousness, to seal both vision and prophet, and to anoint a most holy place." (Daniel 9:21-24)

To Zechariah to announce the coming of John the Baptist—
"And there appeared to him an angel of The Lord standing on the right side of the altar of incense. And Zechariah was troubled when he saw him, and fear fell upon him. But the angel said to him, "Do not be afraid, Zechariah, for your prayer is heard, and your wife Elizabeth will bear you a son, and you shall call his name John. And you will have joy and gladness, and many will rejoice at his birth; for he will be great before The Lord, and he shall drink no wine nor strong drink, and he will be filled with the Holy Spirit, even from his mother's womb. And he will turn many of the sons of Israel to the Lord their God, and he will go before him in the spirit and power of Elijah, to turn the hearts of the fathers to the children, and the disobedient to the wisdom of the just, to make ready for the Lord a people prepared." And Zechariah said to the angel, "How shall I know this? For I am an old man, and my wife is advanced in years." And the angel answered him, "I am Gabriel, who stands in the presence of God; and I was sent to speak to you, and to bring you this good news." (Luke 1:11-19)

To Mary, the mother of Jesus Christ, one of the most famous passages of The Bible—

"In the sixth month the angel Gabriel was sent from God to a city of Galilee named Nazareth, to a virgin betrothed to a man whose name was Joseph, of the house of David; and the virgin's name was Mary. And he came to her and said, "Hail, O favored one, The Lord is with you!" But she was greatly troubled at the saying, and considered in her mind what sort of greeting this might be. And the angel said to her, "Do not be afraid, Mary, for you have found favor with God. And behold, you will conceive in your womb and bear a son, and you shall call His name Jesus. He will be great, and will be called the Son of the Most High; and The Lord God will give to Him the throne of his father David, and He will reign over the house of Jacob for ever; and of His kingdom there will be no end." And Mary said to the angel, "How shall this be, since I have no husband?" And the angel said to her, "The Holy Spirit will come upon you, and the power of the Most High will overshadow you; therefore the child to be born will be called holy, the Son of God." (Luke 1:26-35)

Michael

Michael is a righteous, very powerful, high-ranking angel of God—the only angel who is specifically called an "archangel" in the Bible. Michael is prominent, although not often mentioned, in Bible History Satan fought for the body of Moses, and in Prophecy where he is mentioned in both of the major prophetic books of Daniel and Revelation. He is described as having command of a large force of angels that defeat Satan and a multitude of demons, and as the "great prince who has charge of" the nation of Israel. Michael is the one who gets it done!

Just Prior To The Return Of Christ

"At that time shall arise Michael, the great prince who has charge of your people. And there shall be a time of trouble, such as never has been since there was a nation till that time; but at that time your people shall be delivered, every one whose name shall be found written in the book. And many of those who sleep in the dust of the earth shall awake, some to everlasting life, and some to shame and everlasting contempt. And those who are wise shall shine like the brightness of the firmament; and those who turn many to righteousness, like the stars for ever and ever." (Daniel 12:1-3)

The Body of Moses
"But when the archangel Michael, contending with the devil, disputed about the body of Moses, he did not presume to pronounce a reviling judgment upon him, but said, "The Lord rebuke you." (Jude 1:9)

War in Heaven
"And the woman fled into the wilderness, where she has a place prepared by God, in which to be nourished for one thousand two hundred and sixty days.
Now war arose in heaven, Michael and his angels fighting against the dragon; and the dragon and his angels fought, but they were defeated and there was no longer any place for them in heaven. And the great dragon was thrown down, that ancient serpent, who is called the Devil and Satan, the deceiver of the whole world—he was thrown down to the earth, and his angels were thrown down with him." (Revelation 12:4-9)

Revelation 12:6-12
"And I heard a loud voice in heaven, saying, now the salvation and the power and the kingdom of our God and the authority of his Christ have come, for the accuser of our brethren has been thrown down, who accuses them day and night before our God. And they have conquered him by the blood of the Lamb and by the word of their testimony, for they loved not their lives even unto death. Rejoice then, O heaven and you that dwell therein! But woe to you, O earth and sea, for the devil has come down to you in great wrath, because he knows that his time is short!"

Where there is battle and a war to be settled, Michael is there. Jesus in Revelation will certainly call him. He'll deal with his old buddy, Lucifer and this is a fight he has longed for. Then, it will be done . . .

Lucifer

Who? **Satan!** When you are driving and in traffic, surrounded by idiots, honking their horns, angry because they're late or they just drive crazy anyway, how would your patience be graded? Do you grip the steering wheel and get crazy with them? Do you talk to other cars in traffic? Do you give in to the temptation of anger that gets your "dander" all twisted up? This is only one example of how he reaches out and lures you into his world. If he can get you here then he can get you anywhere because everyone experiences traffic problems and everyone encounters their share of idiots. That idiot is sent from the depths of hell just to break your resistance and your faith to God. How good of a job does he do on you?

To understand life and a Christian's struggles we need to understand our adversary. Lucifer, the fallen angel, in Hebrew is translated as "Helel", whose name literally means "morning star" or "star of the morning". He is the serpent and is the worldly delight in this life as he practices deceit and temptation to keep you from eternal life with God. This is not a movie and not Halloween, it is reality.

Isaiah 14 tells the story of a fallen angel, star of the morning and son of the dawn, as describes an angel that was created by God and once was held in high esteem in the heavens. This angel was probably the director of music in heaven as he described the music in his harps. Lucifer challenged God's authority and put his power to the test by stating he would ascend to heaven, raise his throne above the stars of God, would sit on the mount of assembly, ascend above the heights of the clouds, he would make himself like the most high and other statements that truly illustrated the ultimate act of <u>envy</u>, <u>lust</u> for power and <u>pride</u>. Now do you see why God hates these three ingredients in your character the most? God sent Lucifer and his band of angels crashing to what was then created and established as the depths of hell.

The Serpent of Old
Revelation 12:9 "And the great dragon was thrown down, the serpent of old who is called the devil and Satan, who deceives the whole world; he was thrown down to the earth, and his angels were thrown down with him." Who throws him down? None other than Michael and his angels!

The Great Deceiver
Genesis 3 begins the awareness of Satan and his "crafty" ways of attracting us to this world. In Chapter 3 verse 4 and 5 he says, "You will surely not die! For God knows that in the day you eat from it your eyes will

be opened and you will be like God, knowing good and evil". I believe this to be one of the most important passages in the Bible that helps us to understand what Satan is, who he desires to be and how he plans to accomplish his dreams, visions, and goals.

The plan to twist your reality and illustrate how good this life feels.

The plan to deceive God's heavenly plan, which you cannot see with that of what you can see, touch, smell and hear. Again, it is the fleshly desires of this world and everyone experiences them. And many fall because of them.

The use of power, want, persuasion, passion and fleshly desires is his temptation on us. If it looks good, feels good, tastes good, smells good and makes you physically happy then it must be okay. That's what I said and it hooked me! Let me tell you, once you embrace this world it is a tough struggle to let it go. Have you ever tried to kick a smoking habit? How about sticking to a diet? Each of us has complete control over what we allow into our heart and into our mind. Each of us takes in learning lessons and we allow some to stick and some to pass by. Some of these learning lessons are a cancer to our spirit and corrupt our heart and mind. If the cake tastes bad it means that the ingredients were bad. If the soup tastes bad it means that something you put in it was bad. If the pie tastes bad then something you put in it was bad. Your immediate ownership of the outcome is to ensure what you take in is as pure as it can be. To live a Godly life, stay in John 14:6 as your pure belief and remain faithful with a daily walk in the Light of Christ. Change the ingredients and the outcome will change.

**Put in what is the likeness of God and what will come
out will be like God.**

Once you fix your ingredients and walk in true faith then know well that you become a larger target for Satan, his band of demons and the fools that walk around with a taste of life that is incredibly impure. Will you be perfect and walk on water? No, but you can stop being a victim also. If you are weak in faith he will be strong in temptation. The stronger your faith becomes the more he will try to break you down. You must commit, then step in His Light and stay the course of Christian faith. Your faith will be tested in the same way until your last breath and how you study and train will determine how well you defend yourself against temptation. It is your Shield . . .

In order to understand your faith, you need to understand the forces against it. There will be information and documentation in this book as well as many others that speak of a faithful belief in God's will, following His divine plan and the path to eternal life with God but if you don't believe in the dark side, you certainly can't believe in "His Light".

You must believe that God is the supreme authority and Satan will test this daily with <u>doubt</u>. Satan provides your thoughts with a lure of "you are what you own" and God says, "Leave this world to Satan and come spend paradise with Me." I truly love God's plan.

You must believe that Jesus was born of God to a virgin Mary who was filled with the Holy Spirit of God, lived without sin, died for your sins and was resurrected to Heaven where He prepares eternal life for you. Say these three points out loud!

- ✝ He created salvation on the cross for the penalty of my sin.
- ✝ He provided salvation on the cross for my presence in sin.
- ✝ He promised His return so I could depart this world of sin.

You must establish a sound trust that God is **ONE** and He is the Father, the Son and the Holy Spirit. That Jesus was born of this world to die on the cross for all sin. That He arose and ascended with a promise of His return for all who believe and accept. Your faith will be tested but <u>your trust must never waiver.</u>

You must believe that Jesus is the Christ and He will return, for those who have already passed and those who will be alive on the day He returns. At His predetermined time not ours.

Your belief is by faith alone because we were not here to witness the walk of Jesus, His death on the cross or the resurrection of His body. This is the reason for your Sword & Shield. Read for yourself, study His word, learn from the many eyewitnesses and listen to His teachers.

Follow no man! If any man says, "Follow ME"→ RUN! If you hear a TV evangelist from Texas say, "Who will follow ME?" Answer him by saying, "NOT ME", and then RUN . . . When you hear things like this, think of a snakes tongue and it will help you understand which way you need to go.

I heard a story awhile back from Ravi Zacharias that is appropriate for this message.

A sheepherder was looking for a lost sheep up high on the side of a mountain one day. The weather was cold and became colder as he searched further up the slope. He saw the sheep up a little further and as he got closer he saw a rattlesnake coiled but unable to strike the sheep because of the cold temperature. The sheepherder picked up the sheep and turned to walk back down to his herd when the snake spoke to him and said, "Please help me, for it is cold and I am unable to crawl down the mountain to warmer soil." The sheepherder said "surely not, for I know you would bite me." The snake pleaded by saying, "surely no, for I am in no position to bite the hand that cared for me." The sheepherder said, "no I cannot for I fear you will bite me." The snake again pleaded and promised an oath that he would not do harm.

The sheepherder took the snake at his word and placed him inside his shirt so he could carry the sheep with both hands. The three made the trip down the slope and back to the herd. The temperature was much warmer at the foothill so the sheepherder placed the sheep back to the herd and retrieved the snake from inside his shirt and placed him on the ground.

Suddenly the snake struck with all his might and bit the sheepherder on the hand. The snakes poison raced through the sheepherder's veins and creating pains through his body. The sheepherder cried out,

"Why did you bite me? You promised!" The snake replied, "Yes, but you knew who I was when you picked me up . . ."

Sound unfair? Get over it! Those who are weak and out of God's grace will surely fall prey to Satan's way. Again, do not follow any man, only Jesus who paid the price for man. Satan is already a depleted and cast spirit and he is constantly seeking companionship. Misery loves company.

Demon's and Satan's Deceivers

Most people think of a demon as a spirit that posses your body and makes a little girl sit up in bed, spin her head around and spew green chemical stuff all over the room. Some see a young boy named Damien that has deep dark visions of death and creating harm for those around him? This is Hollywood's attempt to sell a ticket to a movie and it worked very well. Just how strong must your shield be to defend against Satan, temptation and demonic spirits that seem pleasing to the eyes?

1) First understand that Satan and demonic spirits have no right over your soul. Satan tempted Jesus when He was in the wilderness and Satan failed because Jesus was of a pure heart and spirit. As long as you walk in His word you will understand how to avoid temptation and not fall prey to the evil one.

2) Next is Satan and demonic spirits having a spiritual right to temp and pursue you with all their spiritual powers but they cannot touch you physically. Adam gave this right to Satan when he lost his battle with temptation of Eve and the fruit. The sly serpent was Satan and his ways of persuasion are very crafty.

3) Satan and demonic movements become more active when you are at your weakest moments. This is similar to germs when they are more harmful to you when your immune system is low. As an example, if you were a victim of a crime you become spiritually bruised and tempted to hate, be angered, and be revengeful instead of passive and forgiving. The flesh makes it difficult for the spirit to overpower.

4) Next is a family tradition. Satan and demons are passed on from your family. Example would be if the parent or parents are child

abusers then so the children would grow to be abusers as well. Or, daddy beat me so I am going to beat also. This is what they teach Physiologists in school but it is based on mans theory or opinion. If my parent beat me then I know how it feels and I would not want to lay that burden on my child. It is a choice we make and in Jesus name you will not blame this on anyone but yourself. He will judge you and you will represent yourself in His courtroom.

5) Last are earthly mind benders like narcotics, drugs, alcohol and stimulants that weaken the body then the brain. How many crack heads and cocaine addicts are *truly* Christian? The true answer is ZERO. If you are hooked on anything but Jesus, you are not a Christian. You may have walked forward and said a little prayer when you were a child but as an adult you are lost in sin. You don't need to take twelve steps until you kneel where you stand now. Yes, and sometimes the truth hurts! Get over it and fix it!

The sad thing about these satanic and demonic issues is that there are many physiatrists and physiologists that stir and simulate this way of thinking. Medical mental witch doctors will place blame on the family, the environment, on the temperature, on the season and the world for the evil that is possessed by an individual and the acts they portray. Charlie Manson planned and influenced his cult following to slice and murder people but the mental medical community would like to paint old Charlie as a victim of society. Old Charlie should have been shot between the eyes on that swastika years ago and old Charlie would be a dead Satan worshiper today. You see, old Charlie made a conscious decision to be this way and still does. He has been asked if he knows who Jesus is and he spits on the name of Jesus. Old Charlie will not hear "well done" from our Savior but he will be well done in his temperature settings . . .

Most pastors especially in the more traditional churches stay clear of speaking of Satan or demonic temptation. They are content to speaking to the saints rather than digging deep and pulling a saint out of an *ain't*. I did some research recently on a group that is divided in spiritual methods but united in confrontational intent and they are the "Children of Whoredom". This group is rapidly growing and now has the following of Indian tribal war parties that are armed to the teeth and really ready for an opportunity to fight. One such soldier in the war party is "Spotted Wolf" and he is the big talk of weaponry and the willingness to pick a fight. He is packed up with a dude named Prince Zebekiah that preaches from the Bible and talks about lost books of the 1st Century and the only thing the Bible talks about is love and submission to the white man. There is another sprout from this group called "Underground Metro" and these people use God as an avenue for forced vengeance of 500 years of oppression. These are militant groups much like the "Black Panthers" but there are very specific facts that these groups look over.

1. The Bible is about love and it is beyond a love for self or worldly possessions and it is a love for the Lord your God.
2. There were many battles illustrated in the Bible and the point to every struggle was the men who walked upright with God, remained upright.
3. Greedy buffalo hunters, railroad tycoons and gold rush idiots mistreated the American Indians. The Indians of today have free land, no taxes, are allowed to operate gambling casinos tax-free and sell cigarette and alcohol in these establishments. They have more rights today than an African American ever thought about having. The big difference is that if the missionaries had not traveled westward and preached the gospel of Jesus Christ, the Indians would still be praying to birds, deer, trees and rivers.
4. The parallel that the "Children of Whoredom" make between themselves and the Black Panthers was that the Panthers were opposed to the spiritual approach taken by Martin Luther King Jr. But it was Rev. King's approach that ultimately got him killed and created strength in equality. Rev. Martin Luther King Jr. had a special gift from God and these groups would be wise to look closely at what he lived for and the standards for which he died.
5. Lastly, no follower of Christ would make a threat of violence. No follower of Christ would harm a child of God. No follower of Christ would shed blood when Jesus shed enough for the world. Their motto should be "To protect and serve".

Go back and read Matthew, Mark and Luke when they spoke of the suffering that Jesus endured so that you would have eternal life. Then read 2nd Peter 1 and understand that these standards of a disciple are non-negotiable. Then understand that 1st Corinthians 13 was not written in passion as it was written in Christian spiritual love. If you are not living a lifestyle of Christian faith, belief and confidence in commitment then you are outside the will of God. Speaking of outside the will of God.

Stephanie Meyer, author of several books in a demonic vampire series, has become very successful in this world. She awoke one morning with dreams that seem to linger in her mind so the demons had her stay in bed all morning thinking, dreaming and conjuring up tales that turned into "*Twilight.*" The movie, "*Twilight*" released in November of 2008 and she said it grossed around $70 million. The base line of her story is vampire fascination, the attraction to the scent of blood and the taking of life in demonic pleasure. That is it! Blood, the taste for blood, the desire in different fleshly pleasures in taking ones blood and the daily romanticizing of how they are going to drink it next. The lead character in this product is Edward, a dashing young man who gives the impression of perfection. Yes, this is the image that all the girls want in a dashing young prince, a perfect man that says the right things and does the right things, always a gentleman and always gentle while curiously wanting more than the physical sense. He wants their soul and consumes the dreams of the darkest hours while being created by a stay at home mom of her three young boys. I wonder what the three boys were doing while Satan talked her into lying in bed with him and conjuring up details of demonic pleasures. I also wonder how proud she will be when one of her boys turns teenager, paints his fingernails black, blacks out his eyelids, powders his skin pale, dresses in black and begins to sacrifice the neighborhood pets. Then he becomes deeper involved in satanic rituals of burning candles in demonic patterns and worships satanic figures like Bael—Head of the infernal armies of the 66 legions, Abigar—demon of 60 legions, Leonard—demon in sorcery-black magic, Pyro—prince of falsehood-lies, Adramelec—arch demon king of fire, Zepar—grand duke appears as soldier which commands 26 legions, Hecate—queen of the witches, Shax—duke of hell commanding 30 legions and so on. These legions are bands of demons recruited into his world and the numbers are staggering. And where did we begin? We began with what appeared to be innocent pleasures of the flesh, innocent games on a witchcraft board, innocent books of romance, innocent movies of sorcery and yes, innocent youthful games found at your local video game store that lead to deep dark areas of satanic cults. How many Edward's does your daughter dream of and what is she willing to do to have him? If you are too naive to believe then you have been warned and I will gladly move on.

People talk generally of Satan, his demonic acts and evil spirits but after my research, I am convinced Satan has become very savvy after these thousands of years of practice. He has progressed with generations and is always sharp as his forks. We think we can outsmart his temptation but he has been at it longer than we have and he is much better at the game. The truth is that most people didn't start off being rapist, they started as stalkers. Most people didn't start off with murder or manslaughter they began by killing the neighbor's dog or cat. Most people didn't begin with armed robbery they began by stealing a candy bar from the local store. Most people didn't get hooked on drugs until they smoked their first joint or popped their first pill. Most people didn't become obsessed with Internet porn until they began with nude magazines. Most people didn't get hooked on casinos or web gambling until they began with a scratch ticket. The subtle temptation is that the smaller act felt good so the next big thing should feel even better. It is mental intoxication!

That next ticket could be your jackpot!!! How many of you play the lotto? It's not like it's gambling, right? It is for the school children, right? The money goes to benefit the schools, help with their curriculum, buys books, furnishes pencils, buys paper, and so on. Right? Then why do we need an Education Czar to help bail them out? Why are teachers some of the lowest paid professionals on the planet? Why are schools struggling to provide so many school items that you still have to shop retail stores for "Back to School Specials?" Why are classrooms still so very crowded? Why are schools around the world still not able to provide security for the ones who are not practicing satanic rituals or members of a gang? Why do taxpayers still pay school taxes?

How much money have you spent on lotto tickets, scratch off tickets, power ball, and all the gimmicks the state has laid out? Most people who play spend about $25 a week on all the toys; power ball, lotto, fantasy, mega money, play 4, cash 3, scratch tickets and on and on. If you play just $25 a week this is somewhere around an average of $1,300 to $1,500 a year. How did you do? Did you win? Bet if you added up all your investments you are so far in the hole you can barely see the light at the top. Maybe you are not doing it right. Most lotto's have a web site for education and training on how to play. This is like spending money on training to win a black jack or Texas holdem card game. Don't be drawn into stupidity or be trained to be more stupid! You can't see the Light yet because the Light is not in a gambling hall or store full of lotto tickets. The Light is in your prayers and in the word of God.

I have many years of mistakes with money as well as wasted time. I can think of many times that I have made unwise investments, wasted money on stuff that withered away or memories that were not really worth remembering. Here is a thought that is well worth considering. I cannot think of a single instance, not a single moment, not a single penny ever wasted when God partnered in its purpose. Let's consider this again. Can you think of any investment or money that you have wasted on God? What about a donation that you made, was it wasted where no one benefited from your giving? I would be willing to say no, it was never a waste and this is a quality lesson learned as I shared it with our Pastor as well.

Sometimes Satan and his band of demons do stuff just to tick you off or take you out of your spirituality. Not long ago a guy who jogged and walked every day for exercise decided to change his route. He didn't know why, just changed his route on a whim. The park he jogged down was beautiful and he saw a canopy road that ran beside the asylum. Flowerbeds of blooming roses and lilies lined the curb. Towering oak trees lined the street and could be more attractive for a jog. He turned the corner on a sidewalk along side of a long wood privacy fence and he began to hear; 13-13-13 . . . As he slowed his jog the sound became louder from behind the fence, 13-13-13 . . . He notice a small knot hole in the middle of the fence so he walked up, bent over and peaked through the fence when all of the sudden somebody poked him in the eye. He jumped back and hollered, aaggghh, why'd you do that? Then he heard in a louder voice; 14-14-14 . . .

Sometimes the reasons are "just cause" and have no bearing on your life other than to disturb it. If Satan can take you out of your worship, he will. If Satan can take you out of your family time, he will. If Satan can take you away from your Bible study, he will. If Satan can take you away from God's will, he will.

Another demonic act that everyone who drives on the public highways and byways has experienced is the racecar driver that runs up behind you, drafting you like Tony Stewart at Daytona International Speedway. You have a line of cars in front of you and nowhere to go, but speed racer wants you to move so he can be in front of you. So what do you do?

A. Do you tap your brakes and wave him off?

B. Do you take your foot off the gas, slow and show him the finger equaling his IQ?

C. Do you slam on your brakes just quick enough to make him kiss his steering wheel?

D. Do you choose the Christian way? Drive safely, obey the rules and ignore the evil distraction while keeping Satan behind you.

I like **D.**, the Christian practice is the right choice. By the way, singing always makes me feel better about Satan staying behind me, out of my direct vision. Also, gospel songs tend to blind Satan and really annoy his sense of direction . . . When Satan does finally get an opportunity to pass, make sure you smile and simply say "*God Bless*" as he passes on by. A lost soul will have no idea but it might get them to asking what that means and it will create a great opportunity for you to witness to the demon driver from hell.

A painful example of demons is one from my own home. My granddaughter was 4 and she is the sweetest child in the globe. As a matter of fact I believe she is probably the best child in the universe besides the younger of the two who is one and a half. You probably have sweet children as well but we are not writing about yours so we will allow mine to be the best for this story. One day while in my office the four year old came in playing with a toy stethoscope. She, of course, was wearing the earpieces properly in her ears and could not hear an airplane landing in the yard much less me sitting six feet away from her. In a split moment or a demonic second she decided the piece that should be gently placed over your heart should be scratched back and forth across the wooden case behind me. Seeing the demonic moment and recognizing the misuse of medical equipment like a professional would, I calmly asked her to stop. When the fourth request went ignored I calmly popped the demon on the behind and it immediately left her. Now here is the problem. When I leaned over and popped her on the her left cheek of her behind, that must have been where the demon was hiding inside her cause she turned with a sheer shock on her face and hollered, "Papa!" Then she got me with big tears that filled her eyes. Now what I did not understand is that I thought I would have been heralded as the new hero in her life for striking the demon that had her held hostage but NO! I received no thank you, no little hugs and no sign of any appreciation for quick thinking or quick reactions. Instead, she ran to her Nana and told her that I spanked her for no reason. Here again to illustrate the craftiness and centuries of experience that Satan has. Sometimes a Crusader must be satisfied with no appreciation for their work and move on to slay another demon on another day. That is what I did and I went back to my work.

Who are demons and where do they come from? How can you identify a demon? Some demons are deadly and are seriously secured into the darkest side of our lives. In 2009 the extreme was with 5 people who were burned alive in a ditch in Kisii Kenya for being accused of witchcraft. The incident was video taped and placed on the Internet. Four women and one man burned alive until dead while a crowd stood and watched. They were burned one at a time to draw the drama out. Kicked apart to separate the burned victims and to aggravate the extreme pain that comes with being burned alive. Were they demons or were the demons the ones who lit the match? No one is sure because like the persecution of Jesus they were not permitted due process of the law. Satan was victorious that day.

Some demonic acts are considered witchery. Witchcraft was common in the medieval times and common folk did not understand the crafted powers so they burned them to make sure they did not return. Think of the ignorance of those days as they compare to what we know today. A person with epilepsy and turret syndrome of today would have been tortured and burned at the stake in those days. Some demonic burns were with green wood so it slowed the burn down and prolonged the death. Suffering is man made and some cultures are real good at it. January 2009 a woman was striped down nude, tied to a stake, petrol was poured on her and they lit her up in Papua New Guinea. She was about 19 years old and was gagged so she could not cry for help. She was using spiritual chants and prayers to try and cure the widespread epidemic of aides across the area. Was this demonic spirits at work or a Pentecostal moment of prayer? No one knows because she was not offered due process of the law.

The point is that we are not in medieval times and there is the same evil existing today as there was over a hundred and thousands of years ago. The same demonic acts, hate, corrupt and stupidity that runs wildly among us now was evident then. What have we learned over these thousands of years? How do you draw your Sword on these people?

Santeria is a very powerful form of witchcraft and demonic spiritual behavior and is alive today. This faithful following makes it a habit of sacrificing pigeons, goats, birds, and domestic pets. If your neighborhood animals begin to disappear then you better begin looking for this group to appear. Serena Martin killed a Sayville High School cheerleader, Charity Miranda in a ritualistic ceremony. Santeria originated with the West African slaves who were brought to Cuba to work the sugar plantations. This religious cult following is sometimes called Santeros or Saints. The god of worship and their form of worship has evolved and changed over the years as well as the dance and singing involved. When Catholics tried to convert the faithful followers they adopted several Catholic saints as statues and idols of worship. It can be understood as an example of faux-Catholicism.

On August 7, 2007 Soho high school principle was removed from her job for allegations of Santeria ritual acts that included white robes, elephant plant leaves, candles, live chickens, a knife and the sprinkling of their blood on the floor. She was said to have used the rituals to quote "calm the students down". The New York City School District had her under investigation for some time before her removal. I was thinking that if they had drawn their Sword they could have avoided the entire fiasco! Prayer in school always calmed my spirit.

The calling of spirits, ghost story telling and the search for the afterlife is an age-old interest. You would think that we have enough to worry about in this life to think about looking to the other side. A group that calls themselves "AMC" (Afterlife Media Communication) say they talk to the spirit world and even have a question and answer section to document their communication. They sell ghost-detecting stuff to make detection easier. They also dabble in the demon world as they claim that the demons do not like being asked direct questions. Their method of gaining demonic and spiritual knowledge is to ask demons to email them and then they post the responses on their web site. In one alleged "demon's email" he states, "that they are not servants, companions, benefactors or playthings. Do not attempt to contact, summon or otherwise force our emergence or containment in your world. Please use your organization to warn others." This demon dude sounded firm all the way up until he threw the "please" word out there. First of all I am leery of a demon that sends email messages with a valid return email address and secondly I don't think that a demonic force would utter the word "please" for anything. Why make a good threat and then end it with please? That would be like walking into a gay nightclub with a t-shirt that said, "Kiss me, I'm a redneck." It just doesn't make sense!

Some of these ghost buster, spirit chasers and students of ghost whispering are seriously into speaking with and identifying who these paranormals are. They have tools to use to detect, record and deter ghosts. Some have called on priests to exercise homes or businesses and rid it of evil spirits. Some have created simple remedies for ghost removal like; placing a mirror in the room where the ghost frequents so it will see itself and get scared then leave. Or placing a pair of shoes on the floor with one facing one direction and the other facing the opposite direction. Guess this confuses the ghost and they don't know which way is out. Or maybe you could set up a video camera and record the ghost floating across the room. There are also prayer cards that you can get to recite prayers that scare off ghosts and evil spirits. Or you could get an electro magnetic field meter so you can detect evil spirits whenever you feel the need. Or you could just begin having Bible studies and understand God's word and know that when you die you immediately are passed into paradise or Hades. The ghost you are seeking is not Aunt Darlene that died in her bed and won't leave. You are playing with demonic spirits that are keeping you from God's word and His work.

What about the physics, mediums and communicators of the dead? Are they demonic? If they are speaking to spirits that they cannot see or feel and these spirits are showing them signs with 78 tarot cards, ouija boards, wands, and/or other tools, then yes they would qualify for either the wizard or witch categories of medieval times. Here is a clause of the typical psychic question; "are you psychic?" Look for the underlined words that should really say, "beware of Satan's signature".

"We are All psychic . . . it is our birthright, an innate protective mechanism . . . an inner radar designed to forewarn us of danger. But for eons, being psychic has also been considered wicked, the devil's work, fearful . . . and so the natural ability that exists within every human being to read energy and sense the subtle signals has withered away to almost nothing. Still, we are capable of knowing and being so much more and our universe is so much larger than the geography and astronomy teachers lead us to believe. Being psychic enables us to tap into that larger universe, for a lot of good reasons. Being psychic can save your life—or at least your pocketbook, and all it takes is a willingness to look a little deeper into life, get grounded and to reach for a little more."

The psychic network says you must dream more, want more and be grounded to this world in order to be connected to things beyond in this world. This is the single most important factor in separating the demonic people from Christianity. Demons want you to be connected to this world and the deceased. Christians are connected to eternity by God's grace, the life of Jesus and the inspiration of the Holy Spirit. But in order to understand what you are up against you need to know who you are dealing with. Revelation Chapter nine informs us of those who do not repent will rebel.

The Freedom From Religion Foundation is a fully operational faith based group out of Madison, Wisconsin. They are the faithful followers of Satan, atheistic values and a movement to get people to see their moral view of the world rather than a spiritual appointment. Its foundation uses the religious angle for federal tax reliefs and bases itself as non-profit but is a national membership organizaton that solicits donations for their movement. They have taken "Freedom OF Religion" and twisted the words to mean what they want rather than what it was written for. They claim donation use as the church does in mission work and spreading the word of non-biblical relief from ones conscious spiritual decisions. Dan Barker is a converted minister and evangelist who is now the co-president and main line voice of the foundation. Annie Laurie Gaylor is the other co-president. She is a author and journalist with obvious little value in biblical knowledge or awareness. I can find no business or leadershp qualities in either of these two presidents who share the chair much like a husband and wife or king and queen or god and goddess. Remember that in ancient days people found it easier to follow a god if there was a female god that accompanied the male god. This way they represented and spoke to both groups of diversity. Rebecca S. Kratz is the foundations attorney. Now I find this interesting. The church does hire or retain the protection of an attorney, not that Satan needs one. If the foundation is legitimate, the organization is operating within the boundaries of the law and these are people of integrity, then why do they need an attorney? Their web site is ffrf.org and their supporting staff mounts many degree's, accomplishments, memberships of feminist movements and one even has a black cat named Lucky. It all sounds much like a script for the next Halloween movie.

It is not how much you know about the Bible it is how
well you know what you know.

When Americans wonder where all the grief comes from in saying Merry Christmas, placing Christmas displays on public property, prayers in government meetings, organized church meetings in a public school, prayer in school, saying the pledge of allegance, playing of religious music, playing Christmas songs, displaying the U.S. flag, handing religious literature in public places, religious activities in senior centers, including God in official oaths, businesses offering discounts for church bullitins, or other religious rights that have been observed since the settlers came upon the American shores, you can look find some of these fine folks at the Godless foundation. You can go on FFRF web site and be informed, buy stuff and read the fine print that says their information is simply for informational purposes and not intended to be treated as a legal notice. This is obviously a note from Miss Kratz. I say "Miss" because marriage is the only accomplishment that she did not mention. I also find it interesting that one example the foundation chose to use for a kind donation contributor was one who gave his entire stimulas check of $600 to the foundation. It was his to give, it's purpose is to stimulate jobs and no matter if it did come from tax payer money, he certainly has the right to waste his money on whatever unworthy cause he may choose to serve. Note that any funds the foundation receives may be used to market material such as recently seen on buses and billboards stating that there is no God. A recent Seattle billboard had Santa smiling as if to say, "Yes Virginia, There is no God." I am also sure that Ron Reagan, son of the great President Ronald Reagan made daddy proud by being one of the headliners in the November 6-8, 2009 32nd Annual National FFRF Convention in Seattle Washington. Each one will be judge by God for life's deeds so I truly wish these folks well on their journey for every one they win to their side of the choices we make will be a feather lost on their wings.

The New Age Movement origin dates back to at least to 1875 with the theosophical teachings of Helena Petrovna Blavatsky, and later in the 1920's with the teachings of Alice Ann Bailey. They emphasized heavily the evolution of a self-deified; master Aryan society, and a one world "new age" religion and social order. Today, the New Age Movement looks to be an innocent organization with ambiguous goals or leadership. But beneath the surface there is a definite, secret leadership that is organized and with a strategy that guides the vast movement. The main body of leadership resides in an organization called "The Planetary Initiative for the World We Choose." Here is what my research revealed in their belief and what their strategies represent:

New world order
Universal credit card system
World food authority

World Health authority
World water authority
Universal tax
Universal military draft
Removal of Christianity, Judaism & Islam
One world leader

Take a close look at this group's teachings, plans and goals; many expert political scientists agree that the New Age Movement parallels the ideals and philosophy of Nazism of the 1930's and 1940's. New Age writings claim that leaders such as Adolph Hitler and Jim Jones were models to be compared with. Ya think???

Think of this group when you are studying the Book of Revelation. John was very specific in detailing the events of the apocalypse and these strategies match up with pretty strong evidence. These thoughts and philosophies also compare with some of the 2009 US administrations mission. Satan is in the very center of Socialism and it no doubt leads to communism. Socialism and communism destroy free enterprise and free worship. This is the reason why it pained me to see Barack Obama enter into the Presidency. News correspondent George Stephanopoulos questioned him and George asked him what his religious belief was and Barack answered, "**Moslem**." Straight out and without hesitation! George took a second to catch his breath then corrected Barack by saying, "Christian" and Barack agreed. What a classic moment for a professional interviewer to have a subject take you off guard. You see, if something is strong in your heart, it will come out of your mouth as natural as saying your name. Social and communistic values begin with increased government and martial law. Marx and Stalin were as demon possessed as Hitler was. Extreme Moslems in Islamic jihad call for the destruction of Israel and America. Does the voting public think this is a game?

Today's world is filled with demonic games, warlocks and teleports of demonic circles. Let the world know that this is not a game, it is not a contest of wisdom, it is not a world of cartoon figures, it is not an innocent world wide web; it is Satan's playhouse and his world of temptation into his circle of no return. The phrase "warlock" was used in the TV series "Bewitched". It was a comical character that has become a cult term for male witch or male demon. In medieval times the warlock was the male deceiver or liar while the females were witches who conjured up potions and curses. In today's games Satan uses warlock as a path to a much deeper world, the world of satanic ritualism. If you are playing these games you are being drawn into his cult society. If you feel the desire to discard the thought or battle it, go ahead, that's exactly what he would want you to do.

A fine example of one who walks in darkness is Bill Maher, known as a mediocre comedian and talk show host that is only worthy of cable TV. This is the only way his vulgarity would be permitted. Maher had a film out called "religulous" and in the movie he interviews people, most at random but the theme is to question what people know about their own religion. Bill claims to preach the religion of "I don't know". He takes a few jabs like, "the talking snake in the garden", "your God", interviews folks at the "holy land amusement park", and makes quick cracks at the Bibles teaching. But there was one thing I discovered that became very real to me as I studied this. Bill shows obvious signs that he has never really read the Bible. He may have read pieces, went through the motions in Catholic Church with his mom but it is obvious that he was lost all along the way. In his interviews and on his cable programs he is confused with stories, names, places and meanings. His theme is to make people laugh but generally when you make a movie or write a book you at least study the material you are speaking of. Bill was raised Catholic and was very relieved to have left the church but he is much more concerned with getting a laugh here than learning his fate in the afterlife. He believes that Jesus was just another man like him and probably because he met a man called Jesus in Miami that has a following of people who believe he is Jesus. This guy in Miami brands people with tattoos numbering 666. I don't question that he is out of his gourd but how can you have that many faithful followers of a gourd? And willing to have the mark of the beast tattooed on their body! Bill says a lot of people are on to this scam. Bill is brilliant! Bill says all De Jesus is preaching is doubt. So Bill recognizes people who do not know their subject matter? Did Bill recognize that De Jesus was branding his faithful following with the mark of Satan, not Jesus? Come on Bill study your target! But hey, Bill has his opinion and this great country offers him that right to tell his story just like I am offered the same opportunity here. Bill says he made a movie for the other people and to make people laugh. On Jimmy Kimmel Live, Bill called Sarah Palin a category 5 moron. I wondered who made Bill the authority on morons. I also am wondering what categories one through four are. Is there a higher level than five? If Sarah were a category five where would he be? Would I rank as high as Sarah? But typically people of low self-esteem and who struggle with their identity stoop down to name-calling. Children do this when they feel inferior or struggle in their identity. People with child like mentalities feel this need to rant so go ahead Bill, after all your hard work you deserve a good rant. When inferior people rant they also feel the need to curse. If the shoe fits . . .

There is also an additional thought here and that is that many talk shows in Hollywood helped to promote Bill's satanic work. Bill's work was revealed and promoted by Leno, Letterman, Kimmel and others. Was there a guest invited for a counterpoint? Nope! I believe this is what the left is trying to accomplish through the FCC. They are trying to sensor all talk shows, mainly speaking of right wing radio shows, to make sure if they make a right wing point they would also have a left wing counter point. So if Bill is allowed a satanic point or work that was inspired by Satan then God should have an opportunity at a counter point. I would think that Ravi Zechariah would have made a very good counter point and should have been on these talk shows to illustrate the Biblical answers for Bill's burning questions. If you want the truth then go to a qualified source.

The real problem here is the average listener or person is not a theology expert and when you have an entertainer that challenges the common person's knowledge of the Bible then you end up with confusion. Not to mention that there is a huge difference between being religious and Christian. People need to know what they believe and why they believe it. They need to know how to look up and research for answers. If Bill sincerely wanted to ask questions of the library that is between the covers of the Bible then he would go to experts who could explain it and support it with facts. But then that wouldn't be as funny now would it?

But Bill, who is an obvious agnostic thinker, believer and doer selected the most popular thing in the world to do a movie on and that is ignorance of God's word. His ignorance of biblical truths and faith is not funny, it is sad. But also it runs much deeper than you think. Bill did this for the money and the intent is the foundation of greed, which is the center of earthly wants. Worldly desires and wants are what keep you grounded to this world. According to www.quotqationspage.com, here are some famous last words of a few fools about greed:

* ✘ Edgar Allan Poe—"All religion, my friend, is simply evolved out of fraud, fear, greed, imagination, and poetry."
* ✘ Friedrich Engels—"From the first day to this, sheer greed was the driving spirit of civilization."
* ✘ Erich Fromm—"Greed is a bottomless pit which exhausts the person in an endless effort to satisfy the need without ever reaching satisfaction."
* ✘ Michael Fox—"I don't think that fundamentalism has anything to do with Jesus Christ. They call themselves Christians, but if that's Christian, count me out. Fundamentalism is built on fear and greed. They're telling you to give them your money otherwise you're going to hell."
* ✘ Frank Lloyd Wright—"New York City is a great monument to the power of money and greed . . . a race for rent."
* ✘ Sandy Duncan—"we've been raised to compete, to want more! More! More! It's a way of life. It's about greed."

I was also amused at the comments made by Sharon Osbourne about Sarah Palin. Sharon has been on many different talk shows and documented in her comments in fields outside of her own expertise. But what is her expertise? She was married to a drunken rocker that was so consumed with drugs that he has all but completely fried his brains. Sharon was heralded on her ability to hold her family together during her reality shows, "The Osbournes" but what I saw was a sad reality of a wife who acted more as a mother to her mentally challenged husband and a mother who had no control over her children. Jack has tried his attempts at suicide from an obvious dysfunctional childhood and Kelly has been in/out of rehab several times from a long drug addiction to painkillers. With a family fortune and record deals, what sort of pain could you experience other than inflamed family pains. This was ever so obvious in the Osbournes living room because they invited the film crews into their home to witness the sad state of what a Godless family looks like. When you place your life and inside your home on public display then you are a fool to show just how dysfunctional you really are. What example are we truly trying to communicate? Boy, my life doesn't suck like I thought it did—just look at them! But she as appeared as a <u>judge</u> in talent contests when she has no talent and she is relying on living with Ozzy as her expertise. Her standard response to poor talent is, Sweetie, I just love you, then she makes a heart using her hands. Awe . . . Sharon was overly dramatic in bad acting as she took stabs at Sarah Palin in her candidacy for Vice-President. What I thought was entertaining was just the fact that major networks paid her for her opinion on what it takes to become skilled and educated in professional leadership when she has no skill, no expertise in leadership, no ethics and little class. Her embarrassing state of conduct was recorded on the public TV's reality show X-Factor as she all but performed a lap dance on Simon Cowell. Sharon Osborne is a very good example of someone who has no amount of experience and sets a poor example to be giving any comments on someone else. At age eighteen Sharon began her managerial roll for Ozzy and he is the result of her fine leadership abilities. He is now a walking vegetable and she enjoys over $100 million in residual wealth. Congratulations Sharon, you should be very proud of your deeds. But here is my real point: God will forgive every single sin and forget them all if she would just give her life to Christ. Then her life, like mine, becomes a living testimony for others. God's word becomes alive when we speak His name. Sharon, like many today, is living in risk of losing her eternal soul.

When we live a lie, we risk losing our lives . . .

Greed and envy sets the centerpiece to most disasters, divorces, bankruptcies, suicides and failures. We live in a material world and keeping up with the Jones has never been more evident and real. Maher is a great example of mockery and an attempt at creating doubt. I hate to burst Bill's bubble but he isn't the first to try this and he will certainly not be the last.

There is several greed filled men who have at one time held the top of the list for the richest criminals of all time. Pablo Emilio Escobar was the head of one of the largest drug cartels in the globe and gathered a wealth of about $9 billion in US dollar value. He had mansion estates, submarines, planes, and cars in his own empire in Columbia. Carlos Lehder was a co-founder of the Medellin Cartel along with Pablo and his net worth was around 2.7 billion. Susumu Ishii was head of the Japan underworld in the 80's and his wealth grew to about $1.5 billion. Anthony Salerno, also known as "Fat Tony", was the crime boss of the Genovese family and he worked his way up through the ranks to grow an estimated net worth of $600 million. Meyer Lansky was a Russian immigrant and grew in strength as a gambling operator in Florida and Cuba. He began making and laundering so much money that he had to build his own offshore bank in Switzerland to house around $400 million and change. But that was all before the king of Wall Street crime arrived on scene. Bernie Madoff made off with almost $65 billion in fabricated gains and $18 billion in actual losses to his clients. His Ponzi scheme landed him 11 felonies and 150 years in prison. But you can get just as grounded to this world as these men, maybe not as much money but with just as much greed.

Are you as grounded to this world as these men were? Remember, it is not just the act but what is in your heart. There is a simple survey that you can do and to give to those you know as well to determine if you are grounded to this world or if you have desires of eternal life in heaven. Take a clean piece of paper and a good pen. Make a prayer request by writing down all thoughts in prayer that you would want God to bless, resolve or answer. Whatever you can think of that you see is important to you, write it down. Fold your survey responses and place the paper between these two pages. We will discuss it later in the book.

The desire is to write off these warning signs as no big deal. The common saying is that you are reading too much into mans ability to bring you down unless you want to be there. There is power in demonistic practices and they come in many forms. To survive and live to tell is to know and walk in the armor of God's word. To understand divine swordsmanship you must understand your advesary and how very effective he is. Now, let's learn more of the Sword and God's word.

The Writers of the Sword

The Bible is a collection of books or letters scribed by either a Prophet or Apostle who was selected by God to write His book. Again, keep it that simple because it really is. God's word and His chosen men scribed the literature that we follow, to the letter. Your Bible is your spiritual guide to any moment or breath in your life. If someone challenges you or is unsure or has a question then your Bible is the sword you should draw before ever forming an opinion. Let God speak to them. He is the expert and He wrote it.

The honorable name "**Disciple**" in the New Testament was used to identify the original twelve men that Jesus selected along with those chosen while he taught. They were directed by Jesus to follow, listen, learn and teach. I believe to be an Apostle you had to be appointed by Jesus and received specific instructions and trusted with His word, His message and His mission. These men have provided us with all the tools and resources necessary to speak to others and win souls for Christ.

Your Sword & Prayer is always the first place to begin your journey. This is a good place to begin in understanding:

> What are true family values?
> How to get involved with mission work?
> How to keep the faith fresh?
> How to protect yourself from temptation?
> How to overcome a drug addiction?
> How to drop a tobacco habit?
> How to stop an alcohol dependency?
> How to repair a broken home?
> How to find your life partner?
> How to overcome grief?
> How to cope with loneliness?
> How to earn employment?
> When to know if you are ready for marriage?
> How to understand prayer discipline?
> How to prepare for law school?
> How to land that great career?
> Who your friends really are?
> How a Christian has fun?
> How to avoid temptation?
> If you are once saved are you saved always?
> Can a woman minister in church?
> What does the Bible say about homosexuality?

Is an interracial relationship against God's plan?
What truly happens after death?
What does God think of tattoos or body piercing?
Is baptism required in order for me to be saved?
Is it okay to have sex before marriage?
What does the Bible say about divorce and remarriage?
If you commit suicide, can you still go to heaven?

The Bible answers all of life's questions and I will do my best to provide scriptures to the most questions asked. But that will be later in the book and my main focus is to encourage you to draw your Sword, open the word of God and read **His** answer to your every question. Again, do not bend His words to fit your lifestyle. Conform your lifestyle to His word and be obedient. Do you have to live like a monk to be a Christian? No, monks do not follow the teachings of Jesus Christ . . . Christians open His word, read, listen, learn, and do.

The Sword is the word of God scribed by his chosen apostles and prophets that laid out His plan according to what He wants. People have always tried to take a piece of His word or a part of a scripture or ignore some scripture so it can be molded and formed to fit the lifestyle they want to have. Sorry, it doesn't work that way and if you were completely honest you would admit to this truth! When you are completely in His word you are safely in His hands. When you begin to pick and choose then you step off the holy path onto a path with many holes . . . To be made whole, you must live holy . . .

The divine word and direction comes from God, the one who created us. Leave your *wants* behind and follow Him. Your worldly wants and desires will change from this world to **His**. Where do angels come from? In the word and in His works you become an angelic to those in need. Angels give and serve. We are not angels yet they are a great example of our direction. Those who crafted the Sword of God carried it with honor. Understand that this honor comes with challenges and his name is Satan. Understand that Satan was cast out for thinking he was more powerful than God. And to my Mormon friends, this occurred long before the birth of Jesus. We'll also dig deeper into this topic . . .

Know that this book is my word and my discipleships mission is to bring the awareness to you. This world is against God, and the measures used today by Satan move you into Christian commission to tell your story or your testimony to others. Jesus warned us if they are against us that they were against Him first. I feel honored that they are against me, criticize my work for Christ and in my faith in God. It's called temptation and causes my desire to strike back. Divine Swordsmanship is an honor to support, defend, and speak the word of God. Knowing Him will prepare you daily for demonic temptation. Get ready to draw your Sword but there is a very important part of God that we need before we begin our training . . .

Prayer is power, prayer is a partnership and prayer is our bond with Jesus Christ. Let nothing impede your prayer . . .

Sword Training

Before you draw your Sword and open it to receive God's word, always pray. A simple prayer like this:

"Gracious heavenly Father, thank you for your blessings. Thank you Father for your gift of grace. Bless me today while I read your word that you may speak to me with understanding and knowledge. I open my heart as well as my mind as I receive your word today.
For all things I pray and praise your holy name,
in Jesus name, Amen."

Prayer connects you with our Father and opens the path of understanding as well as knowing. The Bible contains our historical documentation of the facts to support our belief system. It is God's word. It was scribed as a tool to understand the path from the very beginning and until Jesus returns. Each book, chapter and verse is a living guide through life whether it be the 1st Century or the 21st Century, it all applies. The words of God flow like the living breathing waters in a river.

Bible training consists of several best practices to read, understand, learn and grow. There are many ways that you learn and the Bible contractors have created different ways for you to hear the text, feel it, see it or read it. Before we get to the first study concept, I believe we must be good stewards of the time that we allot to pray to God, to study His word and honor Him in worship. Sunday is already His day and each day you should take time to open the gospel then breathe the word of God. There are several very good daily devotional guides that assist you with your study habits and ensure you spend quality time with God. He is the most important part of your daily planner.

Quality time management is part of many lesson plans created and followed by big corporate human resource and training departments. Time is our most precious commodity and it is the one most wasted. I have instructed many quality time management courses for several years in retail operations, retail merchandising and retail asset protection. I break skilled time ownership into seven separate pieces.

1. Time to train—to learn new skills and/or lesson plans.
2. Time to define quality skills and resources—then reach out and develop them.
3. Time to learn quality communication skills—learn to tell & teach.
4. Time to sharpen quality leadership skills—learn to direct with quality results.
5. Time to experience your role and focus on COEs (corrections of errors).
6. Time to improve in self-development skills—educate yourself to improve.
7. Time to mentor and serve others—pull someone else up with you.

Now, how much time do you have to study, to learn, to develop and to grow? You have the amount of time that God has offered you and today is a great day to dig in. The desire for daily devotion is a sign that you are on the right path. No desire—no confidence in your heavenly destination . . .

Now let us continue to open His word and worship. You should have a high belief that being a witness for Christ and soul winning is the greatest honor of a Christian. Understanding this helps with the way you learn and assists you with why you learn. Every day challenges are the strengths to skill building and the more you talk about God's word the more comfortable you become in it. Your understanding of these scriptures will help you in your beginning. Mark the page number in your Bible as you read these scriptures.

Genesis 1:1 _____

Psalm 139:13 _____

Luke 12:5 _____

John 1:12 _____

John 3:16 _____

John 3:36 _____

John 10:10 _____

John 14:6 _____

John 20: 30-31 _____

1st John 4:10 _____

Then understand God's plan for you and for you to tell others:

1st John 1:8-9 _____

Acts 3:19 _____

Acts 16:31 _____

Acts 20:21 _____

Romans 8:9 _____

Romans 10:9-10 _____

Romans 10:13 _____

Stop . . . Make sure you have read each of these verses several times before proceeding. Yes, it is that important and will help you to draw your Sword correctly. These are just a few scriptures to help secure an understanding of God's will and His word. There are many more but these will give you firm footing.

One solid lesson that I learned while studying is that there are always going to be questions or uncertainties in life that will put one in the dark. The Bible and God's word will answer those questions for you because Jesus Christ is the Light that will walk you out of darkness. This is my personal testimony to you and you can test it if you like. Walk into a completely dark room and flip on the light. Yep, no darkness is allowed when the Light shines brightly.

Proper Sword Training is through study and understanding. Like, beginning with the Book of John before reading the book of Exodus. Reading the Book of Genesis before reading the Book of Matthew. You could try to study on your own but a more affective way is to attend a Sunday school class with a support group that studies. Why? Because in worship service you are not typically going to stand up and say, "Hey preacher, I don't get it!" You could and it would be interesting and may even be captured on video for a "best of" highlight reel but would certainly be a "different" moment for Church. But seriously, Sunday school isn't just for the little kids; it is for us big kids too. It is a smaller focused group that reads Bible scriptures, has a lesson plan and helps to explain the meaning of God's word. The great thing about it is that if a leader in the class cannot answer the question then there is normally an experienced Pastor, associate Pastor or educator that can help. I think a great idea that our church does is that the Sunday school class topics parallel what the pastor teaches in the pulpit. This offers the class discussion time on the topic. The pastor should meet with the teachers occasionally to do a "deep dive" into the understanding that his people are having.

Is it important to learn more about the writer of each book and in which era the book was written? What else was going on in that area of the world when the writer sat to write? Look at each letter/book as an investigative reporter. Pull out who were the eyewitnesses? Who were the main people that made an impact? What level of faith and belief did it take for them to follow God? Answer these questions for yourself as you read the holy word of God.

The Bible is a collection of 66 books, scribed 2000+ years ago, by more than 40 writers. The center of the Bible is Psalms 118, which tells us that God must be the center of our life. The center of the center tells us to trust in our Lord. The King James Version counts the Lord's Prayer as 66 words. The Holy Bible is translated from a language that is difficult to understand, it contains different writing styles, it is not in chronological order and contains a bunch of wherevers, whosoevers, begats, thouests, and so on . . . If you are like me and didn't study well in school then this is really a challenge. If you studied well in school then forget it because you will need a different set of study habits for these translations. Did you like history? How about geography? Or, what about English as a primary interest? Or, what about Americanism verses communism? These subjects are very important to our study of things past, things happening now and the things to come. They are all scribed in the collection of letters written by Prophets and Apostles that were sheepherders and fishermen. God personally chose each prophet because of his belief and his integrity. It took God's divine Holy Spirit with Jesus Christ to grace these words. Once John finished Revelation it was finished. Any book that seeks compatibility or spiritual comparability will be held in contempt in the highest court. You will not want to argue in that courtroom so choose wisely my friend what you buy into.

Have you ever had a morning that you were going to church and something happened that morning that upset you enough that it interfered with you enjoying the message that day? Maybe it was the hair dryer went out. Maybe you didn't sleep well the night before. Or maybe it was a zipper or a shoestring breaking. What about your drive to church? A little argument in the car on the way or someone pulling out in front of you or was driving in front of you 20 miles an hour in a fifty-five! Or maybe the disturbance didn't happen until the pastor started preaching. Like the kid behind you kicking the back of your seat. Or it may have been the lady behind you that was singing off every key in the hymnal. It could have been the two gallons of Brut the guy was wearing in front of you that made your eyes water. Or any number of disturbances in the force!

Yes, little things that would be just evil enough to twist your spiritual focus. These things can happen when you sit to study. A phone call right in the middle of reading your Bible that irritated you would do it. You may have a number of interruptions that occur with growing frequency. Some may believe these are simple coincidences but I firmly believe these are intentional interruptions by Satan and his band of demons. It could be your spouse that makes that one little comment that begins a debate in the car. Men, I will warn you now . . . Never, ever turn to your wife and say, "get thee behind me Satan!" Not out loud anyway.

This is a great time to discuss your time with God. Never, ever allow anyone or anything to come between you and God. Time is the easiest thing to lose and there is precious little of it to afford to lose. Find a place of solitude and where you can concentrate while you study. Are you ready to memorize a verse or a collection of verses? How about a chapter? What about an entire book? Some do and have no problem committing them to memory. I have to make a grocery list before I go to the store or I'll forget the cereal! And sometimes I forget my list! I find more importance in learning where the books are located and how to look up scriptures that I need to answer a question. Memory of scripture is great! My method is more in the mode of research rather than memory. Find what suits your skill level and go with it. You will be blessed either way every time you open God's word.

Here is what I call: **"Planting God's P's"**

- ✓ Practice your Swordsmanship daily
- ✓ People are all sinners and need repentance
- ✓ Peace is in all Christians who have been saved
- ✓ Preach and teach His word as bondservants
- ✓ Positive people create positive solutions
- ✓ Power is behind His every word
- ✓ Place of worship and the mission field
- ✓ Prayer daily is our time with God
- ✓ Purity of His word in every page turned
- ✓ Planting the seeds of His word to anyone who will listen
- ✓ Praise His name daily
- ✓ Prepare through study & prayer
- ✓ Price Jesus paid for our sins and salvation
- ✓ Poor people don't need sympathy, they need encouragement
- ✓ Precious is the name of Jesus

✓ Perfection from His birth to death
✓ Promise of His return
✓ Possibilities are endless in His name
✓ Patience must be placed in God's hands

Use your Sword like a study workbook. Writing notes, underlining impact passages or marking a page for reference. Color pencils work well or a pen so it won't smudge when your fingers roll across the pages. I even use a quality highlighter in some cases but make sure your page quality is high so the ink doesn't bleed through the opposite page. Take your Bible everywhere you go. You just never know when God's word will inspire or comfort you in your day.

Select your study time so that it will be uninterrupted. Reading while the kids are building a fire in the living room is probably not a good time. Environment is very important. I live close to the beach so this is an important area for me to study. I can pause and reflect in God's word by looking at the beauty that He created. If I lived in a mountainous area, I would think this would paint an awesome backdrop for my study. Or maybe down by a quiet lakeshore. Try a park bench with doves around the area. (The dove is the creature that delivered the Olive branch to Noah in a beautiful story of faith and trust in God's word.) The environment that you study in will help determine the message you receive.

As you study, look for related passages and scriptures that compliment one another. There were different Prophets and Apostles that wrote about the same things and described the same incidents because they all were witnesses of God's grace and His divine wisdom. God's word never changes and He is incapable of error.

Use resource tools to help you understand and research God's word. In addition to my study Bibles I use a Bible dictionary, a concordance, pictures of the area I am studying (find them on the web), maps of the area you are studying (find them on the web) and look at 1st century clothing, styles, shoes, travel methods, communication venues and all sorts of tools to help me understand God's message. Then compare those times with today's current affairs. You will find all your answers if you pray before you begin and close your study with a thankful prayer of the time you shared with Him.

There is a story that is fitting here of a man named Jack who moved away from home, experienced the college scene, girls, marriage then had a son. He was into his career and played golf as well as poker on Wednesday nights with the boys. Jack had little time to think of the past as his life had become busy in the pursuit of his dreams. One day he received a call from his mom who lived several states away and in the conversation she told him that Mr. West had died the night before and the funeral was scheduled for Thursday. Wow, he hadn't thought of Mr. West in some time but his memories flashed of a childhood listening to Mr. West read him stories on his front porch as a boy and even after school as he grew older. Mr. West had a unique style of reading and Jack always enjoyed these times. "Jack?" his mom asked, "can you hear me okay?" And Jack said, "Yes, I'm sorry mom, I actually had thought he had died years ago." Jack's mom said, "Well, he never forgot about you. Every time I saw him he always asked how you were then he would ponder about the time you sat on his porch and listened to him read." Jack said, "I remember and I remember all those times he read to me and I just loved that old house he lived in." Jack's mom said, "You know Mr. West was a very good friend to us after your father died. I don't know what I would have done without his helping hand around here. He was a great father figure to me as well." Jack said, "Now that I think about it, I doubt I would own my own carpentry business if he hadn't spent all that time with me in his shop and showing me how to use quality tools. He spent a lot of time teaching me safety and that is a big deal in my business." Jack caught the next day's flight to his mom's home and on Wednesday evening before the funeral Jack and his mom stopped by Mr. West's house just one last time. When Jack walked up on the porch a tear ran down his cheek as he remembered sitting on the step listening to Mr. West read. They walked inside and Jack paused to remember every thing in the house as it was just as he remembered it as a young boy. Jack stopped suddenly and said with a commanding voice, "What happened to the box? It's gone. The box is not there." Jack's mom asked, "What box Jack?" Jack said, "The box! There was a small gold box on the top of his desk. It was right there! It was always right there!" Jack's mom was puzzled and said, "We'll I don't know dear, maybe some of the family may have taken it to remember him by." Jack said sadly, "I use to always ask him what was in that gold box and he would never show me. He said the same old thing all the time, "It's a secret Jack but it is my most valuable possession that I have." Jack walked to the door slowly and said, "I guess now I will never know. I wish we had just one more time together, maybe it would have been the right time." Jack and his mom attended Mr. West's funeral and Jack caught the afternoon flight back home. About two weeks later Jack arrived home late that evening as his usual and his wife said, "Jack there is a post office card on the table that came in the mail today." "What card?" he asked. "I'm not sure. I think you have to sign for it at the post office." She replied. The next day Jack went to work and on his lunch he stopped by the post office. He handed the clerk the signed card and she got the package and placed it on the counter. He picked it up and walked out to his truck then sat for a moment to look at the package. The address caught his attention. It was mailed from Mr. West's address. Jack sat in his truck and his hands began to shake as he opened the package. Inside was the small gold box he had remembered always sitting on the desk of Mr. West and an envelope beside it. Jack picked up the envelope and it read, "Upon my death, please forward to Jack Bennett. It is the most valued thing I have ever had in my life." A small gold key was taped to the envelope. Jack removed the key, his heart began to race and tears filled his eyes as he opened the small gold box. Inside the box he found a beautiful gold pocket watch. Jack removed it from the box, ran his fingers around the opening and opened the cover. Inside the cover he found an engraved message that read, "Jack, thank you for your time . . . Robert West." Jack sat solidly back in his seat and fell apart. The one thing that Mr. West valued more than anything in the world was just my time. Jack called the office immediately and told his assistant to clear all his appointments for the remainder of the week. His assistant was quite shocked and said, "Jack are you okay?" Jack replied, "Better than ever Nancy, I need time with my wife and son." As she began to hang up the phone Jack said, "Oh Nancy, and one more thing. I want to thank you for your time . . ."

The time you spend in the word of God is the most precious time you will ever spend in your lifetime. It will open your eyes to the most valued thing we have and that is our time doing the things that Jesus would have done. To love, to listen, to learn and to tell. Here are some names to take a spiritual look at. Just names to some but to those who believe they are sacred and the very breathe of these names is priceless:

Almighty God

Heavenly Father	**Holy Spirit**
Jesus Christ	**King**
Yahweh	**Lord**
Creator	**Abba**
Jehovah	**Ruler of All Things**
Shepherd	**Rock**
Prince of Peace	**Majesty**
The Lamb	**Redeemer**
Deliverer	**Savior**
Righteous One	**Messiah**
Sovereign Lord	**Glory of Israel**
Helper	**Judge**
Light	**Alpha and Omega**

GOD!

I believe there are over 70 names of **God** in Hebrew however these are most common to me. In my daily prayers I call Him Father, Lord, Holy Spirit and Jesus Christ for it is in these names I find peace from my blessed Redeemer. For those who choose to believe God is more than one or multiple deities or come in any other variation than ONE then simply draw your Sword!

"Thus says the Lord, King of Israel and His Redeemer, the Lord of hosts; I am the first and I am the last, And there is no God besides Me. Who is like Me? Let him proclaim and declare it; Yes, let him recount it to Me in order, From the time that I established the ancient nation, And let them declare to them the things that are coming, And the things that are going to take place."

Isaiah 44: 6-7

"I am the Lord, and there is no other; Besides Me there is no God, I will gird you; though you have not known Me; That men may know from the rising to the setting of the sun That there is no one besides Me. I am the Lord, and there is no other, The one forming light and creating darkness, Causing well-being and creating calamity; I am the Lord who does all these."

Isaiah 45: 5-7

"So they were saying to Him, "Where is Your Father?" Jesus answered, "You know neither Me nor My Father; if you knew Me, you would know My Father also."

John 8:19

"My Father, who has given them to Me, is greater than all; no one is able to snatch them out of the Father's hand, I and the Father are one."

John 10:29-30

Draw your Sword my friend and be very, very careful in who you seek to advise you of Biblical knowledge, wisdom and interpretation. Take time to read and listen to those chosen by God to deliver your small gold box of precious time. I spoke of these leaders in my last book, "*2012 Global Warning*" and they are worthy of mentioning again.

> Dr. Ted Traylor, OliveBaptist.org
> Dr. Charles F. Stanley at In Touch Ministries
> Dr. David Jeremiah at Turning Point Ministries
> Paul Earl Sheppard at Enduring Truth
> Jon Courson at Searchlight Ministry
> Tony Evans, Oak Cliff Bible Fellowship
> Chuck Swindoll at Insight for Living
> James MacDonald at Walk in the Word
> Dr. Chuck Missler at Koinonia House
> Ed Young Sr., 2nd Baptist Church Houston TX
> Ravi Zacharias International Ministries
> Joseph Prince International Ministries

Your Pastor or Associate Pastor would love for you to meet with them and ask for their guidance then validate what they say to your Bible.

Another historical icon in the ministry that is a good study for anyone learning the Bible, the Gospel of the New Testament and the way of the Light is Jonathan Edwards. Born on October 5, 1703, Jonathan was the son of Pastor Timothy Edwards in East Windsor Massachusetts. Jonathon attended Yale University and finished his masters in 1722, then ministered a few churches and married the long love of his life, Sarah. Forced to resign from one church for disagreement in communion, Jonathan was criticized by his firm belief in the doctrine and all of his writings spurred confidence in the Christian experience that you must be born and re-born in Christ to reach salvation. He was a passionate pastoral evangelist and spent all the energy of every fiber of his being to impress upon the minds and hearts of the people of the importance of complete repentance to God and the faithful service in the Lord Jesus Christ. There are several evangelicals around the globe that could take lessons from Jonathan Edwards and if he were alive today he would rock Houston Texas with the soundness of the Gospel and that God is oneness with no different persons. Reference God's Word in Isaiah 44, 45 and 46. Then study John 1:1-5 and then Jude 25. To the only God our Savior, through Jesus Christ our Lord . . . He is One.

A name to be heralded, as one of the late great Pastors is C.H. Spurgeon and his biography and sermons can be found on www.spurgeon.org. Charles Haddon Spurgeon was born in Kelvedon, Essex England on June 19, 1834 and was given his second birth date in January 1850. At the ripe old age of nineteen he was called to Pastor the New Park Street Chapel in Southwark London. Each Sunday Pastor Spurgeon spoke to a congregation from 6,000 to 10,000 people without the aid of a sound system. He also wrote a monthly magazine, founded a college for pastors, two orphanages, a retirement community, a colportage society and opened several missions. It is said that Pastor Spurgeon told his mother that he wanted to be baptized and she commented that she had prayed that he would become a Christian, but had never prayed that he would become a Baptist. Pastor Spurgeon responded to her that sometimes God does above and beyond what we ask . . . But truly one of my favorites is that Pastor Spurgeon was not a fan of long prayers and once said, "Long prayers injure prayer meetings. Fancy a man praying for twenty minutes and then asking God to forgive his shortcomings." The uniqueness of Pastor Spurgeon was that he spoke the gospel according to Jesus Christ and he never wavered from the truth. Never read between the lines, just read His word as He spoke it.

A very recognizable name in today's ministry work is D.L. Moody. Pastor Traylor of Olive Baptist Church gave an illustration of Pastor Moody not long ago in a sermon and the reference was that D.L. Moody had a Sunday School teacher that was inspirational in his life and he then went to hear one of Pastor Spurgeon's messages but during that time Spurgeon's church was so packed out that you had to have a ticket to get inside to hear him. Moody was able maneuver his way inside and Spurgeon inspired him greatly with passion, knowledge and dedication to God's word. Spurgeon made God's word relevant to that day and Moody brought that message back to the United States where he mounted a strong mission of delivering God's word. Moody university and Moody Radio are named after D.L. In listening to Dr. Traylor's message it wasn't about the success of D.L. Moody, it was about the passion in Spurgeon and it was about the great mission work of one D.L. Moody. Dr. Traylor's message was about a Sunday School teacher that took the time to teach and testify to a young man that made such a strong impact on his heart that he opened it to God so God could place D.L. Moody on a path that not only glorified His name but saved thousands of souls from eternal damnation. We thank God for the teachers who inspire children to greatness and preachers who paint a picture of how one person can change a world.

The Gospel is the same today as it was in the 1st Century and it is: Who He is, who He has always been and who He will always be. He is the same yesterday as He will be through eternity. He is because of:

> His spiritual birth without sin
> His perfect righteousness and sinless life.
> His many miracles, healings and grace.
> His death as a sacrifice for our sins.
> His resurrection from the dead.
> His promise to return.
> His gift of eternal life.

A Christian's mission is all about Jesus and He has me inside and out. Say it again out loud!

Hallelujah, Hallelujah, Praise His name and His name is *Jesus* as I give all the glory to **God**, the **Holy Spirit**, my **Lord** and personal savior . . . Amen

And He would probably say, "Thank you for your time . . ."

Continued Sword Development

A Christian without daily devotion is like a sailboat with no wind . . .

This will probably be the most important chapter in this book because it is the most neglected. There are many who say they know God and feel religious. I know who my neighbor is and I feel like we live in a neighborhood. I know where the local YMCA is and sense that I am a part of the community, I feel like I am a member. I am a member of the church so I should go to heaven. These are not new thoughts and the fine church folks of the 1st century felt this way also. There are many who receive the word, believe the word and get saved then get fired up in the Lord's work. But there are also many who allow busy lives and poor time management to allow their flame to burn out.

If you ever want to test your Christianity then sit down with a bunch of heathens and play a game of Monopoly. Ah yes, the game of money, greed, real estate, power and authority over innocent neighbors and travelers passing by. The strategies are focused on buying up all the railroads, utilities, and property with great combined value then go through life avoiding slumlord property and jail. Then making property improvements with houses and hotels on valuable real estate property that is orange, light blue, light purple and/or dark blue. This gives you a life of power, stability, power, board authority and an obvious hideous demonic laugh. Or it does with the people I have played with . . . These are the properties in the better neighborhoods or considered the high rent district. Strategies also include buying a single lot just to keep someone else from dominating that neighborhood. To be successful you must be a strict neighbor and have no weakness when collecting what you so richly deserve. Travelers' stopping by your property pay a squatter's tax and the better the property is improved the higher the homage is to pay. There is no mercy, no grace, no low interest loans and no way to avoid these risks once the dice of life are rolled. You have a chance to occasionally pass "GO" and receive a government stimulus check of $200. If you get thrown into jail you will need a "get out of jail free" card or know a good "bondservant" . . . This is no way of life for a Christian. A Christian would find grace in helping a neighbor with their unfortunate roll of the dice. A Christian would find themselves as a peasant among the wealthiest of kings and queens and there is not a church on the board to be found. Nowhere! This will suck the holy life right out of a religious person that has no sound connection to Christ or Christianity. But you could still call yourself religious because millions do. They play this game in real life then sit in church on Sunday and feel good about their worldly happiness. Remember, when you play monopoly with your life, you will play alone and die very alone. Happiness stays with you as long as you are allowed to breathe God's air but without holiness you will pass with the same thing that you came here with. Not even a top hat or an old shoe!

No Christian is ever alone, no not one!

If you collected charcoal placed them together and lit a match they would burn brightly together. Pull one coal out away from the others and it will slowly get cold and the flame will go out. This is the same with Christianity. It doesn't mean that you have fallen out of grace but you have drifted into dangerous territory of risk, deception and become easy prey for wolves. The wolves look for the weakest or those injured and fall behind the rest of the group. The Bible makes many references to the lamb or sheep. In the flock they are safe but when one wanders away from the others it become easy prey for danger. The wolves are the deceivers and those that would say this is nonsense. Staying with a group, staying in the word and creating good study habits are essential to strengthening your shield from danger. The better your habits become, the stronger your shield becomes. To defend the word means you must know the word and your faith must be constant.

"In order to completely develop, you must leave your agenda behind and place God's needs before your own."

Pastor Jon DuBois,
Olive Baptist Church

Your agenda? Your wants or your opinion of what you need before God's needs? This is like baking a cake with no oven. It is not going to happen! Many people are satisfied to read portions or take a few versus from a chapter and be satisfied that they understand it. This is like that person you know who sings a song with the words all wrong and it doesn't make any sense so they become annoying and you want to wave your magic wand and seal their mouth like the Lions in the den with Daniel. That is, if you had that kind of authority over Lions and I highly recommend that this not be attempted except by those trained professionals like the Sangfroid and Fried show in Vegas. Oh wait a minute, that didn't work out well either . . . . Never mind!

Anyway, practice your swordsmanship and try these few suggestions:

- ❖ Take small books, small chapters and read them over and over, study them, see the image of the story in your mind so it will become more real to your conscious. Get a Bible partner and practice scriptures on each other. Place a clock on the desk/table and time each other in locating the scripture and reading it. Get a Bible on CD and listen to it in your car driving back and forth to work or class. Let's face it; the radio stations only play the top 20 singles so you are just listening to them over and over again.

- ❖ Write down the page numbers that coincide with the books previously mentioned in this book. Use this book and your Bible as workbooks. Write all over them. Pastors teach out of the Bible and provide explanations, definitions and make story's come to life. I love hearing different Pastors place their life's examples in these stories to offer great parallels to their meanings. Find out what Bible your Pastor teaches from. Listen, learn, take notes and then go tell.

- ❖ Talk about what you have learned to others. Meet someone new? Ask them simple questions like, "Where does a Christian go to have fun around here?" Or try this challenge, "My friend and I were having a discussion on Christians. What do you think happens to you when you die?" Don't worry about not knowing it all; the ones who knew it were the writers and Holy Spirit who inspired them. I guarantee the same Holy Spirit that guided them will guide you as well. You will find that the more times you talk about the word of God the stronger your wisdom becomes. Wisdom is acquired over time and the more you know the more confident you become. You will probably be amazed at how much you have learned when you begin talking about it. In whatever you do, just start a conversation and let the Holy Spirit bring them home.

❖ If you go to breakfast, lunch or dinner and you don't have a partner to dine with, carry your Sword. You will find the best partner in the world in your Bible and prayer. Having your Bible open in a restaurant may be the one sign that someone needs to come to or back to Christ. You say hello and He will do the rest.

Understand that being saved is not a ticket to sit back and wait for the Holy Land bus to come pick you up. It is a commitment to tell others your testimony and show them the scriptures that led you to the cross. Being a Christian without serving others is like:

> ! A pencil with no paper
> ! A hammer with no nails
> ! A vacuum with no suction
> ! A truck with no bed
> ! A ship with no rudder
> ! An apple tree with no apples
> ! A guitar with no strings
> ! A pear tree with no pears
> ! A grape vine with no grapes
> ! Got it?

Find your skills by striking up conversations. You'll be challenged but you will meet some awesome folks as well. Remember your Sword is your Bible and your shield is your faith in God. God made the oak out of one little nut. Sometimes a little nut can become great! A very important foundation of Christian faith knows that when you are weak, He is strong. You cannot walk the narrow path alone without Him. It is spiritually impossible. So when you accept Christ you will be on fire to tell somebody and know now that someone is out there waiting that will do his or her very best to blow your fire out. And it will more than likely be someone you know. The friends that you had before may not find your newly found faith in Christ as such a big deal. These are the very ones that need you to testify, tell your story and explain how confident God makes you feel about knowing what is right as well as what is an eternal fact. But never argue or attempt to defend Christ. I assure you, He does not need defending. He has a history of doing an awesome job of this on His own. Simply tell the truth and leave the consequences to God.

The other development I encourage is to review global events that are not Biblical but have Biblical value. In my 1st book, "2012 Global Warning", I took a look at ancient worlds and how they align with today's world. Here are a few ancient societies that paid the price for doing things their own way instead of "**The Way**"!

EASTER ISLAND

Originally discovered by Polynesians around 1400AD they paddled over and called the island TePito Ote Henua which means "Navel of the World". These people grew and flourished until they decided to construct idol monuments around the island. There were over 900 monuments of dead folks that peer out over the ocean. In 1774 Captain James Cook landed on the island and was surprised to find it inhabited. He found the entire monument collection knocked over, destroyed and a population of Polynesians obliterated from an estimated 20,000 to less than 4,000 living in caves filled with fear. Sixteen thousand people gone! Their demise was blamed on overpopulation, starvation, deforestation and cannibalism. In 1862, 900 were removed into slavery and only 15 survived to return. Those 15 brought back smallpox and other diseases. By 1877 only 111 islanders remained alive to tell these stories. All that was left of this culture was broken pieces of stone. Here is a note to take. This culture cut every tree on the island, carved their gods of stone and made platforms with the tree logs for the gods to sit on. The gods were faced away from the island. They turned the stones away because even their gods couldn't even stand to watch the stupidity. God does have a sense of humor.

Mexico's CHICHĚN ITZÁ

This was home base for the Maya Indians and the city that became the center of mathematical and astrology questions, challenges and calendar phenomenon's. The Maya's worshiped several gods and they built a throne on top the Kukulan Pyramid, over 100 feet tall as it towered over the other buildings. The Maya's were also very serious about their tribal sport. The sport was called "Pok Ta Pok" which looked to me a little like soccer, basketball and football combined. But there are some very BIG differences! The losing team's captain was brought center court, taken to his knees and beheaded. The captains considered this an honor and walked through this ceremony willingly. Talking about losing your head over a game . . . But the Maya's were really into bloody sacrifices for their gods and this was a religion beyond compare. A savage people with too many idols and all the wrong reasons to live . . . and die! For a deeper view of this civilization check out "2012 Global Warning." There is a play by play game review there as well.

China's Qin Shi Huang Di

Self made king of Quin at age 13 this kid wasted no time in spreading his strength and flexing his young muscle. His armies battled fiercely and conquered lands surrounding them and widened their real estate by a respectable margin. The main problem with this king kid was an obsession with death or definite fear of it. He commanded several scientists and scholars to find him a potion for eternal life. He also commanded thousands of artists, creative ceramic craftsman and workers to make a temple protected by an army of terra cotta figures. This temple and manmade army of clay would spread over 20,000 pieces. Do you think he was consumed with himself? This massage art gallery became his tomb.

Turkey NEMRUD DAG

Located on the side of Mount Nemrud or Nemrut near the village of Kardadut with an elevation of 7,000 feet king Antiochus Theos of

Commagene built statues of gods around the middle to end of the 1st century. These statues are of Theos, Tyche, Zeus, Apollo and Heracles along with a long white stone used for blood sacrifice to the gods. This site was built and makes declaration that king Antiochos wants the world to follow him and give thanks to these rock gods. It is believed that the eagles would have been on the outside and in the center would have been a flat surface for blood sacrifices. From left to right they would have been constructed as: Antiochos, Zues-Oromasdes, Apollo-Mithras and Herakles-Artagnes. A collection of strong earthquakes shook the mountains and these statues literally lost their heads. Their heads severed from their torso are distinct reminders of scripture and God's authority over this world. Did I mention the flat slabs for blood sacrifices? Human blood sacrifices? Atheist and agnostics claim God's wrath reflects no love for his people. These rock god worshipers placed children on these slabs and butchered them so the rock gods would find favor on the tribe. God shook'em up and dismantled their rock gods. Thank you Lord!

I walked this real estate in 1979. What an experience this was to see the terrain that these people constructed the figures on and the words chiseled in stone! Marvelous piece of work for this terrain but it might as well been daggers in their souls. For each person that knelt to these gods was damned to Hades. Stephen Quayle, (unexplained-mysteries.com) has an artist rendition of what the arrangement could have looked like back in its day. Long before my walk through these ruins, a German engineer by the name of Charles Sester excavated this site in 1881 so I have no collection of data on what the site looked like before Charles snooped around but Quayle has a good image that is awesome to look at yet deadly to consider the hundreds upon thousands who died because of it. However in 1987 this site was made a World heritage location by UNESCO. There are overnight tours out of Malatya and if you eat at the little outside café with the dark green apron across from where the statue of Stalin still stands, tellem' I sent you and maybe they will offer you some free coffee, fresh bread or a leg of lamb. Maybe . . .

The Euphrates River, beautiful clear clean water. That is, if you are upstream of the camels.

Beautiful bends in the Euphrates open to lakes that would have been used for drinking, bathing and fishing. This river will be completely dry in the end.

This river bend was typical in offering an oasis of food, shade and comfortable living. It served as a article of war as well because clean drinking water was scarce.

This is the base of Nemrut. The people of the 1st century would have made this climb on foot, with donkey, camels and pulling their tools and resources up the mountain.

Halfway up the mountain the air begins to thin. Walking up this terrain with a bottle of water and a camera was a challenge by itself. I can't imagine making this climb with tools and dragging a screaming sacrifice behind me. Man, what a haul!

As we got to the top this was our first sight of the rock gods with no soul.

I found it odd that the many earthquakes experienced in these mountains only severed the heads from their torso. God shook 'em just enough to watch their heads pop off. I love His great sense of humor . . .

Headless stone gods do not seem very commanding. I have always wondered how a rock could be confused with spiritual deity with life sustaining messages. I once had a pet rock and I could not get the purpose or the point. It did ultimately make a good paperweight.

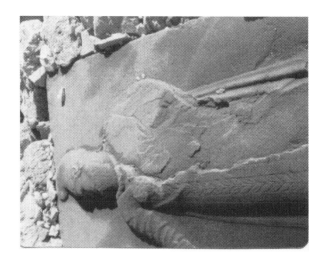

This might be the lid of a king's tomb? It was difficult to tell just where its original position was located. There were stones tossed about all over this area.

Notice the skill it took to cut and place these large stones into their proper placement. The writings were absolutely straight across and they didn't have any lines on their paper to guide them either. And we can't get along without excel, word docs and spell-check . . .

Here is a lion with its head and the bird without. Maybe the lion got hungry all alone on the mountain and ate the bird's head. I asked him what had happened but like the lions in the den with Daniel, he wasn't saying much.

I got a close up view of this wall and it said, "Do not build stupid rock gods or God will shake your heads loose!" Okay it probably didn't say that but that's what I would have written!

Gazing across the feet of these stone gods is where many lost souls knelt to pray to worship while living in lost-ness. Legends say many religions that worshiped idol gods also placed their own children at the foot of their gods and killed them. Murder, manslaughter and a horrific death committed, all in the honor of a rock!

Mean looking eagle! I wonder how many prayers he answered. I wonder if this stoned eagle actually spoke to anyone. I wonder if people understood eagle back then. I was just wondering . . .

India KHAJURAHO

The Hindu people built this monument or temple to honor their goddess Kali. The other two gods of India Hindu's are Brahma the creator of wisdom, Shiva the destroyer ~ fertility dude and Vishnu preserver of the universe. This temple is over 800 figures and some of which are the most vulgar positions ever seen in public without somebody being beat with a reed. Playboy, Hustler and Penthouse magazines are required to cover their cover to block obscene images from minors. I guess this is an exception to the rule cause these figures are ancient art. Obama mentioned Hinduism in a practical sense at one of his White House dinners. He could not have had any idea of what he was quoting. I don't have any pictures of this monument. This ain't that kind of book . . .

Here is my take on these civilizations. **Do not take the Lord's name in vain!** They had no value for God and they tried to find peace in their idols and objects. In the end they ceased to exist and their gods became broken pieces of wasted efforts. It was a choice they made of two separate paths and they chose poorly. God made you and loves you no matter what you choose to do. I also believe that He has an awesome sense of humor. He has the sole ability to shake the earth, play dominoes with stone and rock idols to illustrate where the power and authority comes from. He also has control of the floods, the hurricanes, tornadoes, tsunamis, volcanoes and other natural occurrences.

Mother Nature is a myth. God isn't!

Please, browse these civilizations on the Internet and follow their lifelines until death they did part. Be involved in your scripture and you will die a wise follower of Christ . . . For more information on how these civilizations parallel our world today read my first book on "2012 Global Warning". If you are going to die you should know how and why.

How many other lost civilizations are there? What ever happened to the Roman Empire? What became of Troy? What became of Hitler's dreams of world domination? What happened to Stalinism in Russia? These empires had no spiritual soul or value. These are not as Biblical as they are interesting studies that will strengthen your faith. However, everything we do is based on your understanding of your Sword and your Shield. Your Bible learning as well as your practice skills and your faith in God's word as well as His divine leadership will provide solid continued learning. If you follow His word you will thrive. If you fail to follow you will fail to survive.

"People watching" is a hobby of mine and is a little like bird watching. You look at the different species, colors and habits of God's creations. You listen to their different voices, mating, eating, drinking and home life habits. I enjoy watching people in the mall and large shopping retail stores. What they wear when they shop and who they shop with. People have habits and many are creatures of habit until they become ruts, deep ruts that are difficult to get out of alone. While we struggle with our heads down, a bird knows its creator and simply looks up. If you are in a habit that has gotten you in a deep rut then maybe you should do as a bird does and simply look up.

> *If you always do what you've always done you'll always get what you've always got . . . Don't fall into the same path as those before you that failed. Everyone today has the opportunity for crowns in heaven and the answer is up.*

God took a sheep herding, flute-playing poet and escorted him to the heart of a battlefield where they, David spirited by God, struck down a legendary giant. This single act energized a people behind a future king. David learned quickly who was in charge. The moment David took his eyes off God and decided to go it alone he fell and fell hard. When David reached out for God He was there. We need a clear understanding that God is not our co-pilot, He is not a co-author, He cannot be your co-writer and will not be co-anything. He must be all you are, all you have, all you will do, all powerful, all knowing, all majestic, all wisdom and He owns it all as well as He created what you see in the mirror. Be the energized saint of your world and He will guide you into His world.

He is very proud of His creation and you should be proud enough to humble yourself in His service. No other religion or denomination makes claim of creation. They either choose not to address it. They don't understand it. They claim a theory of evolution. They take life's origin as a seed, or they just acknowledge God has the universe in His hands but simply choose not to follow His word. How could people know that He is that big yet act so small? How could an average person on the street admit that they believe in God but still smoke, drink, party, act immoral, avoid His house and not speak to Him? If you are one of those who walk in denial, then where do you derive at this permissive behavior? In the space provided below, write three things that keep you from a full commitment to serving the God who created you. If this begins with: "I do not believe", then be bold enough to take pen in hand and write it before God.

1. _____
2. _____
3. _____

If you could wave a magic wand and change your world today, what three things would you change today? That is anything in your world, not the whole world.

1. _____
2. _____
3. _____

Now, here is my last question. A Christian has a firm belief that Jesus will return to claim His people who have acknowledged Him and have faithfully followed Him. Millions and "bazillions" have passed before He has decided to return. A large majority of them hesitated and did not seek Christ in acceptance, belief or commitment. If you were to die or hear the trumpets blow at this very minute, would you at this very moment be accepted into heavens gates?

> **YES**, I have **Accepted** Christ as my Lord. I was submerged in the water as He did to symbolize the removal of sins and my old way and rebirth into a new way. I **Believe** that Jesus Christ shed His blood for my sins. His resurrection gave me life. I have **Committed** my life to the great commission of telling my story to others. His sacrifice was His blood and because He shed blood I have newness of life in Christ. Hebrews 9:22

NO, I have not accepted, believed and/or committed my life to Christ and I have been told of His saving grace and I have chosen not to follow His word. I said the prayer once and was baptized or wasn't. either way, I don't walk the walk or talk the talk of one who is "Christ like".

WARNING: Blaspheme the Holy Spirit and you will spiral out of control and be lost to an eternal death where forgiveness is no more. Matthew 12:30-32.

Yes or **No** and there is no maybe, no sometimes and no part time Christian's. It is a full time commitment and a full time walk, which is each and every day in prayerful devotion with our heavenly Father. This little evaluation of your life and your testimony is real and it is either all about you or it is all about our heavenly Father's business. It takes skill to crusade for Christ and to stand in the middle of a crowd and make claim of being a child of Jesus Christ, Creator of all things. The King that was once crowned with thorns will return with the crown of all things living for Him and all things living without Him. Those who live with Him will be welcomed and those who have chosen a life without Him will be cast away from Him. That is the choice in your life today. Now, let's get some skills . . .

> **"Either make the tree good and its fruit good, or make the tree bad and its fruit bad; for the tree is known by its fruit."**
> Matthew 12:33

A YES commitment is a fruitful disciple of Christ. A Christian is known his/her heart, seen by his/her character and felt by his/her giving. Anything less will not make the narrow path and if you think this is not fair then stop thinking and start following . . .

Skilled Swordsmanship

Everyone has God gifted skills and if you don't know what yours are then it simply means you haven't asked Him yet.

Skilled swordsmanship is the next step in our path/walk and provides the confidence needed to field challenging questions as well as confidence to face the world filled with stupidity. If you are Spanish speaking, the translation might be "el'stupido" . . . I say this only because mixed into the legitimate questions one may have of God there are those who really test the realm of sanity. The ones who test it are very foolish . . . Let us walk through several key skills needed. These questions are in no particular order and they in no way capture all questions in the universe but will hopefully give you a guide to give quality answers or be able to show the people how to find it themselves. Get ready to draw your Sword!

The most common legitimate questions are:

- ❖ <u>What Bible should I read?</u> There is only one Holy Bible however there are several translations of the Holy Bible. Ask your Pastor of his translation used then review the options I mentioned previously in this book. It adds clarity to study the same Bible translation that your Pastor is teaching from.

- ❖ <u>Are there study guides?</u> Many translated Bibles have study versions available. I used three versions and a Holman Bible Dictionary. You can get great advice from fellow students in a Sunday school class and on the web. Be careful of the web and seek the advice from your Pastor.

❖ <u>What are the differences between religions?</u> Religion is an institution of belief in a supreme authority that is <u>broad based</u>. You could begin a new religion today and worship a frog. Wouldn't be wise but this world would probably be able to produce some frog worshipers that would follow it. I recommend you research the New Testament as you study God's word then compare religions AND denominations to God's word. You will find that the disciples and apostles were not "religious" as they were Christian. If this were not so then the Romans would have called these followers of Christ "religians" . . . If you find yourself in a church or Bible study where they are not reading out of God's Holy Bible then get up, walk out and find one that does. I find comfort and guidance in prayer as well. I settled in the Southern Baptist because I believe this is my calling from God and the Baptist doctrine follows God's word. Test yourself and test your religion against God's word. On the **Day of Judgment**, each of us will be tested against His word and the judge will be Christ.

❖ <u>What is the belief of Christianity?</u>
Draw your Sword—
Genesis 1:1 God the Father.
Matthew 1:18 God the Holy Spirit.
Matthew 28:6 God the Son.
God is our Creator, Redeemer and Spirit of truth. Christ Jesus alone has full and complete authority in heaven and on earth. **A**→ **B**-→ **C**. **A**ccept, **B**elieve then **C**ommit to follow Jesus Christ and Christians carry the name of Christ and no other doctrine. No other can compare . . .

❖ <u>What church should I go to?</u> One that teaches the gospel as God wrote it and does not add to it or take away from it. A Pastor who teaches/preaches from an open Bible and its Holy Scriptures. God authorizes no other book in the pulpit.

❖ <u>How do I pray?</u> Draw your Sword—Matthew 7:7-8 People have prayed on their knees, standing, with hands out, palms facing to the heavens, on their faces in humbleness, eyes wide open, and/or eyelids closed. You pray how you are led as well as least distracted from the world around you. And speak to God directly. You don't need someone to pray in your behalf. Prayer is your personal relationship with Jesus Christ and He would love for you to call on Him as often as possible. I speak to Him several times a day and it is mostly to thank Him.

There was a traveling salesman a while back that began a journey of city-to-city sales reviews of a new product line. As he drove he traveled through Chicago he saw a church sign that said, "The Golden Phone is here talk to God for only $10,000 per minute." He thought that was rather odd and an expensive call too, then he continued his journey. In Detroit he saw the same sign on a local church. "The Golden Phone is here. Speak to God for only $10,000 a minute." He traveled to New York, Washington DC, Nashville, Atlanta, Tallahassee, Orlando, Miami, back up through Tampa, then to Pensacola, New Orleans and saw the same sign in every city he traveled through. He crossed the Texas state line and immediately saw the Golden Phone sign but this one was different. It said, "The Golden Phone is here today for only $5.00 per minute." Now he was a good businessman and understood profit and loss but this was a big deal. He traveled to Dallas and saw the same sign. "The Golden Phone is here and only $5.00 per minute." He could not travel a mile further without knowing so he stopped at this church and went inside. The pastor met him at the door and asked, "Yes sir, how may we serve you today?" The man told the pastor of the travels he had made and the difference in charges to speak with God. $10,000 to $5.00 was a heck of a difference. The pastor looked at the man and said, "Sir you are in Texas and it is a local call to God from anywhere in Texas."

✦ I've said little prayers and big powerful prayers. <u>How do I know what to pray for or about</u>? Draw your Sword—Matthew 6:7 and Ecclesiastes 5:2. Tell God what is on your heart and for the Holy Spirit to speak through you. And it is always appropriate to thank Him for all He does. He made the sun rise this morning and the oceans tide roll in-out. He is the energy of our universe and can crush it with a single breath or caress a single flower pedal and it never fall off its stem. Thanking Him for the flower pedals in our lives is a very comforting prayer but include the worst for He has the hands of mercy and grace.

✥ <u>How do I know when God speaks to me?</u> First, don't expect the voice of James Earl Jones or Morgan Freeman. Second, stop talking and listen. God speaks in several ways; your consciousness, it may be through someone else, it may be through your Pastor, or other sources. Have you ever been in a situation where you were searching for an answer and when you least expected it someone said something and you said, "It's almost like they knew my thoughts." They don't but He does . . .

✥ <u>When will I know that I am ready to be saved?</u> Draw your sword—Matthew 1:21, Matthew 11:28, Matthew 13:44, Matthew 16:25, and 1st John 5:12-13. Every second that ticks away takes you further away from the truth, the Light and eternal life. It is your time today so read His word, then speak to Him each day and ask for the fulfillment of the Holy Spirit to fill your cup. First know you are lost then learn how to be saved . . .

✥ <u>Is there really a Heaven?</u> Draw your Sword—Revelation 15 then Revelation 22. Jesus also told the criminal that hung on the cross beside Him that <u>today</u> you would be with me in paradise. TODAY! If you died today and were saved, you would immediately move from your physical body into heavenly paradise.

✥ <u>What is a bondservant?</u> They help Christians get out of jail. Just kidding . . . Draw your Sword—2nd Corinthians 4:5-6 and 2nd Timothy 2:24. No leader can lead without understanding how to serve. To serve is to give of you. It is the simplest form of humble offerings.

Now here are a few questions that only God could love:

✥ <u>Can't I get the same result watching church from home?</u> You can't watch church. You can watch people. At home you will die lost and alone! If you are at home, who will know you? Your dog? And if that doesn't get your attention, draw your Sword—Matthew 10:32 Christ is the head of the church so if you are Christian then you are His church. Go where Christians unite.

✧ <u>Why do I have to be baptized?</u> Draw your Sword—Mark 16:16, Jesus was immersed so why wouldn't you want to follow His example? Is it required? No, Jesus will come into your heart the very moment you ask Him to take over your life. The criminal crucified next to Jesus never made it to the river to be cleansed of his sins but Jesus promised him that he would be with Him in paradise that very day. Jesus was fully submerged as a symbolic example and He expects His people to be obedient to follow His example. I wanted to follow His footprints and be obedient. I was fully submerged in 1968 in Thomasville Georgia by Rev. Earl Justice at Calvary Baptist Church. Just like Jesus, I came up out of the water as it is written in Luke 3:21. When John baptized Jesus it began His ministry. When you are baptized then your ministry begins as well. Ministry is to tell.

✧ <u>Is there really a devil?</u> In Genesis he was an angel created by God in the beginning then tossed out of the Garden of Eden but he is not the one that is typically shown with horns, a pointed tail and a pitchfork. Hollywood is Satan's playground for giving flare to his existence. Draw your Sword—Isaiah 14:12-14, Ezekiel 28:12-15, Revelation 12:10 and there are others as well. Think of temptation & deceit and there you will find him . . .

If he fools you then have you become his fool?

✧ <u>Are there different levels of sin?</u> You mean like murder verses adultery? Like a little lie verses a big lie? Sin is sin! But think of a lie in this way. If your body were able to tell you a lie, like a little white lie then it would be able to tell you that you that you are not in pain when you break your leg. Or your eyes would tell you the road is straight when there is a dangerous curve ahead. Or drive really, really fast because that stop sign really, really isn't there. A lie is a lie. All sin is the same in God's eyes but there is one that Jesus took issue with and said this is the most important commandment to follow. Do you know what it was? Draw your Sword and read Matthew 22: 29-40

✦ <u>What does the Bible say about UFO's?</u> The Bible speaks of one world, one man and one Jesus who dies for the sins of this world. Draw your Sword—Revelation 21:3-5 is a beautiful promise of Jesus Christ. If you are looking for insight to extraterrestrial spiritual guidance you will need to submit a request to the little green men right after they fit you with your custom made white jacket. The one that I call a *therapy wrap . . .*

✦ <u>What is sin?</u> Draw your Sword—Deuteronomy 9:7 and 1st John 3:4. And at the same time thumb back to the New Testament to Colossians 2:13-14. Read and understand this. Know what a forgiving Father we do serve. He will forgive ALL sin and forget it! Don't get too warm and fuzzy because Jesus told those whom He healed to go and sin no more. Colossians 3:5-10 will express the frustration that Paul had in the churches sinful habits, prideful imaginations, lack of self control and/or daily battles in temptation. Satan would love nothing more than to take down a Christian. That is a "hellascious" celebration! Stay away from those.

✦ <u>Should I feel guilty about enjoying earthly pleasures?</u> Yes and if you remain in earthly pleasure you will remain in earthly sin. Draw your Sword—Genesis 1, James 1:17 Enjoy God's creations and remember, do not place your faith in the gifts but rather in the giver. Never ever place this world between you and God. The blind cannot be made to see if the blind do not want to see Him . . .

✦ <u>What is the Pentecost?</u> Draw your Sword—Acts 2:1, Acts 20:16, and 1st Corinthians 16:8 It is a Jewish feast held 50 days after Passover. The Pentecostal churches will say it is an experience and Pentecostal is a word for movement or experience by the Holy Spirit. It is actually a moment in history recorded in Acts 2 where the people's tongues were of fire resting on believers and speaking in different languages never spoken before. <u>The languages were Jewish, not gibberish </u>because they were recognized as Mediterranean pilgrim words . . .

✦ <u>I am having financial problems, why doesn't God answer my prayers?</u> God is not the 1st National Bank of I Want, He has no need for cash and He didn't spend it to owe it. You did! Draw your Sword and review Proverbs 11:28, 1st Timothy 6:17, Job 31:24 and Luke 16. Yes, the whole chapter! Place your life in God's hands and He will deliver you to peace. The sacrifice is that you give it all to Him and He will then see that you are ready to serve Him completely. Then ask and it shall be given. I have been in these shoes and they are uncomfortable. It is like walking with a small stone in your shoe that you feel is not removable. Take a deep breath, add what you owe and add what you make. Take every credit card out of every wallet; purse and cookie jar in the house and cut'em up. Don't argue; just cut all of them up! Then stop wasting your income on junk and junk fun! Peel the layers off of the painful process. Pay cash for what you need and once you get out of debt, stay out of it. It is truly liberating.

✦ <u>Where was God when I needed Him the most?</u> Open both hands and place your Holy Bible in your hands. Now open the door (open His Holy Word to Matthew 7:8) and ask Christ to fill your heart, soul and mind with His Holy Spirit. It is an amazingly eternal transformation and you will never wonder where He is again. But if you don't open the door, walk in and stay in, you will not hear His voice.

God will not speak to a back turned so stop walking away . . .

God please let me score this touchdown! God please help me hit this homerun! God help me pass this test! God please don't let this cop pull me over! God please make him ask me to the prom! God make this car start! God help me hit the lotto! Yes I have heard plenty more examples and I am sure you have also. It is really amazing what people ask God to do for them. I am also quite sure that anything they have received was never truly appreciated enough for a quick prayer thanking God. You may have even heard God's name called while someone was hugging cool porcelain in the bathroom . . . He generally doesn't hear these requests if they do not glorify His name or the purpose of saving eternal lives. Again, the facts bring Jesus Christ in as your center and anything physical cannot enter heavens gates.

Have nice things. Enjoy traveling the country or the world. Enjoy the world that God created. But we make fools of ourselves with selfish prayers and "help me" calls to the God of our universe. We laugh at the 911 calls made because the pizza guy messed up the order or the cashier shorted them $1.10. False calls to God are no laughing matter. Jesus had a few very specific things to say about what He expects of us. Draw your Sword and read over Luke 6:20-45.

Trust, faith and healing . . . Draw your Sword and read Proverbs 3:5-6. When you place more trust in your money, in your job, in your car, in your own judgment or in your whatever it is before God and you will surely fail then fall. Fall on your butt later or on your knees now. Your choice!

Read Luke 22:32 and Hebrews 10:35
Your faith will be tested and may waiver when tempted but your trust in God and the Lord Jesus Christ will never leave you or fail you.

The foolish are all around us and they don't frustrate me like I allowed them to do in the past. It is truly sad how some think and how some speak out of ignorance to God's word. I do enjoy browsing through the Internet chat rooms to look at some of the responses to questions that real people of this world come up with. Here are a few comments that I viewed on the Internet so you may form your own opinions to theirs. Remember, these are not my statements, but from the voice of those who walk among us as they have recorded their brilliance on the web. Let it be known that I did clean some of the language up so I could sleep at night posting it here but left their fingerprint so you may feel their voice. Yes, their grammar is worse than mine . . .

- Here are three questions that were posted for open web response:

How many Christians know they are truly saved?

- O Bible Believers, why not you reveal your god that Jesus has paid the price of your crimes and sins?

Most of culprits, sinners, alcoholic, adulterous and transgressor Christians are being afflicted with painful torments like STD (Sexually transmitted diseases) including AIDS, Hepatitis. Why not you tell your god that Jesus has paid the price and do not afflict us due out sins, crimes and transgressions??? Or your sins, crimes and transgressions exceeded than price paid by Jesus?????

- I constantly question God's Word . . . not because I don't believe it, but because I want to understand it better. For every rule in there, there has to be a better reason than "Because God says so." For most of them, I have found at least one good reason that has nothing to do with God—for the rest, I trust his track record and take it that he knows what he's talking about.

- This is great (and you appear to be an honest Christian, not many of those around). Anyway it's good news because we'll be able to continue attacking Christians in hell. Well of course we will have to admit we were wrong about their god, but right after that we give them living hell forever.

  Goody, then the pagans, Wiccans and atheists won't be all alone. Though none of us believe in hell, it is nice to know that you guys will be there too.

- Speak for yourself. I trust God's word and do not doubt His promise of salvation through faith in His son.

- No one can prove that they are truly saved to anybody but their own inner sense of belief, so the answer to your question is that it's flawed in itself. No body can absolutely prove they have been saved in the same way that no one can claim they are in danger of hell verses anyone else. The proof of the pudding in this case is in the eating and that means death.

- That's just a ridiculous statement to me. Having doubts from time to time doesn't make a person an unbeliever. It makes them HUMAN.

Jesus' only requirement into heaven is to believe in Jesus. So we are human and we doubt then this is impossible. It's really not that big a jump to grasp this unattainable Christian logic.

How do I become a born again Christian?

Responses:

- Well if you are serious . . . Believe without a doubt and don't just say you do, that Christ died for you, to take your sin away, because he loves you and doesn't want you to live in sin. Confess and know that you're a sinner and let God have your life, to shape you to prosper for him.

- You have believe theres only god and he has no partners childeren or family. Hes the creator of all things u must accept islam if you really want to be saved or born again islam is the way of life. NO you cant do whatver u want you have to abide by the rulz.

- Luke 10:25-28 On one occasion an expert in the law stood up to test Jesus. "Teacher," he asked, "what must I do to inherit eternal life?" "What is written in the Law?" he replied. "How do you read it?" He answered: "'Love the Lord your God with all your heart and with all your soul and with all your strength and with all your mind'; and, 'Love your neighbor as yourself.'" "You have answered correctly," Jesus replied. "Do this and you will live"
. . . a true believer has no doubt . . .
. . . when doubts exist one goes astray . . .
. . . to be reborn again is to believe without doubt . . .

God doesn't answer casual inquirers. He only responds to sincere seekers. You may think you can joke or quip your way into heaven, but God isn't playing games.

-   He paid and exceedingly high cost for the souls of men.

-   Basically you walk around and look down at everyone with a holier-than-thou attitude
    Is it much work? Do you actually have to do anything? If it's quite easy, I fancy giving it a shot; Am I right in saying that when one is saved/born again, you can do whatever the hell you want without having to worry? Sounds pretty good to me like.

What or who should I believe when it comes to religion?

Responses:

-   My parents grew up Catholic, but don't really practice any religion I was never baptized and I really don't go to church at all. I have been leaning towards atheism or being agnostic, it really doesn't matter to me I believe in science . . . I always have believed that all religions are stories told by people from a time when we knew nothing about the universe and world around us.
    Believe no one but yourself. just listen to yourself everyone is going to tell you their religion is the best and some of them may be right i do like Catholics my parents are too very nice religion.

-   I would recommend learning more about the major religions, both Eastern and Western, read at least part of their central texts (if not all), and explore the arena of spiritual thought. This is what I have done myself, and I happen to be an atheist. My rejection of magic is not an uninformed one . . .

-   Well exactly what you believe is up to you. Atheism is nice because it doesn't ask anything of you but to be yourself. All the details of what it means are up to you to decide. It also makes for a strong sense of ethics since you're directly responsible for who you help or hurt.

- Just listen very closely to everything Rush Limbaugh recommends, and then do the exact opposite . . .

- I recommend praying the rosary regularly. You can definitely trust the Virgin Mary. She is Our Lady of Good Counsel, and will lead you to the truth.

WOW! Can you believe the different responses that are given and little effort is made to simply answer these questions by opening a Bible. We are such a world of opinionated people and will accept what we hear rather than the rock solid proven evidence. Are you really ready to face this world as Today's Christian Crusader? It is not a part-time title.

Nowhere in the gospels does Jesus Christ tell you to pray the rosary beads, pray to the Virgin Mary or trust in Mary for your salvation. The rosary-center.org has several disturbing statements that I find difficult in their historical or spiritual value. If God didn't record it in the Bible then why are millions of people relying on these traditions to comfort them in their time of need? Here are the prayers to Mary as listed on their site.

- Joyful Mysteries, Luminous Mysteries, Sorrowful Mysteries and Glorious Mysteries? It is quoted that Pope John Paul II suggested that the "Joyful mystery" be said on Monday and Saturday, the "Luminous" on Thursday, the "Sorrowful" on Tuesday and Friday and the "Glorious" on Wednesdays and Sundays. There are some stipulations to the holidays.

There are no mysteries in the Bible about prayer or whom you pray to.

What scripture validates a prayer to Mary for any reason?
a) None

Say how many Hail Mary's? *Holy Mary, mother of God, pray for us sinners, now and at the hour of our death.*

a) What scripture supports this prayer?
b) What scripture says to hail Mary?
c) What hail Mary will offer you repentance?
d) Is there anywhere in the Bible that says Mary is part of the Holy Trinity?
e) Is there a scripture that assures me that Mary is a path to eternal paradise?
f) Will Mary deliver the New Jerusalem?
g) What part of the heaven throne does Mary hold?
h) If Mary is of prayerful importance, then Peter and Paul should be as well.

The answer is zero validation so how can this tradition be practiced in a church body that openly reads God's word? I love Mary because she is the mother of my Savior and blessed Redeemer. I can't find reason for praying through her or lighting a candle in her behalf or kneeling before a statue of her. This tradition might be in one of the additional books of the Catholic Church that does not impact the bloodline of salvation. Many, many books and letters were written since the dawn of time but the books in the Holy Bible follow the blood of Christ. It was because of the pure holy blood shed that you have the choice today of life or an eternal death.

Make the sign of the cross and say the apostle's creed.

- ✧ Where is the apostle's creed located in the Bible? In one of the additional books? I cannot find a valid answer on this traditional practice. Paul never spoke of a creed. He spoke the gospel.
- ✧ Where does it document that Jesus ever descended into "hell"? In one of the additional books? 1 Peter 3 will speak directly to this and there are several interpretations. I'll ask when I get there because until then this topic is over my pay-grade.
- ✧ Making the sign of a cross on your body or placing a fish on your car doesn't get you into heaven. Have faith, accept, repent, be cleansed of your sin, obedience and get busy doing God's work. That is all in the God's Holy Word!

The prayer to "Our Father" is correct and can be validated in Matthew 6:9-13 but I cannot find where you have to make a pronouncement of a "mystery". There are no mysteries and Jesus Christ was never mysterious. Jesus Christ is majestic, not mysterious.

These are the fifteen promises of Mary to those who recite the rosary and it is said that this ritual came from <u>St Dominic in the early 13th century</u>. The *13th* century? St Dominic of the Dominican Republic? It is said that this is the way to become a Catholic. There are arguments to the content of the fifteen promises but I have no argument with any one promise. I argue them all as a ritual to be said on specific days, in a specific way and to lead people to a way that is and was not taught by Jesus Christ. Read the fifteen and do your own research.

1. Whoever shall faithfully serve me by the recitation of the Rosary shall receive signal graces.
2. I promise my special protection and the greatest graces to all those who shall recite the Rosary.
3. The Rosary shall be a powerful armor against Hell, it will destroy vice, decrease sin, and defeat heresies.

4. It will cause virtue and good works to flourish; it will obtain for souls the abundant mercy of God; it will withdraw the hearts of men from the love of the world and its vanities and will lift them to the desire of eternal things. Oh, that souls would sanctify themselves by this means.

5. The soul, which recommends itself to me by the recitation of the rosary, shall not perish.

6. Whoever shall recite the Rosary devoutly, applying him to the consideration of its sacred mysteries, shall never be conquered by misfortune. God will not chastise him in His justice, he shall not perish by an unprovided death; if he be just, he shall remain in the grace of God and become worthy of eternal life.

7. Whoever shall have a true devotion for the Rosary shall not die without the Sacraments of the Church.

8. Those who are faithful to recite the Rosary shall have during their life and at their death the light of God and the plenitude of His graces; at the moment of death, they shall participate in the merits of the saints in Paradise.

9. I shall deliver from Purgatory those who have been devoted to the Rosary.

10. The faithful children of the Rosary shall merit a high degree of glory in Heaven.

11. You shall obtain all you ask of me by the recitation of the Rosary.

12. All those who propagate the Holy Rosary shall be aided by me in their necessities.

13. I have obtained from my Divine Son that all the advocates of the Rosary shall have for intercessors the entire Celestial Court during their life and at the hour of death.

14. All who recite the Rosary are my sons, and brothers of my only Son, Jesus Christ.

15. Devotion to my Rosary is a great sign of predestination.

God gave these fifteen to St Dominic in the 13th Century? If St Dominic had done this in today's society he would have been labeled a fraud and the leader of a cult. Truly Mary was important to the path of the developments that was in God's plan. David was important. Abraham was important. Solomon was important. Moses was important. So why would we not hail these Prophets for their faithfulness to God? Cause we only hail one God and no one stands before or between me and my God. This is Biblical and God wrote it in stone.

To place anything or anyone between you and the Lord your God is SIN.

Chains bind those many people who walk up to a statue of Mary, rub their beads and pray for forgiveness will still be in chains. Those beads can become chains and those who teach this to others will be held accountable for their teachings. I am not saying that there are no Catholics that are saved nor am I challenging the Catholic Church, The Vatican or Catholic theology. I am challenging those who believe that these traditions and practices are part of the plan of salvation. Jesus was very specific in His teachings and He never spoke of these in His teachings. If He did not say it then it is not so.

"And the devil who deceived them was thrown into the lake of fire and brimstone, where the beast and the false prophet are also; and they will be tormented day and night for ever and ever."
Revelation 20:10

Who is leading these people to this statue or to this practice? These are teachers, priests, and ministers of a few of the Catholic religions. They are leading these people to hell and the percentage that I use for those who are actually saved may be too high! If you believe that Mary will save you, you are scriptural misguided and part of that doomed percentage. Mary carried the Gospel for around nine months and as the Mother of Jesus we "honor" her, not "worship" her. If you are a Catholic and believe that Jesus Christ is the way, the truth and the Light then I will see you in paradise. Jesus is the Gospel!

"So that whoever believes will in Him have eternal life. For God so loved the world, that He gave His only begotten Son, that whoever believes in Him shall not perish, but have eternal life."
John 3:15-16

If you believe you will have salvation by rubbing beads and saying hail Marys, you are wrong because it is not Biblical. To all those who have an ear, mock if you will, slander if you may, but Jesus did not teach, die and rise to save a religion. He did this to save all people who needed a sacrifice for the sin we are born into. Denominations rose from church dissention and murmuring. Man couldn't get along even in church. Religion is man made and Christ is the grace of Christianity. It is the gospel truth and without Christ there is no righteousness!

> **"Jesus answered, "Truly, truly, I say to you, unless one is born of water and the Spirit he cannot enter into the kingdom of God."**
> John 3:5

I did a little research after listening to a radio interview where a Catholic Priest had recently converted to Catholic from Southern Baptist. This is an incredible switch of faith and it captured my attention. I sincerely wanted to know what moved a gospel southern preacher teacher from what he had taught for years and all of the sudden he felt the need to stop preaching teaching the Southern Baptist philosophy and begin preaching teaching Catholic philosophy. Here are some of the topics he focused his decision on and part of the discussion on his faith-based transformation.

* He struggled with "once saved, always saved" philosophy but would rather teach Catholic philosophy that even if you die an unsaved and non-accepting death then several "Christian Catholics" could gather and pray that soul into heaven. It would be a prayer based on the group's strength in Christ as well as their reliance on His mercy. The recently converted Catholic priest rejects the Biblical track that eternal security is the work through Jesus Christ, which guarantees the gift of salvation based off of **His** sacrifice and not the works of any person. Draw your Sword and read John 10:25-30.
* He struggled with life after death before the return of Christ, not that you would pass but where you pass. He appreciated the Catholic version of paradise and purgatory. Paradise was heavenly until Christ ascended and took all the souls into heaven with Him. God never mentions purgatory, so this is man made myth.
* He struggled with Southern Baptist philosophy of sanctification when Catholics work on salvation from the cradle to the grave. Catholics practice occasional confession to a priest, which gives

them a fresh slate to move forward on. Christian faith is based on salvation through Jesus Christ and it is a mature decision that I will follow Christ. The disciples of Jesus were the best example of making a decision to stop thinking of me and follow Him. Christians believe salvation comes from what Christ did on the cross and from the tomb. Draw your Sword and read Matthew 4:18-22. Draw your Sword and read Mark 8:34.

❋ He struggled with some scripture so he publicly said there were scriptures that he ignored then and ignores now. To ignore any of God's word is to ignore Him. If you don't understand it then this is common and man was not created to understand all of what God does or what He has in store for us but we are never to ignore or discard His word. The parish that this converted pastor has should be very aware of what comes off his lips.

❋ He struggled with Jesus Christ being the only Way, the only Light and the only Path to salvation when he stated that it was the Holy Spirit that saves, not Jesus. This priest is very unwise to discard acknowledgment of the Trinity as One and it was Jesus that was nailed on the cross. Christ ascended and said He would send the Holy Spirit in His name as our comforter, helper and teacher. Draw your Sword and read John 14:23-26.

❋ He struggled with his congregation going directly to God with questions and not gaining the answers they needed. He sought the wisdom of Catholic tradition of a man as the father whom a follower would seek their advice and he called himself a "spiritual therapist". His order of authority is way off Biblical structure and I don't have enough space to quote all the scriptures to tell him that God is sole authority over all living things and the earth they live on. There is only one Father and I refuse to call a human being "holy father". Follow them if you want, listen to them if you will but there is one Holy Father and His Son guides my way with His word and His helper is His Holy Spirit who guides me along my way. If you can't feel it, hold it, have it, read it, hear it and see it then you have not experienced that moment of sanctification that moves you from a physical consciousness into spiritual righteousness. By His grace, not by our works.

Each of us has a gift that Jesus died for. To receive His love and saving grace simply believe in His word, take up your cross and follow Him. Do not follow any man, don't even take my word but open the word of God and pray to Him for understanding, faith and grace today. Say what you will, think what you might and know that all of what you say and do will be answered for. When you thought no one was looking, He was there . . .

A skilled Swordsman would know this well.

The Sword of Discipleship

Today's Christian Crusader is commissioned to tell, not to save.
Saving comes from our Savior and the divine work of God's Holy
Spirit . . .

Jesus said, "Peace be with you; as the Father has sent Me, I also send
you." And when He had said this, He breathed on them and said to
them, "Receive the Holy Spirit."

John 19:21-22

Several surveys agree that about 33% of the world is Christian. Within
the Christian category, these surveys lump Catholic, Baptist, Pentecostal,
Jehovah's Witness, Latter Day Saints, Mormon and several other groups
under one umbrella. Although, many of these denominations separated
for one key reason; several believe that "works" is the passage into heaven.
Draw your sword and study Ephesians 2:8-9. The only groups that can
call themselves "Christian" are those who follow only Christ, worship only
Christ as our risen Savior, acknowledge that only Christ is the only path
to eternal salvation and know that His word is the complete and final
authority. This just separated a few of these denominations from the group
and I call this denominational clutter. Denominational clutter confuses
people and creates questions of what direction to follow as well as in who
should one listen to. The Holy Bible in its entirety and completeness
prevents scatter. Man causes it!

If the rapture happened today and all God's people just in the United States
alone were called at this very moment, then probably about 75,000,000
of the total population of 300,000,000 would instantly disappear. This
means that about 225,000,000 would still be here. And that is probably
being very generous but still *an estimate* just for conversation sake . . . So if

we consider that at least 225 million folks are headed for hell, what is our roll as disciples? Jesus said to tend to His sheep and this calls for a mission of discipleship. Discipleship is to learn and tell the gospel of Jesus Christ. As we mentioned earlier, Southern Central Turkey was Paul's homeland; his family legacy and these folks are the ones who should listen closer than anyone else, but the king constructed a massive monument for these people to worship rock gods. There are about 75,000,000 just in that area and about 98% belong to the nation of Islam. How many are truly saved? Well how many people today in the United States alone have not heard the word of God spoken through Paul? Could there be one mature adult in the United Stated that has not heard or read about the word of God? It is difficult to imagine a mature adult in the U.S. that has not heard the gospel.

Let's take a look city by city and use some common sense mathematics to get an idea of who would answer the call if Jesus returned today. We'll use some estimates in census and population averages as illustrated by US and City populations on census.gov for 2009. I can't wait to hear from the critics on my estimated number of lost souls! It is basic math and common sense. So some intellects will struggle . . .

Los Angeles CA is home to about 9,862,049 and if 493,102 people are saved then **9,368,947** people will still be here. The demographics state there are 1062 churches and a total <u>membership</u> of 820,834. Understand that most churches have less than half of their members actually attend worship services. A few more may attend on Easter Sunday just to say they did. This feels good . . .

Chicago IL, President Obama's last home town, is home to about 9,780,854 and if 489,287 people are saved then **9,291,567** people will still be here. This number would probably be higher if it were not for Reverend Right teaching it all wrong.

Atlanta GA, city limits is home for about 537,958 and if 26,898 are saved then **511,060** will still be here. This may be real low since Dr. Charles Stanley is there ministering the gospel.

Detroit MI, the city of high crime, city limits is home to about 912,062 and if 45,603 are saved then **866,459** will still be here.

Seattle WA, the most liberal city in the nation, is home to about 602,000 and if 30,100 are saved then **571,900** will still be here. Is 30,000 born again believers in Seattle a stretch?

Washington DC, city that includes the White House is home to about 591,833, when session is not in and if 29,592 are saved then **562,241** will still be here. If the legislators were in session then the ones still here would probably be around **563, 241**. Give or take a few backsliders . . .

And **Rio de Janeiro**, not part of the U.S. but is the location of the 2016 Olympics, also home of one of the highest homicide rates in the universe has a population of 14,387,000. If 719,350 are saved, which is a BIG stretch, then **13,667,650** people will still be here.

Do these numbers offend or surprise you? How far do you think I am actually off? Remember, this count is only mature voting adults. How many in these counts have never heard the gospel? It is said no one really knows the matters of the heart but without a plan and a goal then you simply have no target for your base. But if Christ is in your heart and in your life then your lifestyle would reflect a life like Christ. Let that settle and marinate in your heart . . .

Ask yourself this question: How many people at my work are not saved? How many people do I know that are not saved? Now, understand that your salvation is a personal commitment between you and God. So you may argue that a personal commitment would not be known. Try this, take a piece of paper out and draw a line in the middle of the page from the top down to the bottom. On the left side title it "The Saved" and on the right title it "The Lost". Take a few moments now to write down the people you know. First names only, this is only for your benefit. Place them in the category that **best fits** their <u>character</u>, their <u>lifestyle</u>, their <u>testimony</u>, their <u>language</u> and their <u>life's habits</u> as a Christian or not so much. This should be easy so stop reading now and resume reading when you are done.

Remember; what is in your heart will be revealed in your character so if Christ lives within you then you will act like Him. I mean, act like Him all the time, not just on special occasions . . .

Okay, are you done? You aren't cheating are you? Are you reading ahead without doing your assignment? You do know that Jesus is the teacher that never leaves the classroom right?

All righty then . . . Just checking . . .

So how did you do? Total each column down at the bottom and see which total is higher. This is not only a good way to understand that your character should reflect your faith but it also provides you with a witness list. The folks on the left make up your witness team and the folks on the right are who need your testimony. Remember, those who deny the Father on earth Jesus will deny them in heaven. Also, if you were saved then you would be obedient to God and witness as His disciple. If you are saved then you have invited Jesus into your heart and your life. If Jesus is holy then you are filled with His holiness and would remove the things of this world that are unholy. Now, do you still feel uncomfortable about the number of saved and lost? Now here is one final question on this assignment; if both your neighbors, on either side of you, were to make the same list, which side on their list would your name appear?

God's word is not to be pointed at anyone but to be reflected upon . . .

~~~~~~~

"Marriage is to be held in honor among all, and the marriage bed is to be undefiled; for fornicators and adulterers God will judge."
Hebrews 13:4

At the time of my research, gay marriage had become legal so far in Vermont, Iowa, Massachusetts and New York. I am really not sure why they do not select a state, declare that state "The Freedom to Sin State" and offer all who want separation from God's word to live according to hippie type freedom laws in that state. Utah seems to be a good state to do this in since many folks there are already committing adultery with several wives, so gay-lesbian marriages would be appropriate there. According to the gay skippy dippy dot org church, there are over 5,700 gay churches in the United States. These churches could move to Utah and establish their own rules of living. They could even rename Utah and call it; Sodom & Gomorrah . . . The church denominations that recognize gay and lesbian people in the ministry and believe it abides by God's holy word are manipulating God's word into their own. How many gay and lesbian people would that be, 200,000? This is certainly not a majority of anything but I wonder just how many out of that population truly believe they are saved? Saved according to ALL of God's word, not just the words that fit your lifestyle . . . Yes, Jesus loves all people, Jesus died for all sin and He made a promise to take all those who believe in Him to heaven but here is what separates the saved from the unsaved and the sheep from the goats. If you are a saved man/woman you will abide by His holy word. He expects every Christian to be obedient to His word and "Christ like". It always comes back to His word, His will, His way and not our own. This topic is not up for Christian debate so all who desire this way of life should read Romans 1:24 through 32. Remember, **Today's Christian Crusader** is to tell and offer God's word as THE final authority. He is in complete control and He will be glad to hear any justification around His word. The last time God was tested; He burned a city down and turned a young lady into a pillar of salt for even looking back at the wickedness. God is not fair, but He is just in His word!

"Before they lay down, the men of the city, the men of Sodom, surrounded the house, both young and old, all the people from every quarter; and they called to Lot and said to him, "Where are the <u>men</u> who came to you tonight? Bring them out to us that we may have <u>relations</u> (sex) with them." But Lot went out to them at the doorway, and shut the door behind him, and said, "Please, my brothers, do not act wickedly."

Genesis 19:5-8

Think of a smaller scale of people you see every day. Do they behave as born again believers in Christ would? How about the impatient shopper in a line at the register or the aggravated customer standing in line to order food? What about the customers in a parking lot jockeying for a parking space, murmuring and pointing fingers? What about the people you see in rush hour traffic; on they're horn, with their finger out of the window or cutting in front of you? What about the mobs who gather outside a courthouse screaming for justice? Where do you see people organized and rallying with hate or anger in their voices? When would you draw your Sword of discipleship? If you were a born again believer in Christ you would recognize it in their character, right? If you recall the same survey you did earlier of the people you know to the people you don't know but see in every day life, what category would they fall into? Tomorrow morning carry an index card or a scratch piece of paper with you while out in public and use the same format we used earlier to mark the saved and unsaved. The only difference will be that you don't know their names so just place a check or an X under the category they would fall into. Remember again, your character as a Christian, is not like a "religious jacket" that we can take on and off as we please. You are either a born again believer in Christ or you are lost. God called the selection process like separating the goats from His sheep . . .

But according to the scriptures all will know the very moment they are saved by the receiving of God's Holy Spirit. Your covenant with God and the witness in your character reveal it immediately! Are there any arguments with this statement? Can you be nice and still not get into Heaven? <u>Yes</u>! Can you attend church regularly and not get into Heaven? <u>Yes</u>! Can you be a generally good person and miss the call to heaven? <u>No</u>! Jesus is calling every day. I promise you this, if you attend church this Sunday morning, rise and sing with all your heart, dedicate next Sunday too really listen and I <u>guarantee</u> the Holy Spirit will speak to you. If you walk into any room with your eyes closed you will walk into a wall. So walk into God's word with your eyes open and He will speak to you. When the alter call is made you will feel a tug, a nudge saying today is the day . . . Take a step out into the aisle and walk to the front and He will meet you there with all His love. Yes, **He will**! Or you can sit and listen to the argument inside your head. Then step outside the same doors you came in, just as lost and hopeless as you are today. You take a big risk on not making it to another service to claim His love for you and proudly take stand for Him as He did for you . . . If you do not understand any other statement in this book please understand what you just read. I would encourage you to read it again. This will remove all walls so you will never walk blindly again.

"Enter through the narrow gate; for the gate is wide and the way is broad that leads to destruction, and there are many who enter through it. For the gate is small and the way is narrow that leads to life, and there are few who find it".

Matthew 6:13-14

Think about those two little verses for a moment . . . Was Jesus exaggerating? Was He Just saying this to pressure people into going to church? I would say not. But if the lost numbers have still got you going, here are a few other statistics to think about. There are many who still live in denial of Hitler's oath to rid the world of Jews. Yes, there are still those blind, deaf and dumb folks that deny the Holocaust, the estimated 15,000 prison camps where Jewish people were held captive and the estimated 4,465,000 died in just 8 camps. The Auschwitz II, Belec, Chelmno, Jasenovac, Maly Trostinets, Sobibor and Treblinka. Death marches took place where large masses of Jews were placed on trains and moved to camps. In January 1945 one trip of about 3 miles from Auschwitz to Wodzislaw reported 15,000 deaths, just on this trip. In other camps 13,000 lay unburied, 10,000 lay dead of typhus or malnutrition, 180 children had been used for experiments by doctors, and gas chambers held about 200 people each so when canisters of gas would be dropped into the chamber for a mass kill, German ammunition would be saved.

Here are a few estimated Jewish populations exterminated that get or recall your attention:

    -Poland had 3,300,000, and 3,000,000 killed
    -Baltic's had 253,000 and 228,000 killed
    -Germany had 240,000 and 210,000 killed
    -Bohemia had 90,000 and 80,000 killed
    -Slovakia had 90,000 and 75,000 killed
    -Greece had 70,000 and 54,000 killed
    -Netherlands had 140,000 and 105,000 killed
    -Hungary had 650,000 and 450,000 killed
    -Byelorussia had 375,000 and 245,000 killed
    -Ukrainian had 1,500,000 and 900,000 killed
    -Belgium had 65,000 and 40,000 killed
    -Yugoslavia had 43,000 and 26,000 killed

-Romania had 600,000 and 300,000 killed
-Norway had 2,173 and 890 killed
-France had 350,000 and 90,000 killed
-Bulgaria had 64,000 and 14,000 killed
-Italy had 40,000 and 8,000 killed
-Luxembourg had 5,000 and 1,000 killed
-Russia had 975,000 and 107,000 killed
-Denmark had 8,000 and 52 killed
-Finland had 2,000 and 22 killed

Why? Because of one man's hate that influenced fellow leadership that spread to a country and an order was proclaimed then fulfilled. Over 6 million people eradicated from the Jewish population. The same Satan and his demonic following are still present in today's society. The Arian nation seems to be the core but there are many, many more!

We have been faced with evil for generations and it began with one really big sin!

The Plague of Athens occurred around 430BC, returned in 429BC and again in 427BC. Recent research has pointed at Typhoid fever as the cause, but the exact death count is unsure. The many massive graves had the deaths in the thousands.

The Antoine plague or Plague of Galen killed an estimated 5,000,000 in 180AD. As it lowered the population it also killed many Roman solders.

The Bubonic plague or Black Death swept through Europe in the 1300's that would kill you in less than 7 days. Around 12,000,000 died but took an estimated 75,000,000 lives worldwide.

The Great Plague of London occurred around 1665 and killed an estimated 100,000 people.

The Third Pandemic began around 1855 and was active until around 1959. It claimed over 12,000,000 lives in India and China alone.

The Smallpox is recorded to have claimed over 300,000,000 lives from 430BC until 1979. Grasp that number for a moment.

The Spanish Flu claimed just fewer than 100,000,000 lives in 1918 to 1919.

The Malaria Fever kills an average of 2,000,000 every year and is most deadly in children under the age of 5.

The Aids Virus has killed over 25,000,000 people since the first case in 1981. There is an estimated 37,000,000 people walking around with aides today.

The Cholera disease is transmitted though waterways and our global water supply is its haven. I could find no reliable statistics to the death rate caused with the exception of 20,500 just in the year 1947 in Egypt. Many countries don't bother to count in mass graves.

These diseases take lives quickly and some have no chance to repent. Non-believers hang their hat on the theory that most people who attend church are hypocrites and this is the reason why choose not to go. I wonder who the non-believers ask for mercy when they experience a plague, an illness, a cancer, a traumatic medical experience or other trauma. What about a hand carved little fat Buddha statue or a rabbit's foot? There are also those who hug a tree . . . The truth is we have many church leaders who have given the non-believer and the followers of Satan plenty of darts to throw at the Christian community at large. Some confuse being "religious" with Christianity. Here are a few examples of church leaders who stepped outside the will of God and offered that single moment to Satan and he ran with it!

- Wayne Bent arrested for allegations of sex with children in New Mexico. Not to mention more severe sinfulness as he claims to be the messiah of the Lord Our Righteous Church. He has a bigger court to face and the judge will probably throw the book at him!

- Phillip Hodge sentenced for battery of Police Officers and fleeing from the scene. He said he was the deacon for the 2nd Baptist

Church of Elgin. Hodge also had a previous record of robbery and burglary.

- Warren Jeffs, sect leader, polygamous and alleged child molester as well as the head of the Utah based Church of Latter Day Saints. He was also on suicide watch while incarcerated.

- Scientology leader convicted of fraud March 1978 including American Founder, Ron Hubbard and received 4 years in prison and a fine of $35,000.

- In 2003 one of the astonishing headlines was when 44 bishops laid their hands on Reverend Robinson who jumped out of a confessional booth (or a church closet) and announced he was gay in Durham New Hampshire. Well, the scriptures do not say you can't be gay or lesbian and be a priest. The scriptures do not say you can't be gay or lesbian and get into heaven. The scriptures do not say that you can't get into heaven as a cross dresser. The scriptures do not say that you cannot get into heaven with a sex change. The scriptures do not say anything about Internet porn, cyber porn, sex toys, blow up dolls, the cowboy ranch, and 900 squeeze me telephone numbers or other intimacy outside **the marriage of a man and a woman**. Same sex partners are biblically immoral, period. Immorality is sin, period.

- Matthew Hale was the leader of Creativity Movement and was sentenced to 40 years in prison for soliciting to murder a federal judge. Christians are encouraged to speak the gospel for Christ, not to shoot it at them!

- Luc Jouret started the Order of the Solar Temple and was convicted of conspiring to buy illegal guns. When you walk outside of God's will you will find a darker walk.

- William Kamm thought he was Pope Kamm and was sentenced to prison for rape and sex with minor children. He found a very dark place within himself.

- Ervil LeBaron, leader of a Mormon group was convicted for 2 counts of murder and planning another. First he leads people down a doomed religious path then he finds an even darker path to walk. Satan will lead you astray then dump you in a darkened grave!

- Howard Porter was a pastor at the Hickman church and was convicted of murder.

- Paul Schafer, leader of Colonia Dignidad convicted of sex abuse.

- Alice Lenshina, leader of Lumpa church convicted of battery and violence that began with tax issues.

- Jim Baker of the PTL was convicted of fraud and conspiracy. Adultery was an issue and disgrace was his label. His ex-wife Tammy Faye died after battling inoperative cancer. These two led many people in confused directions.

- Mary Hubbard, leader in the Scientology group convicted of conspiracy against the U.S. Government.

- Ron Hubbard, creator of Scientology for illegal business practices as well as false claims of having the ability to heal the sick.

- Henry Lyons was president of the National Baptist Association and was convicted of grand theft and racketeering.

- Jimmy Swaggart sex scandal with Debra and Catherine. Back on the pulpit, teaching and preaching almost everyday. Forgiveness is abounding grace.

    o When you remove the pebble from your shoe then you feel more like walking! I believe this stumble made Jimmy stronger in his covenant with God and I believe his non-denominational ministries have brought literally thousands upon thousands to Christ. Remember that David once stepped away from God in adultery and murder. David was a great king before and after forgiveness. Peter denied Jesus three times and he was a great prophet before and after Jesus forgave him. Repentance and forgiveness is not optional. Listening to The Swaggart Ministries will provide great detail in God's word for they know it well.

Here is a quick note of worthy review. Sometimes we place our pastoral leadership on such a high pedestal that when they fall they fall hard and we stand in disbelief! It not only shocks them but it places those around them in shock as well. The immediate physical reaction is to cast them out of the church and be rid of the shock. Believers in Jesus Christ should not have placed them on a pedestal in the first place because they are humble servants. The other consideration is that a fallen leader should not return to leadership but they certainly must be retained and loved by the church. Remember who the church is? Yes, the body of Christ, the unity of Christians, and the first place that a lost or troubled spirit should find an open door. Here is an example of a leader whose pedestal was too high and the body of Christ forgot who they were serving.

> How far should a humble servant have to fall? The distance from your knees to the floor is the closest distance in you and God's open door . . .

- Ted Haggard battled issues with illegal drugs, lying, adultery and homosexuality. Can you get any more overwhelmed by Satan than Ted did? His wife, Gail must be an angel on special assignment and is absolutely Ted's blessing as well as an example of Christian forgiveness! It is not about acceptance, it is about sanctification.

- Bob Jones of Kansas City took the pulpit and confessed to sexual misconduct. There is nowhere that you can hide from God yet no place in life that He cannot forgive you.

- Gilbert Gauthe as a Catholic Priest confessed to 11 separate cases of child abuse/molestation. Five more Catholic priests were convicted later. This behavior in the Catholic Church has grown and continues to be hidden by its leadership. How fertile is the soil where you are sowing seeds of deception?

These folks made headline news. They are on the Internet and their stories are available if you care to look further. We set the hands of time backward every time we offer up leaders of the faith as unclean, unholy and untrustworthy. The bigger concern is that we place people's eternal lives at risk and this is as serious as is gets! There is no excuse for those who know the Lord to step out of His light but it happens. There is another step that a church can take that will darken even the brightest of churches and that is the inability to forgive. When a people step together, hide their heads in shame and look for someone to blame there is a higher consequence than the moment of a sinful act can bear. Oh my, the last group to do this pulled our Savior out of the Garden of Gethsemane, held a midnight trial and lynched Him the following morning. This was the 1st century church and they did not know Him. The church is made up of sinners saved by grace. We continue to sin because we live in sin therefore must understand repentance. The atonement of sin was paid for at the cross. It begins at the cross with, "I'm sorry for my sin, Lord I ask for your forgiveness". Jesus made a promise to forgive anyone who came in true repentance. Jesus also gave a firm command; "follow Me". No hesitations, no reservation, just turn away from sin and follow Him . . .

To the church congregation of The New Life Church in Colorado Springs Colorado: is Jesus proud of the way you responded to Ted's stumble? Christ no doubt shared your disappointment in Ted's behavior in the beginning, but I will tell you that your actions spoke volume by pushing away the very soul that His Holy Spirit used to build the church you sit in. Your discussions since then are a disappointment to your inward Christian soul and are illustrated in your outward character that you are hypocrites. How does that statement taste? I chose to pick on you because you were the most vocal about your inability to forgive, forget and welcome Ted back home with your loving support. James Dobson said he would counsel Ted then later backed out and turned his back on someone he once called a friend. How proud Christ must have been when James stepped away from a friend in need and a fellow Christian who had stumbled. James, the easiest thing in the world to do is to stumble and fall. I can't image your heart and the hearts of every member of this church so pure as to be without sin. There are hundreds of thousands of unsaved souls that watch and learn from the lessons that Christian's teach in their everyday walk in this world. Christ would never turn His back on a person in need. Christ would never turn away from someone because they sinned. Christ would never refuse to embrace a person who is earnestly trying to make their way back to the cross for forgiveness. Christ never required anyone to beg for forgiveness. You just simply ask, repent your sin and He will invite you in so your new life can begin. Hear me now and hear me well; the one single confession of a sinful man derived from a temptation of Satan that created a fall that offered an opportunity for a church to stand before a nation and say; he is our friend, we will embrace him, help heal the wounds and walk with him to the cross. This was the very opportunity that Christ looked for in His people. What a missed opportunity to witness to the world of true Christ-like love. What a testimony that would have been of sincere Christian faith in a most gracious heavenly Father who forgave Ted the mere moment he hit his knees and asked for it. If you were a part of this Colorado group that moved in anger and turned your back on Ted then I will look you in the eyes and tell you that you do not know my Jesus. You do not know my Jesus who healed the sick, raised the dead and called for brotherly love. Jesus who forgave a prostitute in the streets surrounded by hate, accusers and ill will. How many Ted's are there that stumble or fall and Christian's allow them to keep falling, drifting, even after they reach out in regret and ask for forgiveness? If you cannot forgive them then you are questioning the very authority of God in His ability to forgive, even though He placed His Son on the cross to forgive the very sin you cannot. If you are struggling in your forgiveness then you are struggling in your faithfulness . . .

Peter denied Christ three times and our Lord called him the rock in which He would build His church upon. Paul stood by and approved the death of Stephen at the bottom of a rock pile and our Lord called him to record His word for all to follow. A thief hung on a cross beside our Lord while He was in universal pain and suffering but still He forgave this sinner his debt in full. Forgiveness; it is at the very center of Christianity.

Draw your Sword and you will understand.

Read Nehemiah Chapter 9:17 and ask yourself; "Who am I, that my Father would forgive me but I cannot find forgiveness in my heart for another?

Again, how far off am I on the number of people across this big world that is truly saved? How many are there today who call themselves Christian and cannot forgive, cannot love, cannot give and cannot testify before man that they indeed walk in God's word every day? No one really knows and the numbers I throw out in the open are merely for discussion and speculation. There will be those who will struggle with the numbers and they will miss the entire message of the cross. The decision to accept Jesus Christ into your life as your personal Redeemer is personal. However, Jesus said to confess your sins in this world and He will confess them before His Father. Christ fills your life with holiness so that your faith is what others will see in you; in how you walk, in how you talk and in how you tell others of His saving grace. And, those who accept would also follow the teachings of Christ. Christ must be transparent in your character. We have had enough stuff come out of the closet so maybe it is time for Christians to come out as well. Stop hiding and start testifying . . . The test is in your completeness. Completeness leaves no room for a questionable character.

Now feast your eyes on this lucrative business that people turn a blind eye to and that is the world's sex trade. This will make your brain explode at the immorality! In Cambodia alone it is estimated that 80,000 women and children have been sucked into this business. This is the story out of many of one of those unfortunate young girls. At age 14 her aunt invited her to a garden party. She wore her best dress and was so excited about going. Her aunt picked her up and drove to a home she was unfamiliar with. Once they arrived they went inside and the aunt told Din of Cambodia to wait there for a few moments, as she needed a few things from the store for the party. Din sat alone for a few moments until the door opened and a man entered, bound her hands, gagged her then raped her. Din's aunt never returned for her and she was mentally and spiritually crushed. The man kept Din, held her against her will, used her as his sex toy, was held captive as his sex slave, then the man released her after 4 days and gave her $10 to find her way home. Din had an aunt that sold her into slavery knowing the abuse she would endure would be horrific. This is only one story . . .

"No wonder, for even Satan disguises himself as an angel of light. Therefore it is not surprising if his servants also disguise themselves as servants of righteousness, whose end will be according to their deeds."

2 Corinthians 11:14-15

There are many stories of many little girls and boys. Southeast Asia is estimated to have **300,000** women and children in the sex trade slavery industry. Japan is the major destination for trafficking, as this is more extreme in Thailand and the Philippines. The city of Angeles City, Philippines is said to have 200 brothels with 60,000 children as sex slaves. It is estimated that 500,000 women and children are sold into the sex slavery industry in Central and Eastern Europe. Please read this paragraph again. These numbers are staggering and we are only focused in on one area of the world. Now grasp your discipleship heart around this mission field and the number of unsaved involved not only in the sex trade industry but also in the thousands of sex trade customers.

In small locations and tourist destinations like Costa Rica prostitution is legal and flourishing at its highest when the economy is at its lowest. Costa Rica has a variety of women from various countries like Russia, Europe, Asia, as well as homegrown Nicas or Ticas. The price for sex is <u>advertised</u> as $5 for a quickie and $10 for longer. If she speaks English the price moves up $10 to $25. In most cases the girls cannot leave the premises. Pimps do not want to lose their property . . . If the pimp has gotten enough use out of his property then $300 would permit you to purchase his property and the girl can leave with you. Street girls are already set free from pimps and have no value to them in this part of the world. Most street girls do not have the money to travel and do not know where to go if he did. The majority of these girls are consumed in a world of drugs to escape the shame they live in. Lost souls on both sides of the business are multiplying and rapidly growing. And the U.S. is worried about the Middle East . . .

In Las Vegas Nevada the U.S. approves of prostitution and the sex industry. In Hollywood the porn industry places it on film. The world has embraced sex and porn across the World Wide Web. Think of how many lost souls are lost in this industry as well as those many in sin that use and promote it. Who is accountable? Now let's take a look at those behind bars. Think of the people who got caught and how overwhelming these numbers could be:

What is the population of our prisons, around the world? The **US** Bureau of statistics stated there were **2,310,984** prisoners in federal, state and local prisons as of June 30, 2008. Women in prison had increased by 1.2% and men increased .7% from 2007 to 2008. The media highlights prisons as violent, drug infested, prisoners making weapons, prisoners in organized gangs and riots as well as regular territorial and/or racial fights. How many prisoners are born again believers in Christ? I don't know but Paul and John the Baptist were saved and imprisoned. All prisoners have the opportunity to repent then become a witness like these two men did. Listen, learn then tell. It is that easy even when you are in jail . . .

How many people attend sporting events drinking and shouting obscenities along with violent behavior? Not sure but most stadiums will pack out 80,000 fans. Out of 80,000 how many are drinking, arguing, fighting or just acting a fool?

How many athletes are into drugs and/or alcohol then show violent behavior? The world's urge to compete drives you to think that you cannot perform well without them.

How many people drive the highways and roads angry, drunk, drugged up and termed dangerous on the road? How many lives are suddenly ended by these strains?

How many people live in their cars, on the streets, under a bridge, in the woods or roam from shelter to shelter? An MSNBC Life study in 2007 estimated 744,000 homeless just in the US . . . Our job rate was up then too. Wonder what this years numbers are like since so many are without work? How do you count them? Where do you begin to count?

How many girls are away from home, on the run or under the gun? Turning tricks to survive or under the strong arm of a modern day pimp. There is a church with a pastor with people who care placed everywhere. Today's Christian Crusaders must care . . .

~ ~ ~ ~ ~ ~ ~ ~ ~ ~ ~ ~ ~

How many people attend concerts with drugs, alcohol and violent behavior? Fayetteville North Carolina police seized nearly one ton of marijuana, 26 kilograms of cocaine and more than $3 million in cash. In one bust! How many across the country are missed? Are these born again believers in Christ that are farming it, making it, bagging it, cutting it, selling it and using it? Can a person sell or use illegal drugs and still be filled with His holiness and walk a holy walk? The correct answer would be **NOT LIKELY**.

How many riots have occurred just because their team won or lost a game? On **May 24, in Lima, Peru,** more than 300 soccer fans were killed and over 500 injured during a riot and panic following an unpopular ruling by a referee in Peru vs. Argentina soccer game. It was the worst soccer disaster on record. How many born again believers in Christ attended the game and the riot that followed?

How many news stations and reality shows does it take to show the amount of people in trouble, in pain and lost? What value is reporting with no reaction or solution? How do reporters sleep at night when they live in constant depression? How much would a paparazzi photographer get paid for one candid nude photo of Miley Cyrus or Selena Gomez? Millions! And they would be exploiting a child! How many born again believers in Christ would look?

How many people are involved in the sex business from videos, to DVD's, to telephone calls, to the Internet, to actors, to participants, to the perverts, to the abusive, to the stalkers, to the lookers and to the restaurants promoting half naked girls to sell their food? Our commercial industry knows that sex sells and retail knows how to sell it. Victoria Secret is allowed to place mostly nude mannequins and pictures facing the malls main traffic walk areas. Am I being prudish or is this appropriate behavior placed in our children's face? Is their a born again believer in Christ that approves of these displays?

There are small shops like Spencer's in the malls that have sex toys, sex pictures, sex games and sex clothing that do not stop minors from entering the store. The merchandise they sell reads like a Penthouse forum. Now that I think about it, children are clerks running the registers and stocking the shelves. Would Today's Christian Crusader hire a child in their business to display, promote and sell sex merchandise?

How many sex abusers are caught, sentenced and do their time only to be released and abuse again? How many children have to die of abuse and molestation before we either save the soul that did it or put them where they will never do it again? Prisons protect society from harm and ill will and prisons need Christian witnesses too. Prison ministry is biblical and many disciples had first hand experience there!

What about all the religions around the world that do not recognize God the Father, God the Son and God the Holy Spirit as a single being of authority? Remember, religion is a category of many organizations that create an order of worship. What does your religion worship? Do you have a religion to call your own? Would Christ be proud of your witness?

How many talk show hosts, television stars, movie stars, pop stars, rock stars, country stars, soap opera stars and starving stars are in rehab, again? How many times must they break before sincerely asking to be mended? "Oh God please help me get out of jail" was not what I had in mind. Many are more mad or sad about getting caught than they are about getting help!

How about all those who believe in evolution? The monkey theory verses the Creator? Both efforts take faith. My Creator has never evolved and He is the same God of Adam that is for you, today. Not to mention, that even Darwin had no explanation for the seed of man in its origin or reproduction. Could it be the miracle of creation? If it was created and was part of a creation then it is a given that it must have had a Creator . . . Duh!

What about the scientists, astronomers, alien followers, and astrologist that do not follow the teachings of the Bible? Natural men believe only in man made theories and man made results of man made tests. They take measurements and calculations then count dirt rings and dig some fossils then make some really uneducated man made discoveries then give them man made names. They believe that when you die you turn to dust and POOF, you cease to exist. They pull out pieces of scripture and create denial. Most live in the past and guess at the future. They deny the spirit and bank on physical data. The debacle of global warming and dating Neanderthal man has been two areas where man has proven beyond a heavenly doubt that they cannot be sure of the data they create, the resources they create or the predictions they create from the Creator. It is all because man made the testing process that tests the tests. An intellect will be too proud to admit this is true!

What about all the people who blame God for their problems or situations instead of following God's word to get out of their sin? This is like blaming the mailman for the credit card bill you keep getting! They blame God because they cannot understand His love for them. We do not own ourselves; we belong to God so when we die we literally go home. So far there have been over 2,000 years since Jesus rose and thousands of years before His birth. So really an average life span today of 80 years is merely a speck of time! We are a blip on the radar or one star in the sky of gazillions. We are here but for a blink of an eye. So just how many blinks do you have left? The next time you drive across any bridge, look at the black marks on the sides of the bridge. How many made that mark and are still alive today to change their way of life? How many do not?

How many have committed suicide and truly thought this would accelerate their path to heaven? It is reported that there are **70** suicides every 24 hours in the world today. Seventy individuals that made a conscious decision that life holds zero value for their life, their contribution or their worth. Today, the suicide rate for individuals under the age of 30 has grown over **300%**. Think of this, if you must be forgiven for your sins after you have actually committed the sin, how do you ask for forgiveness for murder before the murder is officially categorized as a murder? Suicide is murder of self. You do not own yourself. You belong to God. Can you forgive yourself then fly a plane into a ship or building? Can you ask for forgiveness just before going on a shooting spree, killing innocent people, and then turn the gun on yourself? Can you ask for forgiveness just before pulling the pin on explosives that killed innocent people? Can you ask for forgiveness just before kicking the chair out from under your feet with a rope around your neck? You can ask but your answer is in the request and not in the act. Once you act then you will face your answer. Thou shall not kill!

How many people work for or support the ACLU? How many people are involved in ACORN? They are working for the removal of Christianity. No way a socialist organization trying to remove prayer from school or deliberately falsifying government records to allow a prostitute federal aid could ever convince me they are Today's Christian Crusaders, born again followers of Christ. It took only two young adults to bring shame to these people and those who supported them.

How many terrorists are there in the world? How many of them hate Christ! Dude, there are not 72 virgins waiting for you on the other side. By the way did you know that when you exit your physical body and become a spirit in Christ or in Hades, you are neither male nor female? Those thoughts are of a physical nature and physical paradise may include a man and woman but in heaven we will not be married. Even though we will recognize each other when Jesus gives us our spiritual bodies we will have no need for reproduction. Stop thinking physical and understand that we will move into eternity transformed as spiritual beings with Christ as Christ has prepared for us. Many take great care of their physical body but neglect their spirit. Which one will last longer?

How many hate groups are there in the world? How many gangs, radical groups, gay/lesbian groups, followers of false preachers, or pro-abortion rights groups are there? There are groups that mildly make their point and there are groups that violently make a statement of their beliefs. There are countless across the world and everywhere you have a point you will always have two or three counterpoints. Again, Satan has become very talented and experienced over the years. The similarity between groups and gangs are the organized faithfulness in their cause. It is a brotherhood and sisterhood beyond compare. Some groups and gangs are complete civilizations with orders that when given are followed without prejudice and carried out without thought of consequence. Many of these groups operate inside and outside of prison walls. From the terrorist groups to smaller hate groups, God sees an opportunity of repentance in them all. These groups are the extreme challenge even to the veteran disciple but

God still loves them so we must learn, listen and tell the gospel to all who will lend an ear.

Now let's move on to bigger gangs. How many people support dictatorship countries? A communist country with a committed team (gang) is a force to be respected like China or Russia. Once you do not respect them then you become weak and we have discussed what Satan does with weakness. Russia once had this authority and to Christianity they were a force that was greatly feared. Now Russia is calling for help from the United States to spray poisons across the opium fields located in Aphganistan. Heroin hauled from Aphganistan is killing Russia like a cancer from within. Where there are major drugs there is normally a supply line to terror of some sort. Even a weak communist can be torn apart by the very source of their own nation's corruptness.

How many people support removing the Ten Commandments from any public place?

How many people have placed lawsuits to suppress Christianity? How many lawsuits have been filed to remove a cross from property? How many lawsuits have been filed to remove a U.S. Flag from property? How many attorneys support and fight these fights? If you are an attorney and you say it is your duty to defend the scum of the earth then you are struggling with your civil duty and your duty to obey God's word. Jesus Christ would not defend any criminal that does not repent of his/her sins. He would love them and be ready to receive their repentance but He would not, therefore could not defend SIN. Defending SIN in any court is defending Satan. These are radical people that love to argue and fight just for the sake of a good fight. Some will march and rally for every cause out there and their faces are seen in every news camera on every channel. These people are typically too loud to talk to so hand them a tract and move on. Attorneys on the other hand are different breed altogether. Many spend so much time getting people out of trouble they lose sight of the real judge in charge. Your civil duty is to act according to God's laws first so you may understand and receive His amazing grace.

How many people stick a needle in their arm every day to get high? Too many! How many of these people need Jesus in their veins? All of them!

How many people live in an alcohol bottle or beer can every day just to get by? This is the largest and easiest deception of Satan in the world. I call it; Satan in a bottle or Satan on tap! Choose your poison! Just the other day I stopped at an interception where every corner and median was occupied by a person holding a sign for help. Underneath the street overpass were three persons handing a quart bottle of beer to each other. If you are supporting these lost souls then you are feeding the beast within them. If you stop feeding the beast the beast will leave and the lost soul will find a shelter and Christian love. It will blow your mind of how many kids get their cigarettes and alcohol from their own home. If the parent's party, smoke and drink do you really think they can keep track of the alcohol and cigarettes that move in and out of their home? Many parents would stand in your face and say; "well if they are going to do it I would rather them do it at home where it's safe." How many parents believe a small amount of this activity is really not important? If drinking and smoking are not critical to ones salvation, then you will be able to do them while on your knees in prayer.

Resolve to know that Jesus Christ does not have a twelve step program. He has one! John 3:3

How many people light a joint every day? How many sell a nickel or dime bag of weed every day, all day? How many are involved in cocaine? How many people are involved in cutting it and bagging it? How many people are involved in getting it in the U.S.? How many people are involved in farming it? This was important enough to mention again because I know first hand of the trafficking that is involved. As a prior Law Enforcement Officer of the State of Florida I have seen it from Miami to the panhandle of Florida. It is dropped from the air, driven down the highways and moved across the water every day with no fear. The prisons can't holdem! And there isn't enough funding to catch all of them. The enforcement officers make a huge dent in them but for every one they catch there are two or three that get by. Some are arrested, charged, convicted and if they have no prior arrest record they are sent out on probation. That is a free pass to begin moving it again and the more they fail the better they get along the way. How many of these people are born again believers in Christ? Not one and because of their career they are very difficult to witness to. One successful trip from the coast to New York City will pay more than you and I will make in years.

How many people are hooked on meth or crack cocaine? The back streets are filled with addicts. Many upper class snooty patooties do not have a clue what I am talking about. Some never drive down the streets of depression or alleys of death but they are there and no reality series could portray the pain when the sun goes down. We have one cure, only one habit that we need and that is the grace of God through Jesus Christ and the Son must rise in your life every day you wake.

How many of these addicts are involved in prostitution, theft and illegal acts to support their habit? We should have two pictures of these people: one as a child and one taken today. They would look very different but the question I would have is at what age did they choose to take the trip to hell? These lost children of God need to get off their back and get on their knees then bow to the only authority we have. Once clean they are the children they once were. They are filled with promise and inspiration of becoming a nurse, a policeman, a fireman, a doctor, a pilot and so on.

There is no hope when you constantly look in hopeless places . . .

How many people are hooked on prescription drugs? Michael Jackson loved, lived and died for the need of a prescribed high that relieved him of the pain in his mind. Elvis Presley was handed prescription pills like they were candy. Even the king of pop and king of rock-n-roll couldn't shake the evil of an experienced deceiver. Many believe they can live with a snake and it will never bite them. When it does, they act surprised. Shake the need and subscribe to daily Bible prescriptions. Are you afraid to ask for help? Then write it down, send a note, write an email, place a card in the offering plate, or whatever you need to do, but stop talking about it and do it. Every second you wait is a second wasted. First you must admit your need for help.

How many people lay out of church and make a conscious decision not to worship God? You cannot be fishermen if you are not close to the water. You can't score a touchdown if you never get on the field. You can't hit a homerun if you are still in the dugout. You can't tell a loved one that you love them if you never open your mouth. You can never say I'm sorry if you don't step over your pride. You can never forgive a friend if you never speak again. You can never make a mistake if you never ever try. Stop making excuses that have sealed your fate in eternity. God already knows your sin and your shortfalls so all you need to do is ask Him to forgive them then forget them. Because He loves you and He died for you, He then will embrace you into His kingdom. But if you are sitting in the grandstands you can never claim victory as a player on the field.

How many Hollywood stars need to be on the cover of a trash magazine for them to understand their fate? They become angered when they are slandered but they have not figured out that the life they chose and the choices they have made places them right in the cross hairs of a camera and a world instantly anxiously waiting for the mud to sling. Generally the shot they are captured in is not a favorable one so why give the shooter the ammunition to take the shot in the first place? Live righteous and the shooters will move on to the unrighteous. If a Christian's life is too boring to make the trash magazines then the Christian life must be the **right** life to live . . .

The trash magazines, propaganda mongers, paparazzi, and tabloids do not want a picture or story of you going to church, attending a Bible study, praying for the needy, serving soup in a shelter, helping the poor, blah, blah, blah. How boring is that? But place yourself at the point of risk, in an immoral situation, in the wrong place, at the wrong time and you become famously pictured for the world to see. On top of a pedestal, famously known, earning the largest income in major sports today and squeak when you walk and you will crash when your world gets the slightest pinhole leak. Not long ago the Tiger found himself deep in the woods when one affair led to another, then another then another until the Tiger was but a scared kitten hiding in his mansions and yachts and trying his best avoiding the public curiosity. All the wealth and all the fame and all the support of this world cannot hold or save your soul when it is spiraling out of control. Buddha can't do it and the immaturity of a boy lost in a man's body came to the surface. If you hide then the world will make up stories and place ink where it wants it to be, rather than where it actually was. There is nothing like standing in front of the world and saying: 'I am a man, born a sinner of Adam and I have wronged my

God, my wife and my family. My time now is to ask God for forgiveness, then my wife for a humble renewed opportunity from regretful sin and to lose everything I own to keep those who matter the most: my God, my wife and my family." Then publicly take all the rock, marble and stone Buddha's out of your life and place them in the dumpster. Then the Tiger will be blessed with his growl back and he may return to his game with a humbled heart. But sometimes Tiger's don't listen and they begin to blame others for their own sins . . .

One lost soul comes to mind that is the perfect example of zero humbleness is Alec Baldwin. On December 20, 2009 60 Minutes aired an interview with Alec and the many dumb things he has said and done. His fame is typical for his style and arrogance in his discipline with his daughter should have been regretful but when you are not humbled before God then you have no measurable value to seek the value of unquestionable love. His daughter no doubt loves him because he is her father and no doubt she will distance herself from the things that do not love her back, unconditionally. Alec is an example of what every father and dad in the globe should not be. Get your heart right and your tongue will speak respectfully, honestly and righteously. Some hearts may be too hardened to desire a pure blood transfusion. Life changes only by the holy blood of Jesus Christ.

> **"But no one can tame the tongue; it is a restless evil and full of deadly poison."**
>
> James 3:8

How many liquor stores and tobacco shops do you have in your neighborhood? How many of them need a stimulus bailout? Probably not many! These folks are making a killing while killing the community. No community ever thrived with hate, wickedness, drugs and alcohol on its corners. But then again, how many born again believers in Jesus Christ are patronizing these stores? Beer is sold out of your corner convenient store for 20% more profit margin than the grocery store down the road. And they sell a ton of beer and tobacco! There is nothing you buy, sell, use and/or consume that you would be ashamed to share or show Jesus. Would He be honored to receive it from you? Guess what? He already saw it and knows you have it . . .

How much money does the US Government flat out waste on the stupid ideas? What would you think about spending $79,000,000 to launch a rocket into the Moon to see if it has water? NASA did! The World Bank reports that 80 countries have water shortages that threaten health and economics. More than 2 billion people, have no access to clean water or sanitation. (This data is posted at ag.Arizona.) But we shot a $79 million dollar rocket at the Moon for water exploration. Not once but twice!! If they found water, how much would have cost to go get it? Maybe if there is water, we could run a water line to the Moon and have fresh Moon water. We could attach the first lunar moonwater pipeline with a pump station and bottle the lunar water for the rich and famous. That will be a great blonde joke in the future. Then you will have to explain the whole earth turning on its axis thing and draw a picture of the hose choking the life out of the globe . . . ☺ That's funny, I don't care who you are!

~ ~ ~ ~ ~ ~ ~ ~ ~ ~

How many people would rather look at filth magazines and Internet porn than their Bible? Oh sheltered one, this is bigger than you think and I would be willing to bet that no person in the world has ever searched the Internet and not come across a porn site, even if it was just a pop-up ad. And it is the fastest growing business in the globe. This is one of the biggest reasons for divorce more than any other thing today. Yes, more so than FaceBook! I didn't have to take a survey to make that assumption either. It is mainly a man's deception and it is an open door to the gates of hell. Have you ever landed on one of these sites by accident? It is easy to do and so easy to get caught up in it. Some sites will lock you in with one click and one click opens a never ending loop of porn. One leads to another and then some require you to clear your browser before you can rid yourself of the filth. This is a global problem that only God can deliver us from.

The TV, radio and Internet are full of reports and clear indications of unsaved civilizations of today. On US soil and abroad many unsaved and lost souls turn to look for someone to turn to. People in financial trouble turn to this world to get them out and they end up trusting in false hope. People who live in lostness are swallowed by this world and many do not realize they are lost. The people lost greatly outnumber those who are truly born again believers in Christ and completely surrender their walk in The Way of God's word. "**The Way**" is the path described in the New Testament and is the truth and the light in Jesus Christ. Your discipleship is a key ingredient to witnessing to others for Christ and your story is similar to many. We all struggle and we all understand the walls that are before us. We need to ensure these walls do not come between us. We certainly must remove all walls that stand between us and God.

Have you ever needed a do-over? Golfers would call it a mulligan. A chance to undo something you did? A chance to say, I'm sorry, will you forgive me? Peter and Judas certainly did.

In John 12:3-8 Judas criticized Mary for using expensive perfume to wash the feet of Jesus with her hair and was corrected by Jesus.

In Luke 22: 47-48 & Mark 14:43-45 Judas showed the priests and men where Jesus was for 30 pieces of silver and identified Jesus to them by kissing Him on the cheek.

In Matthew 27:1-8 Judas tried to return the money and went into a field only to hang himself for the betrayal was too much for him to bear. Shameful unforgivable suicide.

Judas would have loved to have a do-over; a mulligan or a 2nd chance to undo what he did to Jesus.

In Matthew 26:69-75 Peter denied knowing Jesus not once, not twice but three times. Jesus had told the disciples that one of their own would do this and on the third denial a rooster would crow. His prophecy was right. Was Peter forgiven?

In John 21:15-17 Jesus asked Peter three times did he love Him and all three times Peter said he did. Jesus forgave him and said, tend to my sheep. This means you are forgiven now go take care of God's work so that all may hear His name. This is His instruction to us and we owe Him our obedience. It is a parental responsibility to ensure your children are cared for both mentally and physically. You would not allow them to eat out of the garbage can or drink from the toilet then do not allow them to be exposed to the filth and vile things that "this world" considers of value. Be responsible and set a good example of godly values.

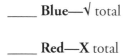

As Today's Christian Crusader, you must know what you are up against! The pleasures and deceptive pull into this world are incredibly powerful. Things of this world are very attractive to the eye, the touch and the smell. Remember the survey you completed earlier? It should be folded in the book. Let's pull it out and review. Follow this simple guide:

Take a **blue** marker or place a √ mark by every blessing request that <u>does not</u> directly impact you.
Take a **red** marker or place an **X** mark by ever blessing request that <u>does</u> directly benefits you.

____ **Blue—√** total

____ **Red—X** total

The **BLUE** total is your thoughts, prayers, wishes for others to be healed, made well, be blessed, or otherwise affect the improvement of someone else's life.

The **RED/X** total is your desire for self-improvement. "Help me, save me, work with me, tend to me, guide me, buy me, give me, I want, I need, and so on." These are requests made for your own life's well being, for your own benefit, something physical that you want or a self-blessing.

The bluer you see the closer you are to understanding God's will. Take a closer look at anything in the red. If you chose not to do the exercise then here again we discuss discipline and obedience. If you didn't do the exercise you probably don't exercise God's word in its completeness. Don't mean to be mean, just want the truth to surface in your heart so your life will see Light . . . Romans 1:5 and 1st John 2:3-6

~ ~ ~ ~ ~ ~ ~ ~ ~

Being a Christian is being a friend to others. It is a need to give or to offer help for another. It is offering a prayer for someone in need. It is caring for their world and their sufferings. It is being involved with others. It is a desire to <u>want</u> to help others. It is a no hesitation offering of ones self to someone else in need. A born again believer in Christ and Today's Christian Crusader must live between the boundaries of His mercy & grace . . .

Being strong in your Christian faith will allow you to have nice things, drive a nice car, live in a nice house, eat good food and be secure in this world while never ever allowing anything of this world to come between you and God, Ever . . . Will these things fall from the sky like manna in the Book of Exodus? Probably not!

And if you think being a Christian isn't tough then do not go outside. Stay in your monastery, behind your walls, on your mountain and stay safe away from the world. But then again, how will you witness? How will you do God's work? How will others see what God has done for you? How will a child's life ever be better if you don't touch their lives? How will you show your discipleship? How will you tend to His sheep? It would be impossible unless you are waiting for the fish to come to you. But then again, how will you control the thoughts that Satan places in your mind? Being alone without fellow believers in Christ is a dangerous place to be . . .

The history of the Bible includes many battles, many wars and many bloody incidents. It is full of wickedness and sinful behavior. Beginning with Cain's murder of his brother Abel, we have been in brutal days and will see it increase. It began in Genesis.

"Then the Lord saw that the wickedness of man was great on the earth, and that every intent of the thoughts of his heart was only evil continually. The Lord was sorry that He had made man on the earth, and He was grieved in His heart."
Genesis 6:5-6

It takes courage to step out into an aisle and take the walk of faith to the front of a church and take the hand of God's servant and say; "I seek God to take control of my life. I ask Jesus Christ to forgive my sins and I believe in the blood He shed for me. I ask to receive His Holy Spirit and His gift of grace for eternal life. I ask to baptized and cleansed of self so I may commit my soul to doing His work. I believe, I accept and I will follow." Know that the world is wicked and in this wickedness you have a chance for refuge. It is God's grace . . .

"Whoever claims to live in Him must walk as Jesus did. Dear friends, I am not writing you a new command but an old one, which you have had since the beginning. This old command is the message you have heard." 1st John 2:6-7

The Courage of Discipleship

"From that time Jesus began to preach and say, "Repent, for the
kingdom of heaven is at hand."

Matthew 4:17

The original dozen, the first disciples were summoned together by Jesus
and were listed in order that they appeared beginning in Matthew 10 verse
1 and they were:

1. Simon Peter
2. Andrew, Peter's brother
3. James, son of Zebedee
4. John, brother of James
5. Phillip
6. Bartholomew
7. Thomas
8. Matthew the tax collector
9. James, son of Alphaeus
10. Thaddaeus
11. Simon the Zealot
12. Judas Iscariot, the one who betrayed Jesus

These men, the original twelve, received specific directions from Jesus:
where to go, who to witness to, whom not to speak to and even specifically
what to say. The key verses for me were in chapter 10 verses 16 and 17:

**"Behold, I send you out as sheep in the midst of wolves; so be
shrewd as serpents and innocent as doves. But beware of men,
for they will hand you over to the courts and scourge you in their
synagogues."**

These two verses give clear and present warning of the dangers in following Christ then and the same dangers faced in our work today. There are still those who have made it their mission to deceive, detour, disturb, deny and destroy our work. Jude 10 gives a telling statement, *"But these men revile the things which they do not understand; and the things which they know by instinct, like unreasoning animals, by these things they are destroyed."* But the verse just before makes a profound statement that we need to learn and understand. Know when to step away from those who refuse to listen, have reason or deny God's gift. No one will receive God's Holy Spirit by force. Simply say, *"The Lord rebuke you and I have done my calling"*. Step away and move on with confidence that God will take over from there.

The message of the disciples was very consistent and constant. They spoke of Jesus, as prophesy of His coming, the fulfillment of this prophecy, the healings, the raising of the dead, the lessons He provided, and the required path to Heaven.

Matthew, Mark, Luke and John all speak exactly the same life path. The simple part of this message is the difference between this life and the promise of the next. A born again believer in Christ places all their faith in God, His Son who came to die for our sin so that we might have everlasting life and the Holy Spirit who walks with us every step of the way. God is not concerned with our looks, our height, our hair (or the lack thereof), our fame, our fortune, our awards, our popularity, our career path, our titles, our trophies, our plaques, our gold medals, our super-bowl rings, our golden globes, our Emmys, our Pulitzer Prize, our golden calf, or our whatever you call it that recognizes worldly accomplishments. If you receive recognition in this world for anything it should compliment God who made it possible. I am not speaking of those who praise God for helping them secure a championship season! Heavenly recognition with eternal rewards is impossible without God's blessings.

~ ~ ~ ~ ~ ~ ~

It is easy to see that atheists, agnostics and anit-Christ religious believers are opposite of God's Holy Bible. Opposite of it's sole authority over life to death and every word from a single Creator or single Being of Father, Son and Holy Spirit. If a born again believer in Jesus Christ dies, we have but one way to move and it is an eternal life with our Redeemer. Those who oppose this belief die and believe they will simply cease to exist.

If Christians are wrong we will all simply cease to exist. If Christians are right then those who are not born again believers in Jesus Christ will fall according to their faith. That is an eternal gamble with your life!

It never helps when you have an evangelical that stumbles and falls hard. I spoke of Ted Haggard being wrapped up in adultery, sex scandals, suicidal tendencies, gay affairs, and many, many lies. I believe that Ted feels that God tests His people and provides them with opportunities to recover. Ted continues to struggle with being accepted but he is very confused about who tested him. God does not tempt nor test but He does provide His word so you may test yourself to His word. God is very forgiving and mends broken souls before He will call you to service. I think Ted returning to church is right but returning to teach to soon might be a risk. Teachers, pastors, ministers, chaplains, bishops are held to the highest of standards. While God's people forgave Jimmy Swaggart, Ted's congregation abandoned him and the media slammed him. Ted is beginning a new church. The world will continue to question and watch this process very closely. If Ted can bring the Holy Spirit into his voice, God will not allow him to fail. If Ted is doing this without the Holy Spirit then we will know soon enough. When you feel the love of His healing then you know the love in His grace as well. Blind your physical sight and see with the holiness of your eternal spirit. Try seeing through God's eyes and see His forgiveness with clearer brighter vision.

It is easy to get caught up in this world's stuff. Money is the biggest luxury item that everyone would say is hard to come by and most would say they don't have enough of. I call it a luxury item because it never seems to be enough, more is less and less needs more. Good grief, we pay for water in a bottle! Can there be a better example? Other things that most people would feel are "gotta-have stuff" such as: cloths, hats and shoes. I am not talking about the requirement to cover your body. I am speaking of runway model custom designer material, $1,000 suits, $500 dress, and a closet full of shoes that you never wear. Then people would place travel high on their list of "gotta-do stuff". You have got to get out of the city for fresh air. You have got to go to the city to shop? People who live in the mountains want to vacation at the beach. People that live close to the beach want to vacation in the mountains. People who do not like their money want to vacation in Las Vegas. People who like sports don't mind spending $150 to watch a pro football game. Die hard sports fans have to have a $100 jersey to watch the big game on TV. But here is a novel concept; everything you own is destructible, it will all fade away, it will tear away, will turn to ashes or break. But if you truly "deserve" it, then please do not place it between you and God. If you do, you will lose more than you bargained for.

The quickest way to make folks uncomfortable is to talk about money or finances. If you ask for a donation then you have really set them running. Discuss tithe and peoples tempers rise! It seems that everyone has his or her hand out and asking for something. There is a bucket at every traffic light, a bell at every door, a helmet for every kid's football team uniform, a pompom for the cheerleading squad to go to camp, and then there is the Girl Scout Cookies. Now that's something you can sink your teeth into! The coconut caramel bar with the little chocolate stripes is just plain sinful . . . **But** do they need a hand out or a hand up? Not long ago they would wash your car to EARN money for camp. Because parents are busy with multi-careers, multi-tasks, multi-lifestyles, multi-families due to divorce and multi-hobbies that keep them from mentoring their multi-kids. Now everything must be freely given because parents have no multi-extra time to multiply discipline on undisciplined kids. It is not a change in the times. It is lazy worthless sorry no count parents raising their children to place their hands out. Soon there will be the generation of complete dependency. Then the anti-Christ will open the door with all the answers . . . It's not prophecy; it is common sense in basic Bible study.

The favorite line that has stood the test of time is: "Sorry, I gave at the office." When I am approached for donation I look at each group and ask myself, how will God benefit from this donation? The poor, homeless and folks stranded begging for cash need to go to a shelter and/or local church for support. There are some that have worked the same exit ramp for years and it is their full time job to beg.

Do not confuse "I can't" with "I won't!"

God loves a cheerful giver and those who help the needy but if your kid wants to go to summer camp to learn to fish, hunt, swim and tell ghost stories by the campfire light then you pay for it. If he needs a football jersey for the new season then you buy it. If she needs a bus fare for winter tumbling competition then you pack your bags and go with her. If the church youth group needs assistance for supplies, food and fun for Vacation Bible School then pass the offering plate. Does your need benefit God and if we donated to help you, will you in turn help God?

Don't confuse needy with greedy . . .

God has a simple idea of wealth. He is only concerned with our name as it is welcomed in the Lambs Book of Life. He only wants us to place Him before any of the stuff we get. Your cash will not get you in the book, neither will a good deed, an occasional trip to church and nobody can pray you there once you bite the dust, kick the bucket, seal the coffin, drop in a six foot trap, lay for worm food, push up daisies, received your death warrant, reach your final destination, made ready for the fossil farm, bed like compost, out in the bone yard, on the stairway to heaven, snuffed out, taken your last dump, kissed the dirt, dead as a dodo bird, down under, part of the worm farm, reached the zombie zone, out of business, passed on, landed in the eternal cooker, the forever flame broiler, dead as a dog, graveyard dead, on your final snooze and stiff as board. When you are dead, then you are **DEAD!**

We cannot control the wind but we have the ability to adjust our sails.

When Jesus was asleep in the boat with His disciples, losing their minds across turbulent water, He asked them where their faith was. Did they actually believe that anything would happen to the Son of Man? When He stood He commanded the winds and the seas to calm. And they did. Who is this that can make the winds and seas calm?

His name is Jesus and He lives inside you each and every day. If you live with the fullness of Christ within you, you will always know how to adjust your sails during turbulent times.

When you are not able, He is the authority of the heavens and earth.

My studies have also included research in several Internet blogging sites that offer dialog from all who sign in as members. My very first observation was in one site that had a membership of over 65,000 people but less than a tenth were actively engaged in debates. And I do mean a debate. Many are there to create confusion, many are there to argue, many are there to make attempts at offering help, some fail with wise crack comments and others just offer an "amen". Here is the sad result: Several people enter the site claiming the title of atheist yet they quote Bible scripture, quote Old Testament violence, God's firmness with an unruly people and situations that are unquestionably harsh in today's standard. That is, today's middle to upper class standard. These few have not researched the cruelty of men in global nations that abuse, beat, maim, terrorize, burn and murder innocent people. The sex trade is not felt but our borders are being bent. The drug trafficking is not seen but our borders are being bent. Our health care is suffering but our borders continue to be bent. Our current communicable diseases are among the lower class but our borders are being bent. Illegal alien babies born in this country are granted immediate citizen rights and our borders continue to be bent. Our unemployment rate continues to climb but our borders continue to be bent. Our national security continues to be threatened but our borders continue to be bent. Mexico's el presidente stood on the White House lawn and told Arizona it was wrong and President Obama agreed with him. All this while our administration continues to be bent over to man made will. Our nation is filled with unquestionable ungodly people, confused religious people and tested Christians. Our borders just recently went from being bent to being opened in a mutual trade agreement. What happens to any valley when the dam is opened? Unbridled horror floods the valley!

Our faith and love for Christ automatically draws the desire to love Him, to repent our sins to Him, to thank Him, to work for Him and to seek our rewards from Him. A born again believer in Christ best financial plan is to place life in perspective of what is important and what is not as important. Here is a great way to place your life in priority:

> God is always first
> God created everything
> God owns everything
> God provides what we need
> All we have to do is manage it ~ we live on, in and around what He owns . . .
>> If you could not say it, use it, move it, buy it, sell it, trade it, take it into heaven ~ then you don't need it . . .

If we would respect what God provides for us, thank Him for His provisions, and earn what we receive we would have a better appreciation of what we have. There is absolutely nothing wrong with having good stuff and doing fun things as longs as it doesn't own you and/or become between you and God.

Father → Family → Fun

How do I know I am a born again believer in Christ? How do I know that change-repentance has occurred in my life? Here is an example of unselfish unconditional love.

The Window of Dreams

There was a man who was injured in an automobile accident, had surgery and was placed in ICU for recovery. He was informed that the hospital was abnormally full and they were locating a room for him. He rested and was patient, for a while. As he became more aware of his predicament and where he was, he demanded service and to be placed in a private room.

Shortly after arriving the attending nurse came and began to prep him for his trip to his room. He said to her in a grouchy voice; "I must have a private room, a private room I tell you! And a window, I must have a view outside". The nurse smiled and continued to roll him to his room. Upon arrival she said; "Here we are, Mr. Gibson we have a neighbor to keep you company". The injured man said; "No I must have a private room, I must have a window or I will surely die in here". The nurse pulled the curtain so he would have privacy and reassured him that she would continue to look but in the mean time for him to relax and enjoy Mr. Gibson's company.

Mr. Gibson; "hello friend, whacha in for?"

The injured man; "I was hit by a car, damn old woman, she wasn't even looking!"

Mr. Gibson; "Well you'll love it here friend, they have the best food and a real great staff with always a kind word for those who need a little cheering up. What's your name friend?"

The injured man; "Watson, Bernard Tyler Watson, now, what can you see out the window?"

Mr. Gibson: "Window? Well, it is . . ."

Watson: "Stop stallin man, and tell me what you see!"

Mr. Gibson: "Well, I see the blue sky, there's a park, a pond and some birds".

Watson; "Gibson, I am a gardener by trade, I own 16 florists shops around town and I have never been where I could see my gardens or my flowers. I don't what I will do without seeing my garden or blooming flowers."

Mr. Gibson: "Well friend, until you get your own room I would be glad to tell you what I see."

Watson: "Well, if you'll just describe what you see out the window from time to time, I guess that will have to do."

Mr. Gibson; "Sure I will, I look forward to it."

The next day, Watson awoke and hollered; "Gibson, you awake?"

Mr. Gibson; "A, yes, yes, why yes I am."

Watson: "Gibson, what's it look like out there today?"

Mr. Gibson asked; "Well, what time is it?"

Watson; "what time? What do you mean what time is it?"

178

Mr. Gibson: "I don't have a clock over here and I was simply wondering."

Watson: "It's 6:31am man common! What do you see?"

Mr. Gibson: "Ah yes, the morning dew is about to lift off the grass. I see birds flying around pond as calm as it can be. There are beautiful flowers surrounding the pond, yellows, reds, roses, daffodils, gorgeous iris's blooming and there is a slight dew on the petals while I see hummingbirds working the blooms and a beautiful lady sits quietly on a bench reading a book as doves coo around her asking for a snack, maybe a nibble or two. The grass is freshly cut and trimmed perfectly around the flowerbeds and a gardener is fluffing the bedding around the flowers. The walkway winds around the flowers and the trees are filled with green leaves. The walkway is lined with hand laid stones and a gentleman and his lady walk hand in hand under the dogwood and cheery trees in full bloom. It looks like the cherry trees are in early blossom this year and the puffy pink blooms glisten in the morning sun. Watson it's a beautiful morning, a beautiful morning indeed."

Watson lay gently back in his pillow, a subtle smile and expression of peace upon his face as he said: "Thank you Mr. Gibson, I have never seen such a place and I thank you for that. My oh my, I can't wait to see it myself."

The gentlemen both talked this way through the day and the following day.

On the third day Watson awoke and he called to Mr. Gibson as he had the 2 past mornings. In an anxious voice Watson called out; "Mr. Gibson, Gibson, speak up man. How is your window this fine morning?"

The nurse walked in the door and smiled at Watson saying, "Good morning sir, we have your private room ready with a wonderful window view."

Watson: "What, where is Mr. Gibson?"

Nurse: "Oh I'm sorry, Mr. Gibson passed away in his sleep last night. He was very ill."

Watson: "Oh my, I didn't even know."

Nurse: "Yes, his passing was very quiet and peacefully he drifted away in his sleep. I'll get you ready to move."

Watson: "Move me! Move me? The hell you say, you can draw that curtain and move me close to that window on the other side!"

Nurse: "I don't understand". And she pulled the curtain to full expose the entire room. There was a solid wall on all sides of where Mr. Gibson had laid.

Watson: "I don't understand. He spoke so eloquently of the views from a window that was right here. It was right there! A pond! It was a garden, full of flowers and blooms and birds. There were people strolling and walkways winding. Please tell me what happened here!"

Nurse: "Sir, Mr. Gibson couldn't see a thing. He has been completely blind since he was a child. He had no vision. No sight at all."

Mr. Watson sat and pondered the sight of it all. He could close his eyes and see it all. Just as Mr. Gibson said, life was more beautiful just beyond that solid wall . . .

Mr. Gibson had no vision but yet his gift was unselfish to the man who needed his vision to get him through his pain. He gave unconditional blind faith and good will to someone in need. It is very simple, the cost is simple to see but you must remove "self" and replace it with "serve" so others can see Christ, through you and me . . .

"But a natural man does not accept the things of the Spirit of God, for they are foolishness to him; and he cannot understand them, because they are spiritually appraised".

1ˢᵗ Corinthians 2:14

If your natural desires are not pure and do not have the Holy Spirit in them then they are easy prey for Satan and he revels himself in every opportunity to deceive. Your spiritual vision is by the grace of God. Take it, accept it, embrace it and keep it as your shield of protection.

"And God is able to make all grace abound to you, so that always having all sufficiency in everything, you may have an abundance for every good deed."

2ⁿᵈ Corinthians 9:8

Let's break 2ⁿᵈ Corinthians 9:8 down:

And God is, always has been and always will be.

Able—He has the ability to do everything, anything and will, if you have faith and believe.

All—His word leaves no crumbs on the table, nothing to ponder or wonder. All is everything!

Abound to you—it is free to you, a gift without hesitation.

Always—Forever, infinity and beyond.

Everything—This is from a grain of sand to the highest of mountains, the depths of the oceans to a sip of drinking water, and from the tip of the South Pole to the tip of the North Pole and all points in between.

Abundance—Take the description of everything, add it all together then make a multiple of infinity.

For every good deed—Okay wait a minute. You mean that I can't just walk to the front of a church, shake a preacher's hand, and say a prayer then be done? You mean that I can't just go to church on special holidays and sit in my assigned pew? I gotta do deeds? Draw your Sword to Romans 8:28. You are not here for your own goodness for no one is good but God.

~ ~ ~ ~ ~ ~ ~

So many people have issue with being a bondservant but they will stop by the minute market and buy a lotto ticket. They'll stand in line overnight for a store sale to buy something they want. They'll spend the night camped out to get a ticket to a concert they want to see. They'll tail gate a ballgame out in the stadium parking lot and never see the game live. They'll spend $150 to go to a pro ballgame and stand in line to use the restroom. They'll wait tables for $2.10 an hour plus tips and complain about poor tippers.

They'll stand in a unionized strike line of their favorite union that they pay dues for. They'll sit for 2 hours to watch a movie in a theater but won't spend 1 hour in God's house. Why? Because what you put into anything is what you can expect to receive! Expect to have a good time and you will have a good time. Expect to get nothing out of your time and it will be time wasted . . .

Like a marathon runner training to compete in the Olympics they train each day for strength and endurance. You will be challenged each day in your spiritual faith and the challenge will come from non-believers and "so-called" believers. The foundation blocks to build a strong spiritual marathon come from learning your skills, understanding the limitations of your skills, toning your skills and developing your skills beyond a sprint and into a lifelong run. And remember, you don't have to be the strongest or the most talented spiritual soul in the group. Just know that He loves you no matter what you have done. Just know that He is with you no matter what you face. Just be assured that He will be waiting for you when you get home. His name is Jesus . . .

Jesus said;
"I am the way, and the truth, and the life; no one comes to the Father but through Me."

John 14:6

Disciple means to learn and Discipleship simply means go tell somebody what you have learned! The courage of a disciple comes from faith in God's wisdom and trust in God's guidance. Reach out and touch someone lost and when you begin to give then you will begin to understand. Faith has three distinct ingredients:

1) Faith in His promise
2) Belief in His word
3) Covenant with God which is to commit to action

You cannot have completeness without all three ingredients. Our daily fellowship in Christ is secured with daily prayer, daily scripture and daily devotion. Does this sound like too much to do? Then go look in the mirror and ask yourself this question: "If I have no desire to follow

Jesus completely then why should Jesus completely receive me in His kingdom?"

"He who does what is sinful is of the devil, because the devil has been sinning from the beginning. The reason the Son of God appeared was to destroy the devils work. No one who is born of God will continue to sin, because God's seed remains in him; he cannot go on sinning, because he has been born of God. This is how we know who the children of God are and who the children of the devil are: Anyone who does not do what is right is not a child of God; nor is anyone who does not love his brother."

1st John 3:8-9

The History of the Crusades

Today's Christian Crusader is a warrior who is learned, skilled and always prepared for spiritual warfare.

✐ ✐ ✐ ✐ ✐ ✐

"Let your light shine before men in such a way that they may see your good works, and glorify your Father who is in heaven. Do not think that I came to abolish the law of the Prophets; I did not come to abolish but to fulfill. For truly I say to you, until heaven and earth pass away, not the smallest letter or stroke shall pass from the Law until all is accomplished."

Matthew 5:16-18

The medieval "Crusade" was a holy war. For a conflict to be officially considered a Crusade, it had to be sanctioned by the pope and conducted against groups seen as enemies of Christendom. Initially, only those expeditions to the Holy Land (Jerusalem and associated territory) were considered Crusades. More recently, historians have also recognized campaigns against heretics, pagans and Muslims in Europe as Crusades. They were fighting for those who had not heard of Jesus. They fought against barbarianism, for the oppressed and the right to seek God's word. This may sound a little familiar to our fight today. We just wear a different uniform.

For centuries, Muslims had governed Jerusalem, and they tolerated Christians because they helped the economy. In other words, they worked hard, earned an honest living and paid taxes. Then, in the 1070s, Turks (who were also Muslim) conquered these holy lands and mistreated Christians before realizing how useful their good will (and tax revenue) could be. The Turks also threatened the Byzantine Empire. Emperor Alexius asked the pope for assistance, and Urban II, seeing a way to corral the violent energy of Christian knights, made a speech calling for them to take back Jerusalem. Thousands responded to the call, resulting in the First Crusade. And there was wealth behind this mission as well!

Urban II made his speech calling for a Crusade at the Council of Clermont in November 1095. This is seen as the start of the Crusades. However, the "reconquista of Spain" (lasting about 800 years), an important precursor to crusade, had been going on for centuries. Traditionally, the fall of Acre in 1291 marks the end of the Crusades, but some historians extend them to 1798, when Napoleon expelled the Knights Hospitaller from Malta. These again were times of war, lost lives and worship of rocks and false gods.

Who Went on Crusades

People from all walks of life, from peasants, farmers and laborers to kings and queens, answered the call. Women were encouraged to give money and stay out of the way, but some went on crusade anyway. When nobles crusaded, they often brought huge attendants (servants), whose members may not necessarily have wanted to go along. At one time, scholars theorized that younger sons more frequently went crusading in search of estates of their own; however, crusading was an expensive business, and recent research indicates it was lords and elder sons who were more likely to crusade. Either way the rich got richer or the poor stayed poor and died for the wealthy. This sounds a little familiar and close to home in our military efforts.

Crusade Territories

Upon the success of the First Crusade, the Europeans set up a king of Jerusalem and established what is known as the Crusader States. Also called outremer, which is French for "across the sea" or "overseas", the Kingdom of Jerusalem controlled Antioch and Edessa, and it was divided into two territories since these places were so far-flung. When ambitious Venetian merchants convinced soldiers of the Fourth Crusade to capture Constantinople in 1204, the resulting government was referred to as the Latin Empire, to distinguish it from the Greek, or Byzantine, empire they had claimed. Areas were divided up much like the states are in America.

Impact of the Crusades

Some historians, particularly Crusade scholars, consider the Crusades the single most important series of events in the Middle Ages. They needed to explain the reason for the missions. The significant changes in the structure of European society that took place in the 12th and 13th centuries were long considered the direct result of Europe's participation in the Crusades. This view no longer holds as strongly as it once did. Historians have recognized many other contributing factors in this complex time. The more they read the more they reveal. Or is it the more confused they become?

There are no doubts that the Crusades contributed greatly to the changes in Europe. The effort of raising armies and providing supplies for Crusaders stimulated the economy; trade benefited, as well, especially once the Crusader States were established. Interaction between the East and West affected European culture in areas of art and architecture, literature and education. And Urban's vision of directing the energies of warring knights outward succeeded in reducing war within Europe. It was having a common goal and common objective, even for those who didn't participate in the Crusade, brought a closer view of Christendom as a united people. In some areas of the world an army must clear the way for the Word to be heard.

The plot worked better than Rome could ever have anticipated. Even the common folk soon took up the call to arms. Starting in AD 1096, Peter the Hermit and Walter the Penniless led a group of poor, ill-armed peasants in an advance party, which was destroyed either during the trip east or by Muslims in Anatolia. A comparable sight would be the act of any nation taking arms against the Unites States. Every household that owns a firearm would take arms against a united enemy. California and Washington may be taken captive but the rest of the states would fair well. These two states would be called causalities of war and an acceptable loss for the greater good of the nation . . .

The real army eventually set out from France, led by Baldwin of Flanders, Robert of Normandy, and several other nobles. I was always interested in the nobles and their following. Their wealth was by family but also increased as they conquered. This army had many successes, including the capture of Antioch on June 3, 1098 and then the capture of the Holy City of Jerusalem a year later, on July 15, 1099. To the victor go the spoils. Victorious, the Crusaders established the four Crusader States of Edessa, Tripoli, Jerusalem, and Antioch. Maps of old align with maps of new show that wars have been fought on these lands since the beginning and if you study your Bible you will see that they will be the point of battleground in the end as well. The news media does an awesome job of reporting our nation's leader on foreign soil bowing to communist and socialist leaders. They also have done an awesome job reporting his inability to support Israel and the Holy Land.

Unsettled peace reigned in the Holy Land until 1144, when Edessa fell to the Muslims because Jerusalem refused to send aid after the Franks of Edessa refused to accept a woman as their ruler, even as a mere regent for two years. Hilary Clinton, Nancy Pelosi and Michelle Bachelet of Chile would not have been impressed with this rule. Sarah Palin may have been considered a favorite since she is a better shot than most jihad soldiers and she understands Godliness before worldliness.

Two years later, in 1146, Bernard of Clairvaux, Louis VII of France, and Conrad III of Germany led armies to the Holy Land to recapture Edessa. This Crusade was a disaster for Europe, but the Crusaders did manage to retake Lisbon, Portugal from Muslim hands.

After the disaster of the Second Crusade, there might never have been another, had European greed not led to the breaking of a sacred peace agreement. This would also be the case that the colonies felt when Paul Revere made his famous ride. After the Second Crusade ended in 1148, King Baldwin of Jerusalem forged a truce with the Syrian Sultan, Salah-al-Din, whom the Europeans called Saladin. That truce, called the "Truce of God" lasted until 1187 when Reynald of Chatillon broke it by attacking a caravan bound for Saladin's own sister. Saladin responded to this insult at once, demanding Reynald's head, which the foolish King of Jerusalem Guy refused and the battle soon began. In the end, Reynald's greed and Guy's incompetence led to the Arab conquest of Outremer, and the launching of another Crusade from Europe. Again the greed of an individual or nation will lead to ruin. If you begin to live for the wrong reasons then the wrong results are sure to follow.

The first European leader to set out for the East was the German Emperor, Barbarossa, in May 1189. The German army while under this great Emperor's command had many Crusading victories along their road to Outremer, re-opening many Arab-held overland routes. Then in early June of 1189 disaster struck when Barbarossa drowned while crossing a river. The German army more dedicated to their leader than to the Holy War soon turned homeward again. This happens when those who battle are following the man rather than the cause.

Kings Philip of France and Richard of England set out for Outremer in July 1190 taking a journey that was mostly across the water. In the end Richard would be instrumental in the reclaiming of Cyprus and much of Outremer though he would fall short of his goal and Jerusalem remained in Arab hands. The Third Crusade is often referred to as either Richard's Crusade or the Gentlemen's Crusade since both Richard and Saladin claimed to uphold the virtue of chivalry and spent as much time in a battle of manners as in actual battle itself.

A tournament hosted by Theobald, Count of Champagne, was the unlikely breeding ground for the Fourth Crusade. While the Count's motives for Crusading were religious and chivalrous since Outremer had no King and Theobald was the nearest blood relation to the female heir, others had no such chivalry in mind. They were merely escaping the inevitable battling between King John of England and Philip of France. Greed in earthly ownership and pride of who's got what will get you into a fight every time.

This ill-conceived Crusade ended up never even reaching Outremer. Instead of attacking Egypt, as planned by Theobald the Crusaders pillaged Constantinople and captured it in AD 1203. After the Crusaders had moved on there was a citywide revolt causing the Crusaders to return and recapture the city again in 1204. You just can't leave a bunch of heathens alone for a minute . . .

The next Crusade is rarely spoken of or remembered in the undertaken by the knights of Christendom was preceded by tragic events. In 1212, boy-preachers led an ill-fated "Children's Crusade" that would never reach Jerusalem or even as far as Outremer. Some say these events were fictional and were not bands of children but were the poor and homeless marching to reach the Holy Land. It is said that many of these children or wandering poor died of starvation or from hardships and drowning before they were forced to turn back. No matter if it was fact or fictional, their Crusade did fuel the final decision to go to war again in an effort to re-open overland passage to Outremer. This was decided at the Council of Lateran in 1215 which again, the few decided the fate of the many.

Begun in 1217, the Fifth Crusade amounted to little more than a series of raids until late in 1218 when attacks on the Sultanate of Egypt began. In November 1219 after a siege of nearly sixteen months Crusaders captured the city of Damietta. Had the Crusaders had a competent leader they might even have captured Cairo. Instead their venture ended in failure and Egypt remained in Arab hands.

The last three Crusades were not high in either interest or popularity in Europe. Warfare in the East was losing its appeal to the nobility of Europe and morale was at rock bottom in Outremer. These half-hearted Crusades would gain and lose unimportant ground repeatedly resulting in complete and utter failure. By 1291 the Kingdom of Outremer was completely destroyed. In these failures, thousands of men lost their lives in an attempt to free people to worship the living God Almighty, Creator of all things. The issue then becomes the intent of the leader who sends men and women in harms way for the wrong reasons. Is man glorified or is God glorified in the mission?

So what did Europe learn in the course of the Crusades? Crusaders gone East to fight the Saracens learned many valuable things from their enemies whether through war, captivity, or truce. Advances in medicine, warfare, mathematics, anatomy, textiles, and cooking sailed westward with the treasures of war. Also, truce times opened trade routes through contact with eastern merchants opening up a whole new world to Europe through exploration. The opening of trade through the Near East, which traded across Asia and deep Africa, fuelled the European hunger for wealth and knowledge. These desires would prompt Europe into a race to find the fastest trade routes to the Far East, first overland, and then by sea. For the first time in centuries, Europeans sought knowledge, and curiosity had opened the world to them. And if everyone were truly honest they would agree that religion had little to do with any of this. It was mainly <u>greed</u> for more stuff and pride in "I want it first, I want it most and I am willing to walk over you to get it!"

It remains an indisputable fact that the Crusades were a brutal time and left war torn people and destroyed property. However, we must never forget that had the Euro-Centralism of the Dark Age Europe never led to the Crusades it is highly likely that Europe would never have emerged from that ignorant age. But have they become any smarter today? Did they win? If they won, what did they win? Good luck finding two people to agree on this answer! One thing is for sure; wars are costly in lives but bring economy back to life. The battle for Christ is for eternity!

~ ~ ~ ~ ~ ~ ~

Today's Christian Crusader prepares for what type of spiritual battle? The largest in size and highest in priority is Allah. Allah is a religious god/idol similar to Baal except more warrior god than god of fertility. Allah has called for death, suicide, violence, battles and war for thousands of years and it has no appearance of going away.

Jihad, routinely translated as holy war often makes headlines. It occurs now more often than EVER before. This is definitely the case since 911 and the terrorist prevention measures taken since. In May 1994 Yasir Arafat's in Johannesburg called for "jihad to liberate Jerusalem" was a turning point in the peace process. Israelis heard him speak about using violence to gain political ends and questioned his peaceable intentions. Both Arafat himself and his aides then clarified that he was speaking about a "peaceful jihad" for Jerusalem. Yea right!

This incident points to the problem with the word jihad and what exactly does it mean? Two examples from leading America Moslem organizations, both fundamentalists, show the extent of disagreement this issue inspires. I will use much of their language to post both positions correctly.

The C.A.I.R. (Counsel on American-Islamic Relations), a Washington-based group, clearly states that jihad does not mean holy war. Rather, it refers to a central and broad Islamic concept that includes the struggle to improve

190

the quality of life in society, struggle in the battlefield for self-defense or fight against tyranny or oppression.' CAIR even asserts that Islam knows no such concept as a "holy war".

In sharp contrast, the Muslim Students Association recently distributed an item with a Kashmir dateline, '"Diary of a Mujahid." The editor of this document claims to understand jihad and says: "While we dream of jihad and some deny it, while others explain it away, and yet others frown on it to hide their weakness and reluctance towards it, here is a snapshot from the diary of a mujahid who had fulfilled his dream to be on the battlefield."

Does jihad mean a form of moral self-improvement or war in accord with Islamic precepts? There is no simple answer to this question, for even Muslims for at least a millennium have disagreed about the meaning of jihad. If they don't know then how could the rest of the world know? So far to date, December 2009, there have been eighty-eight countries that have documented jihad activity. In my humble observation, these are eighty-eight countries that have been exposed to a group that are pro-Moslem and anti-Israel; Anti-Bible, anti-God, anti-Jesus Christ, and anti-New Jerusalem. Jesus Christ is not recognized as the Messiah in the Qur'an but Mohammed was considered a prophet even though his main role was as a military leader, not a peace loving healer with authority over death.

Muslim today can mean many things by jihad as told by C.A.I.R. "The jurists' warfare bounded by specific conditions, Ibn Taymiya's revolt against an impious ruler, the Sufi's moral self improvement or the modernist's notion of political and social reform. The disagreement among Muslims over the interpretation of jihad is genuine and deeply rooted in the diversity of Islamic thought as well as individual belief. The unmistakable predominance of jihad as warfare in Shar`i writing does not mean that Muslims today must view jihad as the jurists did decades ago. History speak only to, not for, contemporary Muslims. A non-Muslim cannot assert that jihad always means violence or that all Muslims believe in jihad as warfare." Really?

On April 17, 1995 it was reported that Timothy McVeigh pulled the pin on a timer that set a reaction of ignition on roughly 5,000 pounds of ammonium nitrate, some agriculture fertilizer, and nitro-methane which was all carefully placed in the back of a 20 foot Ryder truck. It is said that he drove this truck into downtown Oklahoma City and parked it curbside at the Alfred P. Murrah federal building. At about 9:02am, Oklahoma City shook and a chunk of that building fell. How does one man get this together, have the knowledge to safely assemble each part in the correct sequence, drive this beast downtown, park it in front of a federal building then walk away and not involve but one other idiot to help? I don't buy into this theory. This would not have been associated to an act of jihad until it was revealed that young Timothy spent time in Saudi Arabia and had Islamic terrorist connections. Like it or not, he now can be considered jihad with Muslim association. By the way, everyone remembers the big blast; building material falling and people's lives ending and that many lives were changed forever. But there were two other bombs said to have been larger than 5,000 lbs. Bomb Squads disarmed numbers two and three devices that would have done comparable damage. Timothy and Terry were caught but who wasn't? This was 1995. The Twin Towers were bombed in 1993 with about 1,100 pounds of explosives in a truck that had gained access into the parking garage. Then, on September 11, 2001, nineteen al-Queda terrorists took down both towers and a piece of the Pentagon with aircraft. Some entered the building with commercial airplanes and others fell into a Pennsylvania field with the united strength of a few brave Americans. There were 2,976 people from over 90 countries who died from these attacks. If all these actions are separated then they seem like individual acts of violence but put them together with the same methods used then they become acts of terrorism on a much larger scale. We are fighting the same Christian battles as the Crusaders did hundreds of years ago and we are losing ground all the way to Jerusalem's gates. Israel is God's Holy Land, or has Washington forgotten?

It is also worth stating those Muslim terrorists in jihad suicidal fashions are heard screaming; "Allah'a Akbar" before pulling the pin to commit murder. Men, women and children are murdered in the name of Allah. The Moslem nation at large denies the use of violence but the Qu'ran does not. There is not two Qu'ran books. Just one! Are you okay with this? I have never heard of a single case where anyone screamed "Jesus

Christ" before killing. There are two roads and one is very narrow while the other is wide as a country mile. The narrow one requires belief, faith and obedience. Jihad and murders in the name of Allah are part of the wider path.

The discussions over the meaning of jihad permits deliberate deception, such as the CAIR statement already cited. A Muslim can honestly dismiss jihad as warfare, but he/she cannot deny the existence of this concept. As the editor of the "Diary of a Mujahid'" writes, "'some deny it, while others explain it away, yet others frown on it to hide their own weakness." Infidels! Christianity and religions on the grander scale are similar in doctrinal argument but very different in the foundation of faith. Christianity is following Christ in love, faith and obedience. Being religious can be very radical, fanatical and eternally tragically, which is not grammatical but is dramatically correct . . .

The real issues of Muslim is their core beliefs of worshiping Allah, following a prophet called Mohammad ibn Abdullah founded Islam in June 8, 632 in a temple built in Kaaba and claim all their beliefs are deeply rooted in their bible. Their bible is not the Holy Bible but called "Qur'an." Mohammed retreated to a cave around the age of 40 and it is here where he experienced his visions and "divine inspirations". Sounds similar to Joe Smith's Mormon experience, but Mohammad never received golden tablets. Mohammad fell ill and died in 632AD. The prophet fell ill and died? I thought prophets grew old and went to sleep with their fathers, or walked away with God, or were swept to heaven on a chariot of fire, or were beheaded because of their faith in Jesus Christ, or were stoned to death because of their faithful ministry?

So in Islam, Moslem religion, you must go through Mohammad in order to meet Allah? But of course Muslims are forbidden to question the Islamic faith and are expected to accept its truthfulness blindly without investigation. Muhammad understood that information was the main enemy of his newly invented religion. In many Muslim controlled nations, for example, young men are paid to learn nothing but the Qur'an to the exclusion of science *and* history *and* current world events. They are told this is all they need, but in reality, they are brainwashed and basic world information is deliberately withheld from them. This is their word, not mine. It is the Muslim doctrine. Remember, The Nation of Islam desires Moslem Mosques on U.S. soil but refuses to allow a Christian church to be planted on Arabian soil. Why?

The real issue to this man made religion is fear. Leave the Muslim faith and you will die! Muslim extremists, or far left believers, think that if they sacrifice their life for Allah they will wake up on the other side with 72 virgins. I am uneducated in Islam but not stupid. The Muslim faith has its "idiots" just as some hypocritical Christians do and we are all to beware of false prophets and false statements of the truth. The issue I have is God is not an evil God and does not support evil acts. Anyone who says that God wants us to kill each other and commit suicide by killing is a blasphemer and is driven by Satan. We don't mind if you want to walk out in the desert and strap on some plastic explosives around your head then hit the switch, but please stop taking innocent people with you. Lord knows we love a good fireworks show so let us know when you want to go and we'll come watch you light the sky. There, I said it, so in the immortal words of Mr. Lawrence T. Cable, "get-r-done!"

~ ~ ~ ~ ~ ~ ~

My research has indicated that Dawood Ebrahim or Sheikh Dawood Hassan, translates the Arabic word *hur* as *virgins* and the context makes clear that virgin is the appropriate translation: 'Dark-eyed virgin's sheltered in their tents (which of your Lord's blessings would you deny?) whom neither man nor jinnee will have touched before. The word *hur* occurs four times in the Qur'an and is usually translated as a *maiden with dark eyes*. This is only a virgin if women who lose their virginity have eyes that turn a different color. I have many friends across the Middle East and all their eyes are a beautiful soft brown. What is said of as 72 virgins is insulting to those who walk in true belief on behalf of Islam, Muslims, and all mighty and merciful ALLAH=GOD. Yes, Muslims, of the true faith, say that the living God of Abraham is the same as Allah, which is Arabic for God. Our customs are different and can be compared to denominational differences. Denominational clutter is more appropriate since the Qur'an does not acknowledge Christ or God's Holy Spirit. If you want One you must know all three in One.

Our generation has created so many denominations that they begin to clutter and cross with one another. I believe this is one of the reasons why people shy away from religion, especially understanding the truth in Christianity. So my question is simple, just to clear the air. If Allah is God, and the Qur'an is spoken by the same God as the Holy Bible, then why would Abdullah and Smith feel the need to sit in a cave and write another book when the Holy Bible explains through the Holy Spirit of the Living God the beginning to the end? If they followed the Almighty God, then they would have known that Jesus spoke through John in the scriptures revealed in Revelation 22:16-21? It is obvious they did not, so they felt compelled to create a separate religion whereby creating idolatry as well as blasphemy. This, boys and girls, is an unforgivable sin . . . Draw our Sword! Matthew 12:32

They say true Islam is a peaceful "religion" and that the All Mighty Great Merciful Allah has chosen mankind, for Islam is not here to bomb anything, or kill anyone; or not even the smallest creature, like the ant, would be harmed. Islam is about Peace, helping people/others, and to please Allah in his eyes and be a righteous man/or woman while you are in this world. This is basically the same thing that the Mormons believe. Both religions claimed to have been the creation of a man with guidance from a divine spirit or angel. Both religions created a separate book outside the bindings of the Holy Bible. Their doctrines teach life after death as well as moral concepts. I'm not being hateful or mean, but the truth is simply the truth. Satan's powers of deception have been well documented in the Bible and since Satan did such a good job on Abdullah's extra book he probably felt he might as well try it on Smith. It worked! A bunch of folks bought into it! The biggest difference is no one from the Osmond family have been accused of murder, flying planes into buildings, wearing fashionable back pack bombs, firing weapons in the air or shooting rockets at the moon when they are consumed with Middle West happiness. And the scientology folks are too busy loving life here and hugging a tree to worship an eternal life in Christ. If any of these statements bother you then you are obviously on the wrong path.

Now, how does the world really feel about born again believers in Christ? Here are some incidents that will open your eyes about the hazards of Christianity according to persecution.org:

195

On March 21, 2007 in Nigeria, Muslim students attacked and beat a Christian schoolteacher to death for opening a Bible and giving the class a different perspective than just the Qur'an. I would imagine this is where the U.S. is headed by removing prayer from our schools and moving God from the lips of our children. Soon if you bow your head in class to honor God you may have it severed.

In August 2008 in Saudi Arabia a father tortured and killed his daughter when he learned she had converted to Christianity. The murdering father was arrested and revealed that he works for the government agency that enforces religious purity. I'm not sure if he held the title of Religion Czar or not, but we have one they can borrow. He was held and then freed on his on recognizance.

On June 12, 2009 in Pakistan radical Muslims beat a Christian man to death for drinking tea from a Muslim cup. Ishtiaq went to the register to pay for his tea when the cashier notice the necklace Ishtiaq was wearing had a cross on it. The restaurant owner and 14 employees beat him with stones, iron rods and clubs then stabbed him multiple times with kitchen knives while he pled for his life. Ishtiag lay dead in the street and no peace seeking kind hearted loving Moslem came to his aid.

In August of 2009 Muslim radicals killed six Christian's in Pakistan and burned the house they were staying in. Afterwards, they torched 15 more houses with unknown injuries and fatalities reported.

In August of 2009 in Quetta Pakistan 5 Christians were gunned down and killed then over 100 homes were trashed by radical Muslims. The Muslim law has an anti-blasphemy law that stipulates life sentence or death to anyone who insults the Qur'an or their prophet Mohammed. If you teach or read the Bible, you have insulted and violated this law. These are the facts so be conscious of your tongue and choose your words carefully or be prepared to lose your life.

On September 27, 2009 in Delga a Muslim bus driver stabbed and killed 4 Christians for handing out Christian pamphlets. The driver was honored by his peers as a hero.

In August 2008 11 Christians were killed by Hindu radical group Vishwa Hindu Parishad and more violence erupted in Barakhama with the murder of three adults and one child. This Hindu group must have taken a break away from their peaceful yoga therapy session.

In September 2009 in Baghdad Iraq 13 Christians were killed over a two-week period. Nine hundred Christian families have fled for their life because of these murders and the hate felt by these extreme Muslims. Spread the word, God will kill those who oppress and cause harm to His people. For centuries Baghdad has become very familiar with God's authority . . .

The Vatican reports incidents all over the world and has statistics that the majority of the news stations or media do not bother to research. I use the Vatican website regularly to ensure I am informed correctly in today's information. Again, use your Bible to know what to believe and who to listen.

~ ~ ~

Jesus Lives
Jesus Loves
Jesus Saves

People debate and litigate the Holy Bible from cover to cover but these three facts have never been lost in translation. This understanding will keep you centered in your studies, as Jesus must be at the center of your life. He has sealed your life with His blood.

~ ~ ~ ~ ~ ~ ~

In the eyes of many Muslims, not all, but many, it is moral and right to kill converts from Islam. In nations like Saudi Arabia this is enshrined fully within the codified law of Islamic Sharia Law. Carrying the Sword out in the open is and has been a risk for centuries. Know our surroundings and be ready to take a stand for Him and He will stand for you. If you bow your head to Christ and lose your head on His behalf remember this: the very moment you take your last breath you will be absent your physical body and immediately with the Father.

It isn't how you go, it is where you go.

Do you remember Fox News breaking a story in February of 2002 that 129 Christians had been killed by the Chinese government from a crackdown on churches operating outside the direct control of the Chinese government? There was a Hong Kong businessman imprisoned for bringing Bibles in a communist country. President Bush instructed the Chinese government to release him, and they did. On September 4, 2007 the China Review reported 3,000 Chinese Christians were killed, murdered, since the year 2000. The communist leader, Mao Tse-tung is considered the biggest "mass murder" in Christian history by the murder of over 30,000,000 Chinese people. People, who either revolted against communism, fought for freedom or sought Christ for deliverance. You can be sure that Mao Tse-tung is very well-done by now . . .

On December 7, 1941 the Japanese bombed Pearl Harbor where over 2,400 Americans lost their life in a matter of a few hours. Soon after this announcement Americans began looking at every Japanese American in the US as the very ones that flew the planes, dropped the bombs and killed our soldiers. Over 110,000 Japanese Americans were arrested and placed in "War relocation Camps." Mind you, all 110,000 Japanese Americans had their feet on mainland soil when the attack occurred and they were suddenly snatched from their homes, businesses, schools and playgrounds then incarcerated. About 80,000 of these Americans were born on US soil. What a great Christian act that turned out to be! It was a good thing that George W didn't snatch every Muslim in America for the Twin Towers action. George W and God were damaged goods for going after and killing Satan Hussein as a weapon of mass destruction. I guess the mass graves uncovered in Hussein's back yard didn't qualify him as a weapon of mass destruction and a demonic tool of spiritual destruction.

The Japanese main religions are Shintoist, Buddhist and Christian. Shinto does not have a founder on record nor does it have sacred scriptures like the sutras or the Holy Bible. Propaganda and preaching are not common either, because Shinto is deeply rooted in the Japanese people and traditions. "Shinto gods" are called **kami**. They are sacred spirits, which take the form of things and concepts important to life, such as wind, rain, mountains, trees, rivers and fertility. Humans become kami after they die and are revered by their families as ancestral kami. The kami of extraordinary people are even enshrined at some shrines. The Sun Goddess Amaterasu is considered Shinto's most important kami. This religion keeps the Japanese grounded to this world and the things in this world. Do you see the need for discipleship here? People run with what they see, hear, smell and feel. These are senses of this world and I would rather my census be in the next world. Japanese ancient religions are foundationally very close to Scientology. Very close!

According to the US CIA figures in June of 2008 the population of Japan was estimated at 127,288,416. About <u>86%</u> of their adult population is part of the Shilo and Buddha religion, and have zero faith or belief in Jesus Christ. These are about 109,468,038 souls that will not enter Heavens gates, and this is in one country. These religions are the belief of others around the globe as well. This count was before the multiple earthquakes of 2011 that killed thousands of Japanese people. In seconds, lost souls fell to Hell. I am not being cruel or insensitive to speak the gospel truth. It is what it is.

> The Christian mission is to speak the gospel of
> Jesus Christ to all who will listen!

At last count there were about 1.4 billion people in China and their main beliefs are in Buddhism, Taoism, Islam, Catholic and various Christian denominations.

- Buddhism claims 13, 000 temples, 33 colleges and puts out about 50 different publications.
- Taoism is 1,800 years old and claims 15,000 temples.
- Islam claims 30,000 mosques with around 18,000,000 followers of Mohammad.
- Catholic Church claims 100 parishes, 5,000 churches
- Christian denominations claim 12 churches, 1,800 ministers and about 10,000,000 believers.

1.1 billion People in China are atheist, agnostic, secular, and non-believer or otherwise LOST. Now think about the numbers I reviewed earlier of the saved to the unsaved people. There are only two roads and one is very narrow. Is this becoming a little more in focus yet? Made in China is on virtually everything we see on the store counters and shelves. Made in China is on the vehicles we drive and much of the industry we work in or around. Made in China is reaching dominating levels around the globe. Soon the U.S. mint will read, Made in China . . . I'm not laughing . . .

> Soon the U.S. mint will read, Made in China?
> We already owe them more than we can repay . . .

Some believe that Christians have the market cornered on faith. Oh no, not so. People of all religions, even non-believers, have faith every day. Faith is what you place your belief system into and feel it internally so much where it is no longer a conscious thought but an every day way of life practice. Like when you get on a plane you place your faith in the pilot for getting you to your destination safely. When you get in your car automatically you have faith that your brakes will not fail you. Every day people pick up their fork in a restaurant and trust that the food they will eat is safe. Each day parents drop their children off at school having great faith that they will see their children when they arrive home that afternoon. Employees place faith in their employer that they will operate with integrity and they have faith that you will act with integrity. We place faith in our doctors to perform well. We place faith in our judges and legislators that will rule properly. I have seen incredible blind faith of a mother who leaves her two children in an unlocked car at a gas pump while she goes inside the store to buy cigarettes. We place faith in our judicial system that insane people will be removed from an otherwise sane society. We also have faith in our clergy, no matter the denomination, that they will embrace our children in God and not themselves. As a Crusader, we must be able to recognize the blindness of others and the deception practiced by the evil one. We must be able to recognize a wolf in sheep's clothing . . .

As a Crusader, we also need to take a closer look at the mission field of who or what and where we are witnessing. Again, it is estimated that 33%

of the world is Christian: **born again believer in Jesus Christ**. I guess the rest are lost in their lost-ness? Within the 33% considered ***"Christian",*** divide man or woman into three distinct groups and I recently studied this in messages by Dr. Ted Traylor, Dr. Charles Stanley and the late Pastor Adrian Rogers. This is reality!

1. <u>**Natural** Man/Woman</u>: This group is unsaved, have not accepted, believed or partnered with Jesus in His invitation or commandments. Lost with ample opportunity but procrastinated and have not or did not make the walk of faith to accept the gift that has already been paid for and offered for free. It is a pre-approved gift that was never considered as welcomed and he/she never acknowledge Jesus Christ as King of Kings, Lord of Lords and their eternal Savior. This group is also fascinated by how much stuff they collect and do before they die because they are owed a good life. There are many natural men/women in church every Sunday.

2. <u>**Carnal** Man/Woman</u>: This is a water-down, church going people, who claim Christianity on any given Sunday. They may be in the nightclub on Saturday night. They may down a few beers at a game. They may even look at some light porn on the Internet. They might tell some minor dirty jokes at work. Some may have an occasional playful affair. Some may curse, but only when really angered. A few may sing at the nightclub, do some karaoke and also sing solos in Sunday's worship service. Some may also teach in Sunday school, usher, deacon, may be an elder, or may be the piano player. Some of these folks can sit at a four-hour football game or sit in a two-hour movie and never complain about the time, seats or temperature. The Carnal man or woman is just as lost as lost can be lost. I don't care if you have been dipped or dunked, you are lost and wasting your time until you accept, repent, believe and obey! It is the only way . . .

3. <u>**Spiritual** Man/Woman</u>: This group is born again believers in Christ. Saved by grace, believing in every word, faithful in service, spreading the gospel and partnered with God in doing His work. This group is far from perfect but they are learning, continually growing, studying to become better and getting closer to all the crowns and rewards that Jesus has to offer. This group is also

focused on how much they can do for God because they know and acknowledge themselves as belonging to Him. They worship the Creator not His creations.

Now, let's take a look at religion because it was truly my favorite research project. Why? Because millions of people walk blindly into religions and do not study God's word versus the denominational practices of the church or organization they sit in. Remember friend, when you read over this research that I am not religious; I am a born again believer in Jesus Christ. My research includes the following religious gods, churches and organizations but certainly not all of them. While reading over their denominational statements, traditions or practices, remember that Jesus never made an announcement that indicated any religion was better or greater than the other but He certainly made the rules abundantly clear. But humans got hold of their desires for a "feel better about me" guide for worship practices that suited them rather than honoring our Father. Good intentions sometimes defeat and drown out the purpose. They most certainly cloud every message of Jesus Christ. But before you read further in this book, draw your Sword and turn to Jude and read his 24 little verses. Once you have read it, then read over verses 10 through 13 again. Now read these denominational differences, so you may decide when to say, **<u>"Woe to them!"</u>** I like to refer to these topics as the **W.D.C**— *"Worldly Denominational Clutter" . . .*

Catholic—I have a section in this book with concerns of certain Catholic Churches. The Catholic Church, also known as the Roman Catholic Church is today's largest church in the globe with more than a sixth of the world's population. This means that one out of every six people claim to be Catholic. So the Catholic Church says . . . The Catholic ministry states its mission is to spread the gospel of Jesus Christ. They care for the needy, operate many social programs, own many institutions around the world, own schools, missions, hospitals, universities, shelters and do a tremendous amount of charity work. It has the Vatican which is a nation unto itself! It sees the Bishops as successors to the Apostles although some have fallen into the sins of the world including homosexuality, sexual child abuse and "God complex" in their leadership. The Catholic scholars cite a letter from Pope Clement I as evidence that Jesus founded the Catholic Church, even though there is no evidence of this found in the Bible. There is trouble in some of those who assign themselves as Catholics in that they kiss the hand and touch the cloth of the Pope as if he is sacred or deity but he is a man. He is not a god to be glorified or followed. They are instructed by the church to say Hail Mary's to receive blessings. This places Mary between them and God. They confess their sins to a priest or bishop and this practice places the priest between them and God. They take or offer Holy Communion whether they are saved or not and this goes against the instruction of Jesus. They do not baptize with full immersion as John baptized Jesus but they do sprinkle or tinkle a bit of water, which is less than obedient to the word spoken by Jesus. They practice a "saved by birth" philosophy rather than a decision of conscious acceptance. The church believes in three states of afterlife: Heaven, a substation to Heaven and Hell. The substation is for those who were "good" but didn't practice being saved and requires God's grace along with prayers from friends to get you to the next level. If you gather in a group and pray extra hard for their souls then you feel better that God allowed them to move on to heaven. A practice of this sort is not for the dead but for the living to feel better about who died. This practice is stated in one of the six extra books they have added to what the Holy Bible has in its library but then again these additional practices contradict Jesus in His own words in Matthew, Mark, Luke and John. This may be one of those "earthly feel good" things that make the pill a little easier to swallow. Hope this works well because the judge will be ruling according to <u>His Word</u> not "feel good" "ear tickling" "man made" additions to God's word. One must enter on ones own decision of belief, repentance, acceptance and faith. Righteousness can only be received from Jesus Christ!

Catechism is the doctrine of the Catholic Church and has been changed over the years and as recently as September 8, 1997 by Pope John Paul II. It is the religious instruction in church rules for children, young people and adults. The Roman Catechism was published in 1566 and created as a reference tool for priests. In 1992 the Vatican empowered the United States Catholic Catechism for Adults. It is similar to a college textbook and lists the rules to live by. I would consider the Holy Bible to be the trunk of their tree, then as it grew they adjusted it then trimmed it and then developed new branches for different areas of the world according to the different growing generations. What I lose in this process is that God's word was written for all people for all times in all generations. But then again, there are about twenty-one different catechisms for different areas of the globe, different cultures, different opinions and just different rules. It's just different!

Here is another interesting note about the Catholic Church. If you divorce your spouse, the church requires you to complete a "**letter of reason**" why the divorce was needed. You complete a survey questionnaire about the separation, and then, the church decides if the reason was just, or not. This is in addition to whatever the legal decisions are. If the church decides that there was no just cause then you will be excommunicated from the church. This goes against every living fiber of God's will for forgiveness of sin, of fault or of error that man makes. Jesus forgives as long as you have a breath to ask for it and He insists on brotherly love. But this makes the church leaders play judge and places them between you and God as god. So does the practice of praying to a dead saint. Woe to any priest or saint who dares step in those bounds of spiritual idealistic behavior and steps between God and His people. I know personally of two men this has happened to and there is no need to try and justify pushing anyone away from the church. It is forgivable but I would not wait much longer or you risk the gate becoming too small to enter . . .

"I hate divorce" says the Lord God of Israel, "and I hate a man's covering himself with violence as well as with his garment," says the Lord Almighty. So guard yourself in your spirit and do not break faith."
Malachi 2:16

The Catholic hierarchies also practice the age-old theory of celibacy. The priests shall take no wife and the nuns shall take no husband. I have done my best to try and find this practice in God's word and the only things I keep finding is that God's will is for man to take a wife and walk in His divine word. He created Eve for Adam because in Genesis 2:18 He said it was not good for man to live alone. He also didn't expect for His priests to remain closed up in a church or cathedral or monetary all their lives. He sent His disciples out into the world to tell, unless, Catholic priests are not really disciples, pastors, bishops, or Christians. Jesus was going though all the cities, villages and synagogues teaching and proclaiming the gospel. Then He told His disciples to go and make disciples of all nations, baptizing and in the name of the Father, the Son and the Holy

Spirit. Surely everyone has the same Holy Bible as I do and read this in the gospels; Matthew, Mark, Luke and John!

Lastly is the reference to any leader of the church calling himself HOLY FATHER. I struggle to contain my words on this self appointed title especially when church leaders and church goers bow and kiss this mans hand. This is blasphemy!

Protestant—This is a term used for all Christian philosophy and theology. It is the foundation of Christ's teachings to the gentile for which I am so thankful to be included in. This foundation of Christian belief is then separated into many denominational churches that can not agree in basic traditional practices OR many ceremonial differences. According to wikipedia sources there are over 38,000 different "Christian" denominations in the world today. This means basically that there were at least a minimum of 38,000 Disciples of Christ that could not come to agreement on their own interpretation of God's word and they argued over traditional values. No way we can waste pages by listing all the denominations and all the differences they found to disagree or agree upon but there are several main line churches that are worthy of noting because they consume the large majority of "Christians denominations". In the end, most will find their way back together, maybe not in name but as the world church. Certainly a meeting table somewhere will find a gathering of the leaders of authority that will combine thoughts of the state of the world. I believe that the Vatican will call for this meeting and anyone in church leadership that receives an invitation, airfare and accommodations by the Vatican will be at the airport two hours early to make sure they do not miss their flight. When they do this they will begin the initial stages of uniting a world church. The holy pope will tug on his rope and sound a bell that will ring to unite all churches of the world to form a union under the guidance of one man. This is Bible prophecy. (Find more details in *2012 Global Warning*)

Uniting for what? Uniting against terrorism? Uniting against Islam? Uniting to generalize beliefs and differences of tradition? The World Church will look much like Lakewood Church in Houston Texas which is a smaller version of future worship services. This facility will hold around 16,000 people and oddly enough was the location where Queen played in 1977, Prince played it several times to include a famous concert in 1981 then the facility was home to the Royal Rumble in 1989 where a giant, Big John Studd won the mega royal held by the World Wrestling Federation. A queen, a prince and royal drama in the world federation sets the stage for a non-denominational church format. So, why wouldn't it be a perfect location for the United States World Wide Church Federation to begin? The first sermon could be; All religious roads lead to the same God . . .

In 2005 the facility was leased to the church by the City of Houston with $75 million dollars of renovations and the church has an indefinite lease to its property. The motto "Discover the Champion in You" is the foundation for Pastor Joel Osteen. He holds services six times a week and is neutral in denominational beliefs for this mega church that currently holds the largest congregation in the United States of more than 43,500 that attend each week. The church reported spending around $30,000,000 in 2007 on television alone. It is truly a family business of his wife Victoria, brother Paul, and sister Lisa along with Marcos Witt who preaches in Spanish. I like the facts that Lakewood is neutral in denomination and I am on record several times saying that Jesus was nondenominational. He was very clear in His message of **John 10:25-30**. Many have publicly criticized Joel's ministry but the same amount of criticisms are made of any church or especially "Christian" based ministries that do not preach one cross-one Savior. If Satan can find a way to shake it up, he will. It doesn't matter that they do not have statues, pictures on the walls or curtains adorning the hallways. Who cares? God doesn't! What God does care about is the quality in the message that His people are hearing and do they know the direct path to salvation? **John 3:36**

It is ever so great to know that God wants us to do well and have good things of this world that He created. He also wants us to read His word in its entirety with the message of repentance, in the messages of John, James and Jude. All churches should begin with the message in Joshua then Jeremiah to understand that God **is** love when His people are obedient. I truly love what Joel Osteen has built and I believe he has a solid foundation to launch a gospel of growth similar to or bigger than the Billy Graham crusade ever thought of being. I also believe that he needs to take God's message on the road and reach out to other parts of the nation then the globe. Take God's word in the stadiums and theaters across the globe spreading the gospel more personal than a satellite can do. On one condition . . . Lakewood Church needs a revolution of the gospel like Paul would have administered then Joel can close with a great message of finding the champion within you. The champion within each of us is God and with God as our center point of one direction, then we cannot be defeated. It is a divine partnership that must be told in its entirety and in all languages. Joel will continue to move souls in false doctrine if he continues to minister in false understandings of God's word. This misdirection is in any statement of more than a one way to God's grace. He must define his messages about the cross, about sin, about repentance, about the blood shed by Jesus, about a holy walk and about "Jesus Christ" centered in your life. If not, I will continue to question Joel's intentions and the mixed message he delivers.

But here is the risk that Joel Osteen makes if he begins preaching the blood of Jesus Christ and the cross. The majority of his large congregation will walk away because they can no longer feel good about their sinful life and they will have a clear understanding of repentance and change. Joel's next sermon should be in **Hebrews 9:11-28**!

Eastern Orthodox—came after the 11th century and separated specific things like images, the Holy Spirit nature and the date of Christ's resurrection. Some differences are in the legality of the church practice and some are philosophical differences. Could the form 'icon" have a significant importance to commandment #2 in Exodus 20? "Our Lady of

Vladimir in Russia" and "Our Lady of Smolensk" is similar to Mary being idolized by the Catholic Church. If over 500,000 people of Russia place these ladies between them and God then they are sinning against God. Draw your Sword to Exodus 20:4-5.

Anglican—is not really a religion but more like a church of a religion. Its roots are in the Church of England and bring more proper or ceremonial practices to a denomination. The songs, the facilities, the candle lighting practice and others come from this traditional form. These traditions were practiced in the Old Testament. Not sure that they really realize that Jesus was the reason for the New Testament and that ALL things of old changed in His testimony.

Freemason—This group has a heritage of famous men, historical men, my great grandfather and men of esteem respect in the political arena. But can this be considered a religion? They have an oath that is like none other and states clear instruction of what is to come of a member who lies, cheats, steals, or has immoral affair with a fellow Freemason and so on. The reason why I place the Freemason here is because this oath and this membership call for a god to watch over their oath as well as their daily prayer called GAOTU. This prayer said by one member might be to one god while the man standing next to him may be praying to another. Any man who pledges this oath acknowledging any god other than the Almighty God from Genesis to Revelation and voices an allegiance to man is blasphemy. Our military, law enforcement and fire fighters swear an oath to defend and protect a people. The Freemason swears an oath and allegiance to each other and it is a decree in blood. The only blood that is sacred is the blood shed by Jesus Christ.

Kabbalah—is growing like a weed across the globe and is gaining in popularity because of its "feel good" nature. The Hollywood pop stars are talking about it and the religion takes the Holy Bible and does a few twists to move supernatural into the natural ability of the all-ness. It claims that it was Moses, not God, who parted the Red Sea, which allowed the Israelites to pass in safety. Moses had this ability not because of God's supremeness but because Moses was in touch with all the earth's powers. This religion boasts of 72 names of God but not in the general sense of the meaning but that 72 Hebrew letters combine into a formula of sort that when combined a human being can have supernatural powers. This religion is also based on a belief that you are born with a spiritual mission and if you die before your mission was complete then you are reincarnated into another being until your spiritual mission is complete. Many stars like Madonna, Demi Moore, Britney Spears, Ashton Kutcher, Paris Hilton and others wear the **red string bracelet** that is said to protect wearers from negative forces and demonic evilness. I thought that wild sex tapes, public nudity, extreme profanity, immoral sex acts, gay/lesbian acts and that sort of behavior was demonic or at least satanic influence! Think about this; any religion that states that man has the ability to perform acts of deity without the necessity of God, then go ahead and believe that you will also be your own eternal judge then as well. Also, if you wear the red string bracelet, but don't really claim the religion or embrace its philosophy, then you are a fool. This is not costume jewelry. It is idol worship and blasphemy against God.

African Independent Church—is based out of Africa, has about 110,000,000 followers, and it is similar Bible scripture and the Christian God. Early AICs practiced cultural dancing with massive percussion instruments. I was okay with this and could probably get into it with them but then they mentioned they allowed their members to be polygynous and practice female excision. Okay boys and girls this is where I would hit the doors running. This ceremony removes the sex portions of the female vagina that creates/causes sensation or arousal. The men encourage this so their women will have no desire for other men. Excuse me? If the dominant male wants 10 wives and doesn't want them to stray then this is the practice? Pull this up on the web and you will never want to have sex again! Or, if you think your wife might be wandering the streets at night . . . Just kidding! Since the old days, they have adopted many of the Pentecostal and Charismatic practices. All I have to say is thank you Jesus . . . Wow! Also not sure why the dominant male doesn't get a wife then 9 blow up dolls. They won't stray and would probably have the same reaction to him.

Independent Fundamental Baptist—Baptists, Southern Baptists, Independent Baptists, Reformed Baptists and Independent Fundamental Baptists are people who grow apart and divide God's word into separation of His people. Some claim total Bible discipline while some seek truth in the fundamental purity of the New Testament following. Documentary's and investigative TV programs such as 20/20 have provided documented evidence of corrupt, sick, demented, sexual and abusive behavior from fundamentalist leadership. The Tina Anderson story provided an example of this behavior from the pulpit to church leadership, not only in the acts of perversion but in covering up information once it was made known. In one incident an underage minor female was forced to stand before the church congregation and speak about her sexual conduct with an older adult male. One church is not to be compared to another but when the church body condones a pastor placing a 15-year-old girl in front of the congregation on display, a Christian should have stood and rebuked this behavior immediately. When pastors and elders are charged, convicted and sentenced for criminal acts of sex and physical abuse, how then must the lost find safe haven in God's house? In this case, eventually the guilty were charged and convicted. The sad story continued when the church forced the girl to move because they could not embrace her in the church after such a controversy. Or was it because they could not face their guilt?

A separate incident reported from an Independent Fundamental Baptist church was one of child abuse and pastors were preaching abuse from the pulpit. One quote recorded on 20/20 was; "If you are not bruising your child you are not spanking hard enough." Another witness stated that a child should begin to experience spanking at two weeks of age. These "churches" focus on rituals, ceremonies outside God's word, formalities written by man and pride themselves in submissive behavior. The strict dress of this religion is less concerning as the hearts left hardened from so many acts of ungodly behavior. I am ashamed that these few cast shadows over the name of Christ. You cannot be independent of the love of Christ and be fundamentally in God's word.

Baptist churches at large are as close as you get to God's word with exception of Pastor, elder and deacon selection. A divorced man cannot serve in any of these positions.

> "Blessed are they whose transgressions are forgiven, whose sins are covered. Blessed is the man whose sin the Lord will never count against him."
>
> Romans 4:7-8

Saul committed murder by signing off on the stoning of Stephen before Jesus forgave him and Saul changed to Paul. Paul was a member of the Sanhedrin where a man must be noble and married. Paul was single during his ministry until the day he died. What happened to Paul's wife? Paul wrote Romans and specifically understood the forgiveness of God's grace through His Son Jesus Christ. Jesus forgives and never counts those sins against you again but the Baptist leadership cannot?

Latter-Day Saints—Mormons traveled across the U.S. and Joseph Smith, born in 1805 wrote the book of Mormon around 1830 and he is considered their prophet. Joe says that an angel called him to be a Prophet and told him to re-write the Bible or add to it because of the earth's apostasy. Joe found two gold tablets that looked like they had Egyptian writing. Joe had no formal training in any other language than English. An angel appeared to Joe while he had the tablets inside his hat. Joe may have had this experience just moments after he discovered the new mushroom field down in the valley . . . Many people asked Joe to show them these golden tablets but Joe said the angel took them back to eternity. Now there are several differences of opinion as to who saw these tablets. The book of Mormon says it was witnessed but their own web site described their statement of faith very differently. There are Mormon leaders who have differences in what they know to be factual occurrences in 1830. The major difference is that Joe said he saw an angel who told him what to write. The Bible declares <u>God's</u> word from Genesis to Revelation as the final authority. Joe included in his book that the Holy Trinity is three separate or many gods (BYU Journal of Discourses 7:333), God took on human form before he was God (page 346), God the Father has a wife (page 516), God is not an eternal being and would suddenly stop being God if intelligences stopped supporting him as God (page 175), man was in the beginning with God (D&C 93:29), Jesus was the firstborn heavenly man and is considered our brother (page 127), Adam and Eve did not commit sin they created a deed filled blessing (page 476), Jesus died on the cross so we would have eternal life because before this all men remained in the grave (page 63) and the icing on the cake places Satan as the brother of Jesus since God is the Father of all beings (pages 407-408). Joe did his own bible translations but did not speak or read Hebrew, Greek, Latin or even Swahili! Joe also ignored Jesus in two specific scriptures: Revelation 9:20 in worshiping golden idols and 22:18 adding to or taking from the word of God. Joe was also fond of their men having many wives. Some Mormons are fully involved in Mormon doctrine and some practice parts but not all of Joe's teachings. Again, when you separate from God's word you begin to make up stuff that you want. Several wives might be attractive to some men.

I say marry one wife with multiple personalities!

BYU (Brigham Young University) sponsors a Barlow Endowment concert as a musical celebration in honor of the "prophet", called Joseph Smith. This concert includes songs of praise and worship like; "Remembering Joseph; We Who Press the Path" as the lyrics suggest praise him (Smith) as if it is a call to worship. A concert was held, in his behalf, for 200 years of continued prophesy by Mormon prophets. They worship Joseph and praise his name while at the same time "commemorate the birth of the baby in Bethlehem." I quote from the Mormon Journal of Disclosure 7:289 "From the day that the priesthood was taken from the earth to the winding-up scene of all things, every man and woman must have the certificate of Joseph Smith, junior, as a passport to their entrance into the mansion where God and Christ are—I with you and you with me. I cannot go there without his consent." Underlined is a warning to all who follow the writings of one Joe Smith.

Mormons also believe that there are apostles among them that various angels speak to and tell them to add to the book of Mormon. An ever-evolving book means Mormons have to go and buy the latest version to keep up with times. The book of Mormon that I thought I was using as a study reference was updated in 2008 and is already out dated by several additions. All Mormons need to read and understand Isaiah 44, 45 and 46. God proclaims to His people that He is ONE GOD. To discard any of God's word means to discard all of it.

And to the Mormon apostles that are leading this group:

"But what am doing I will continue to do, so that I may cut off opportunity from those who desire an opportunity to be regarded just as we are in the matter about which they are boasting. For such men are false apostles, deceitful workers, disguising themselves as apostles of Christ. No wonder, for even Satan disguises himself as an angel of light. Therefore it is not surprising if his servants also

disguise themselves as servants of righteousness, whose end will be according to their deeds."

2 Corinthians 11:12-15

To discard or discredit one chapter, one verse, one word or one letter of God's word is to discard and discredit it all. Just so you know this is an eternally unhealthy decision to make.

Evangelical—has four very specific beliefs:

(**1**) Receiving Christ and experiencing a new spiritual birth or born again as referenced in John 3:3. "Received" is based on faith alone and given by God to us as a result of grace alone as in Ephesians 2:8-9.

(**2**) The Bible is the ultimate and final authority from God as stated in 2nd Timothy 3:16 & John 17:17.

(**3**) Evangelism, discipleship, mission work and becoming a witness as stated in Matthew 28:19.

(**4**) The only way to God is through the Son, Jesus Christ and His sacrifice on the cross as the only means for salvation and forgiveness of ones sin as stated in 1st Corinthians 15:3-4. It is also the belief and practice of baptism by full emersion under water as Jesus did in John 3:5. All this is as one in the name of God the Father, God the Son and the Holy Spirit of God.

Jesus traveled about 60 miles; either by foot or by animal, to have John the Baptist baptize Him in the Jordan River. Why this distance and this location? John announced His arrival and the river had enough water to completely submerge the world's Savior. He wasn't tinkled, sprinkled or sprayed, but He came up from the water. To be baptized has nothing to do with denomination. It is an act of obedience to go into the water from an old life and emerge into a new life of eternal salvation. If you are moved by God's Holy Spirit in repentance and baptism then you will know this is the greatest experience you will ever know.

Seventh Day Adventists—small differences from other Christian religions are they hold Saturday as the Sabbath, which is the Old Testament; they believe that God keeps a "family album" rather than "The Lambs Book of Life". They describe the trinity as Jesus, the Father and the Holy Spirit rather than Father, Son and the Holy Spirit. While Jesus was His physical name, Christ the Son is His deity. In Hebrew it was **Emmanuel**, meaning "God with us." They quote "The Lords Supper" as His prediction in John 6 rather than Matthew 26:27 when it actually occurred. Jesus used "fruit of the vine" language in the Bible, not wine or grape juice as quoted in their beliefs. These and other scripture inconsistencies may seem minor but Jesus was very specific in Revelation 22:18. Read it and quote it word for word accurately!

Jehovah's Witness—are controlled by a "Governing Body" and to truly understand the theory of this religion you must read Matthew 24:45; "the faithful and sensible slave whom his master put in charge of his household." Their bible is the "New World Translation" and they deem this the only bible in existence. Although the men who translated their bible that was released in 1950 were Fred Franz who had 2 years experience in Greek and was self-taught in Hebrew, four of the five men had no historical or ancient language experience, period. Franz was asked to appear in a France courtroom to translate the Book of Genesis and he could not. How many people follow this doctrine translated by an unskilled editor? How about an estimated **1.4 billion** people! This religion has no foundational belief in Hades or Hell. I struggled to find their path to Heaven. Franz and his team ignored Revelation 22:18 where it defines both. The Jehovah's Witness believe in one God but reject the doctrine of the Trinity. They claim that Jesus was not God but was God's creation and Jesus was not crucified but placed on a single upright stake. This theory does not comply with Roman crucifixion practices which are detailed in *2012 Global Warning*. Jesus was not established as a King until 1914. Jesus has been ruling since 1914 and it was Jesus that threw Satan and his band of evil spirits into hell. This would mean that Genesis was wrong and God lied. The Holy Spirit is not God but is His active force. No hell exists and they believe that all evil spirits will just be dead, annihilated, cease to exist and so on. The other big belief is that there will only be 144,000 people permitted into Heaven. So, if there are 1.4 billion members but only 144,000 will be going to heaven . . .

The next time a carload drives up to your driveway and knocks on your door just ask, "Are you part of the 144,000 or are you stuck here with the rest of your carload? Then say, "I believe in heaven and hell and if you are not on God's plan you are on Satan's plan. That plan is not permitted in my world so in the name of Jesus Christ who died on the cross for your sins, I call for this church to step away from the book that stands between you and eternal peace with God the Father, God the Son and God the Holy Spirit, who is One. Now, would you like to pray with me?" If they stay, then tell them about Jesus and the glory of God. If they leave, pray for them as they drive away in darkness. Remember, there are two paths but only one Way . . .

Lutheran—Luther's large Catechism of 1529, which is a part of the Catholic separation, speaks of rules of instruction in faithful conduct. On August 22, 2009 the Florida Times Union reported confirmation on a global changing turn in church tradition from Minneapolis where a 559-451 vote in favor of the new policy that allows homosexuals living in committed gay relationships to serve as priests in any Evangelical Lutheran Church in America. This has created cross fire among congregations across this great land and it has accomplished exactly what Satan intended to acomplish. It disrupted worship among God's people. They now have their first lesbian priest and the gay/lesbian crowd is following in groves.

Quakers—is another word for "friends" and their fellowship is not Christian but rather in "friendship". Then there are "programmed" friends and "unprogrammed" friends. Some have pastors that lead the church and some have "silent" services that seek the inward teachings of Christ. Many Quakers do not live by a creed or denominational faith claim however they do have books called; "Faith and Practice" guides that provide inspirational tracts, advice, question and answer extracts and all the Quakers come together in meeting houses or regional meetings. Some groups are called liberal friends who call themselves "universalist" while others call themselves Christian and practice faith in scripture. They have their own web site and you can read what their varied philosophies are, and I wish you luck because it reads like the 1960's diary of a hippie commune or a bunch of flower children that started a church. Their walk is in a belief in God but not through the specific teachings of Jesus or even disciplined to scripture. Their worship services vary but they have a list of "rules" to abide by while attending worship service. Then at the bottom it says not to worry about the rules because an older Quaker may break them at any time. If you want to stay in this world then this is your ticket to a front row seat. While the majority practices peace, most do not concern themselves in the immoralities of the world and you seldom hear of a Quaker in trouble or waiting their turn on death row. Maybe there is something to their "friendship" practice while you are here but friendship will not bring the righteousness of Jesus Christ. I hope they know how to find the cross because they make little mention of the only path to Christ being through the cross and the sacrifice He made for forgiveness of sin. Christ is Christianity!

Assembly of God—is a foundational religion much like the Protestant church with a few distinct differences: The Assembly of God practices speaking in tongues as a sign of anointing, practice "miraculous healings" even though a true physical healing is rare and they will get inspired and motivated in the pulpit in a holy heartbeat. Pentecostal is an emotional and spiritual experience with less water and more emotion. Speaking in tongues and healing were included in God's word. If this is authentic then praise the Lord. If it isn't and they are simply putting on a show, God certainly knows . . .

Many AOS services are very musically based, with great musical talent and most of their pastors use song within their sermons. As an example of several of their denominational practices, go to the Pace Assembly of God website and listen to Pastor Joey Rogers. Pastor Rogers is very skilled and knowledgeable in God's word but strap yourself in, buckle your seatbelt and hang on to your seat! They are puttin' their foot on the devil in this church!

Amish Mennonite—began in Switzerland around 1693 by Jakob Amman and his following became known as Amish. This group migrated to America and began to settle in Pennsylvania and must follow the rules called Ordnung which are many but include no electricity, telephones, automobiles, governmental assistance, insurance or other comforts of modern day living. They practice baptism but everyone is baptized by age 16 to 25 and is mandatory before marriage. Because of their religious beliefs they will not serve in military service but they do enjoy the freedom that our military men and women provide them. I also struggle with their tax laws and even if they pay FICA tax and contribute to the social security.

Good luck because their world is more secret than the FBI or CIA. The Amish do not marry outside their faith, unless they escape, and normal size orders are 20 to 30 families. This has created issues with family trees with little or no branches . . .

Secular, revisions, extensions, and other forms of religions have separated from main line churches for probably many arguable reasons. The main reason is that they cannot get along with each other or they do not desire governing support so they break away and form their own church. The worship practices vary from church to church as well as the messages they deliver. Some churches mix religions to make them feel good and they break away from traditional values or practices. I know one church that is Mormon and Christian so they obtain Mormon Church support but feel better about teaching Jesus. Yes, it is confusing to me and I personally know several who attend this church.

These denominational separations typically begin with a pastor wanting to reform or revise then he/she recruits a congregation, beginning with close family and a few close friends. Then the group worship attendances are based on others who have in the same beliefs. The divisions are where many unbelievers get confused and who could blame them. Put 10 people in the same room and try to select a new wall color. You will get at least 5 different opinions unless you only handed out one paint sample. Church is no different from any other task to perform when people can't agree on the purpose and/or method of reaching designated goals. The end result may be the same but how you get there may take on many different forms.

Remember; Church is not a membership or social club that entitles you to benefits. You are the church and uniting together creates the body of Christ in praise and worship. The facility is simply a building and does not become a church until you get there. When you arrive, you brought God with you. When you receive Christ you become His temple.

God doesn't sit in an empty building waiting on you to arrive . . .

Zionism—gets its name from the word Zion that refers to Jerusalem. Nathan Birnbaum, founder of the first nationalist Jewish student's movement Kadimah with a journal written in 1890, formed the term. The group is formed of five principles beginning with unity, ingathering of Jewish people, strengthening the state of Israel, preserving the identity of the Jewish people and the protection of Jewish rights. In many ways this movement looks more political than spiritual. The easiest way for me to understand this movement is that the international Jewish people are making a connection to Israel. This actually should be extended to the Greek and the gentile as Paul stated so eloquently in Romans 2:9-11. We will soon realize if this movement remembers Holy Scripture.

Israel—The Jewish people are God's chosen people and Israel is a nation that will be the central piece to the recorded Revelation of Jesus, the 2nd coming of Christ. According to Romans 9:15, God has mercy on people because it is in His divine being to be merciful and not just because someone or some people are deserving. ALL have sinned and come short of the Glory of God and ALL must come to Jesus Christ for salvation before He will confess us to the Father. The Old Testament of Isaiah pleads for the salvation of Israel and no doubt God has a plan for the protection of this great nation, just as He always has. I simply feel fortunate as a Gentile to be honored with God's grace through my belief in His word, in His promise and His imminent return. Only God knows His plan for the end and the time of His return. Our obedience is our command and our command is being obedient to His word. Do not get caught up in the language or the argument of translation, just simply obey His word. Jesus is the same in any language you want to speak and it has more power and authority than this world can understand. We are seeing times where nations around the world are backing away from supporting Israel and Islamic / Palestine nations are closing in. When the first rock is thrown at Israel, **look out**! The Revelation of Jesus Christ is about to unfold and the skies are about to open . . . By the way, this is in *2012 Global Warning* as well. Just so you know . . .

~ ~ ~ ~ ~ ~ ~

If you don't like any of these religions then you can start a new one. There are pages and pages of "how to start a new religion" on the Internet. There is a page on ehow.com that will walk you through the steps of breaking away from a main line religion and creating your own. It provides instruction on how to create a new church, and how to avoid your new religion from being called a cult. It tells you how to choose a proper name for your religion, decide on fundamental beliefs, decide on a god to serve, create a book that your people will follow, create a web site that reaches out for new people to follow, get a band together to play music, launch creative marketing campaigns, develop a fund raising system so you can make money, take up charities so your people will love what your purpose is and finally, how to grow the people under your new steeple. But wait, there's more. Yes, you too can have your own religion because let's face it, religion is a form of worship and is a broad based word that includes many, many separate beliefs. Here are a few religions that have already claimed themselves a following of sort. From A to Z there are hundreds, thousands and the count continues on. Zion's Order, Inc, Rainbow Family, Latter Rain Movement, Ghost Dance, Moral Re-Armament, Oomoto, Shakers, Vedanta Society, The Word Foundation, New Kadampa tradition, New Thought, Namdhari, Lucis Trust, Lama Foundation, Jesus Army, United Lodge of Theosophists, Umbanda, Sahaja Yoa, Rama Computer Cult, John Frum, I Am Activity, Grail Movement, Esoteric Nazism, Dianic Wicca, Church of Aphrodite, Bahai Faith, Association of Vineyard Churches, 3HO, Cargo Cult, Confederate Nations of Israel, A Course of Miracles, Freedomites, Jews for Jesus, Manson Family, The Peoples Temple, Twelve Tribes, White Eagle Lodge, Amway, Assemblies of Yahweh, Church of Daniels Band, Dances of Universal Peace and must I go on? Just how messed up do you think this world has gotten? Think of the tribes that were destroyed by the floods when God became fed up with mans inability to follow simple direction. Now go read Daniel and Revelation again.

There are other groups that state without a doubt that Jesus was a vegetarian. Here again we have mankind out of touch with God and His word. There are several leaders who have their opinions stated on the Internet like Kamran Pasha and many believe that Jesus was opposed to animal sacrifice and animal consumption. The animal sacrifices at the Jewish Temple may have been the triggering event that led to His crucifixion. But of course, this type of statement comes from people who are not born again believers in Christ and do not follow Biblical truth. One was identified as Moslem. Animal cruelty is wrong in any religion but Jesus attended many feasts where meat was the main course. He also ate fish, and the last thing He did upon His final ascent was to cook fish for the disciples. Please stop picking and choosing pieces of God's word and trying to make a man made created statement that has obvious satanic hands on it. Only Satan could be steadfast in crafty notions such as this so read it for what it is then know He came to serve as a living sacrifice for your sins and today you are pre-approved for it and pre-authorized to accept it. If you are born again believer in Christ then reach out to a family member or friend who needs this assurance today.

~ ~ ~ ~ ~ ~ ~

In reviewing all the different religions and denominational differences listed over the last few pages, how many times did you say, **"Woe"**? Now understand this, I am not religion bashing and my research wasn't to degrade or belittle as it was to inform and compare. I am not your judge nor am I the judge of 1,000 different religions. But I know who is and according to His word we are not to drift from His word. All these religions and denominations are like a buffet; some look okay, some look good but leave a bad taste in your mouth, some may make you hurl and some may make you run . . . It all can be confusing, so it is important to know your Bible. Ask God for guidance and understand salvation. Jesus did not teach denomination, religion or segregation from His church. He taught salvation, discipline, obedience and discipleship. One day, when we all get to heaven, Jesus will settle the mistakes we've made in doctrine and no matter what you want to call your church, if Christ is the head of your church, Christ is the center of your life and Christ is the One you follow; Christ will reveal Himself to you when your life here is done. He's not looking for labels; He is looking for followers of His word, His will and His way . . .

I used to be *religious*. I believed in God and knew Jesus was crucified on the cross and that the cross-symbolized His suffering for our sin. Yes, I knew it, understood it and went to church where I heard regular messages on it. But not long after I became saved, I became weak and allowed Satan to set me adrift. It was completely my fault! I had not allowed my sincere experience with God's Holy Spirit to inspire and guide me into the experience of fulfillment. That is when I recognized the real difference between being religious and being a born again believer in Christ. I changed/repented and accepted God as the supreme authority, believed in the gift of life through Jesus Christ and committed to remove self and receive all of Christ. Oh my, what a difference this moment has made in my clarity of understanding. The "knowing" is beyond inspirational, and it is divine grace with the fulfillment of the Prince of Peace. In the most turbulent of times, His presence is complete calmness. My message is not about denomination, it is not about ceremonial practices, it is not about tradition and it is not about challenging anyone's book. My message is solely on Jesus Christ and I have mentioned it before and I will mention it again:

"And for those who saw Jesus and believed in Him were treasured but for those who believe in Him and have never seen Him then those souls will be richly blessed by Him."

John 14:6

My conscience is clear with the Way, the Light and the Truth. The only way to eternal salvation is through Jesus Christ. There is no other way but through the cross and by the blood He shed for you . . . It is a choice to make today, forever and ever, Amen.

These are the ingredients tainted or lost in most churches today. The obstacle is either in the pulpit or the people or both. I have personally heard pastors tell their congregation to step forward and say a little prayer and be saved forever. Part of this is true. Public profession is part of acceptance and confession of faith. Then belief and commitment will immediately follow. If you do not walk in Christ then you have not accepted His divine direction therefore, you are living a lie and it will cost you your eternal spirit if you do not settle it today. Stop the "feel good I just wanna be happy" talk and get holy! There will be many sitting in the pews of churches the day after rapture because so many people thought they were Christian.

Many will sit in the church pews the day after the rapture has occurred and they will say, "The rapture couldn't have happened, look, I'm still here!"

If you paint an old empty rusty shed where it looks brand new, you still have a empty rusty shed that rust will later show through! Calling yourself Christian and being a born again believer in Christ is very different indeed. Believers want to be in church, want to be in daily devotion and want to serve Christ. If you fail to follow Him then how can you profess to "know" Him? If you do not follow Jesus faithful in your daily walk then you do not walk with Him. If you are not holy then He does not dwell within you. If this upsets you then stop right now and go look in the mirror because it is the Holy Spirit digging deep. It is your unsettled heart and what you see in the mirror that reflects what lives in your heart. Every time you look in the mirror you should see the reflection of Christ.

Understand this and understand it well. No one gets to the Father before you go through Jesus Christ. No Methodist, No Presbyterian, No Catholic, No Baptist, No Hindu Indian, No Muslim, No Buddhist, No Mormon, No Jehovah Witness, No Pentecostal, and No Jewish chosen, I mean NO ONE. Go on and get mad. Draw your Sword, read these scriptures out of one book, one testimony and one God: John 1:16, John 3:23, John 5:8, John 5:12, John 6:23, John 10:9, John 13:8, John 14:6, John 14:12, John 14:13, John 16:17, and John 16:20. If you are still grumbling go to Matthew 7:13 and 14. Still wandering around kicking mad? Go to Matthew 9:6, then read Matthew 10:32, then Matthew 11:28 and then go back to John, thumb to Chapter 14 and run your finger down to verse 6. Salvation is not by works and it is not a birthright. It is by faith, belief and acceptance that you receive grace in eternal life. The path is narrow because it is a daily walk in holiness. I am not speaking about some guy who climbed a mountain, shaved his head, wears a robe and chants all day. I am telling you to pick up your cross and live in His footsteps every day and then obey every word Jesus spoke. Draw your Sword and live by His shield . . .

Here is another easy way to tell if you are on the right path or not. Walking in the footprints of Jesus is really quite easy as long as you know exactly where Satan is and what his temptation looks like. When Satan tempts the feelings are physical. When Jesus speaks then it is spiritual. When Satan offers you a deal it is typically very short lived. When Jesus offers you salvation it is spiritual. When Satan offers you a drink or a symbol of his generosity it is physical and typically comes in the form of silver, gold, jewels, fresh paint or a mind altering high. When Jesus offers you anything it will begin in the form of service, becoming humble as a servant, it will look like a carpenter made it and it will have eternal implications. When Satan tempts it will come with impatience and have "now" written all over it. When Jesus speaks it is eternal and has spiritual patience of a dove. Satan will want to give it all to you and the greed will make you want more and more until you will be willing to risk everything you have for the gamble of more. Jesus offers you less here and says that by following Him, you risk losing your <u>worldly dignity</u>, risk <u>physical bondage</u> and risk <u>suffering</u> but the eternal reward is a gift of eternal peace. Satan wants you to enjoy your life here while knowing this life is only temporary. Jesus wants you to enjoy His love here and prepare yourself for glorious heavenly rewards beyond this world.

I have friends of other religions and some who are agnostic and one who is atheist. I can't throw anyone a life preserver if they want to risk the dangerous water alone and the Holy Spirit can't rescue anyone from eternal damnation if they refuse to listen or understand. Like the gods and idols previously mentioned in this book, if they choose against God and salvation through Jesus Christ, God will tend to them. I can only offer the truth, which is a life raft in a river of rapid water of sorts. The consistent statement that I hear from people is; "God really didn't mean for the Bible to be His only word" and the other statement is, "you don't think God only spoke to the Prophets in the Bible, do you?" I challenge you to think about these religions mentioned and look for their faith and belief practices on your own. Then look at their worship practices. Then measure the criteria they use to God's word in the Holy Bible. Do they have a:

✟ Complete belief in God the Father, God the Son and God the Holy Spirit as one God?

✟ Complete belief in the virgin birth of Jesus Christ, His death and His resurrection?

✟ Complete belief in those who are born again in Christ spirit, your deaths passage will become immediately absent your body into heavenly paradise with Christ.

✞ Complete obedience in baptism as a symbol of new life in Jesus Christ?

✞ Complete faith that He will fulfill His promise of returning for all those who accepted Him as their personal savior as written in the Lambs Book of Life?

✞ Complete understanding that the Bible is complete and no other Word is acceptable before Genesis and after Revelation?

Then read Matthew 28:19-20 and Romans 1:17.

Jesus is in the Bible at least 86 times in the New Testament and He was announced several times in the Old Testament. His name is written and His words are quoted. It is less about denomination, religion and a title than it is about salvation. The Crusades were not about Catholics or Baptists or Muslims; it was about Christ and the freedom to worship Him. Your prayers center around the name of Jesus and you may only get to God through Jesus Christ who paid the ultimate price so we may have everlasting life. Draw your Sword and answer these following questions:

Matthew 1:25 And His name was called what? _____

Matthew 3:16 And who came up out of the water? _____

Matthew 4:10 And who commanded Satan? _____

Matthew 4:17 And who began to preach? _____

Matthew 5:1 And who taught the sermon on the mount? _____

Matthew 6:9 And who said how to pray? _____

Matthew 6:33 And seek whose kingdom? _____

Matthew 10:32 And confess whose name? _____

Matthew 11:28 And come to who for rest? _____

Matthew 14:19 And who fed over 5,000 with bread and fish? _____

Matthew 14:26 And who was seen walking on the sea? _____

Matthew 16:25 And lose your life for whose sake will find it? _____

Matthew 28:20 And who will be with you till the end? _____

Mark 1:17 And follow who? _____

Mark 10:15 And receive the kingdom of God like a what? _____

Luke 4:21 And whose prophecies were fulfilled? _____

Luke 9:48 And receive who? _____

"Blessed are those who hear the word of God and follow it!"
Luke 11:28

"Jesus said to him, "I am the way, and the truth, and the life; no one comes to the Father but through Me."
John 3:6

What do you believe and where is your faith calling you? Your salvation and the discipleship of witness will greatly depend on your center. Your center is not the champion in you and it has nothing to do with finding yourself. You must lose yourself and surrender your center to Christ. This center means that you have surrendered your control to God and have given all you have to Him. You will turn selfish to service and "me" to "Him". This "change begins at the cross and in repentance of your sins to Jesus Christ, not some priest in a closet or head doctor on a couch.

While people seek better lifestyles, better answers of worldly magnitude, better conditions to live in; God simply seeks the better Christian inside you. Develop an eternal plan that prepares you for an eternal journey that sets sights on achieving spiritual satisfactions of heavenly treasures beyond the worldly imagination.

A—B—C

Do you have a covenant with God?
Have you come to the cross in repentance for your sins?
Do you have a holy walk in obedience to Christ?
Do you live in daily prayer and devotion?
Do you know Jesus Christ as the risen Savior?
Do you believe that the Holy Trinity is One Almighty God?
Do you believe in the sanctification of the Holy Spirit?
Do you walk in His word and in obedience?
Was there a hesitation or skip in your answers to His love for you?
Are you ready to **A**ccept Him to **B**elieve in Him and to **C**ommit to a covenant to Him?
Are you ready for the biggest change in your physical and spiritual life?
His name is Jesus . . .

Today's Crusades
And
Sword of Freedom

Are we living in a generation of people who desire to have freedom **of** religion or freedom **from** religion?

~ ~ ~ ~ ~ ~ ~

"Therefore, having been justified by faith, we have peace with God through our Lord Jesus Christ, through whom also we have obtained our introduction by faith into His grace in which we stand; and we exult in hope of the glory of God."

Romans 5:1-2

The Prophets, Disciples and Apostles chosen by God set the examples, scribed the instructions, provided the evidential documentation and set a straight path for us to follow. Not to follow them but follow God's word, the path of Jesus and His word. There is no man worthy of you following him or her. No, not one! Not when it comes to your spiritual life. Today's Christian Crusader has few obstacles that were different in the days of old but the view sure has changed.

There are many Pastors, Bishops, Ministers and Teachers today worthy of your ears and they are in your local churches, on TV and on the radio. Listen to their messages and music on the radio and watch their messages on TV or Internet between your church services or when you are physically unable to attend. Do not attend church when you may risk spreading germs of colds with flue like symptoms, fever, the plague and the combinations thereof that fall along the lines of the French disease called; "pheel-lak-poopoo". This is when you can turn on the TV or turn on your computer and invite a minister into your home. These programs are for those who physically cannot attend or for added Bible study. But, if you are physically able, you need to unite with God's Church. Let's face it; it is an hour on Sunday morning, an hour on Sunday evening and an hour on Wednesday evening. Three hours out of 168 hours each week is really not too much for you to dedicate to Him. If you can't attend all three, go to two and if you just cannot make two then at least go to one. But here is the ultimatum; a born again believer in Jesus Christ would not, no could not stay away from God's house. If you can, then test your salvation my friend . . . Romans 12:2

Why go to church? Let me throw out some ideas for you:

- o **Learn**—the more you know, the more you will understand God's vision for you and the more confident you will become in His word.
- o **Listen**—to the message, to the sounds of His praise to the testimony of others just like you and listen to the breath of God. If you have not received Christ as your personal savior, I guarantee He will speak to you. It is your responsibility to stop the argument with the deceivers in your head and make the move to the front during the call to the cross. John 20:19-23
- o **Worship**—this is an opportunity for you to thank Him, to praise Him and come to His house to show your respect for Him. The music will inspire you but more important, it pleases God that you would sing praises to Him in worship. Anything you do away from the church body is not worship it is Bible study. There is a big difference.
- o **Unity**—if you attend, others attend and all unite to show God we are one people in His flock. Understand this; worship is not about you. It is about Him.
- o **Give**—**G**od **I**nvests **V**alue **E**ternally. If you invest in Him, He will invest in you, forever . . .
- o **Grow**—your physical life depends on the strength and stability of your spiritual life. Being around fellow Christians will help you with your growth and continued development.

Remember, Satan preys on the weak in heart, weak in spirit and weak in character. If Satan could convince a group of people to shout "crucify Him" for no reason then what gives you the right to a divine shield of protection? Who are the convincing groups of today? What do they look like? Who are the ones pushing Christianity out of the schools and into the courtrooms? If they were canceling your favorite TV program you would remove the courthouse door hinges!

The trials of recent times are similar to those seen in our history. You don't have to be Christian to see the parallels but you must believe in Jesus Christ the Son of God in order to understand the truth in the trials. Jesus came here to die for us and here are the allegations made by a court of people, just like us, but they were certainly not selected of His peers. That was not possible, could not be possible and will never be possible.

Out of 15 years as a certified investigator, here are my findings: The trial of Jesus Christ had no legal precedent or foundational criminal rule to govern by. Jesus was brought before a quick court, convicted and executed even though Pilate found Him innocent of any wrong. Before sentencing was made final, the judge in this case, called out to an angry mob for sentencing. If they had done this in the O.J Simpson and Casey Marie Anthony trials, the outcome would have been: **CRUSIFY THEM!**

> Jesus was taken at night and subjected to preliminary proceeding at night out of the public's eye. According to Jewish law, only daylight proceedings were permitted.

> Jesus was arrested without formal charge of any "illegal" act or criminal behavior. Judges themselves brought the charges with no witness testimony. The comments of the high priests were unfounded and without deposition of proof of any rule of evidence. Not one piece of evidence was logged as an exhibit.

> Jesus was unlawfully held and indicted before sunrise so His followers would not have an opportunity to witness on his behalf. No pretrial witness, no depositions and no jury of His peers. But then again, no one is a peer to God . . .

The group who accused Jesus was the very ones who bribed Judas to falsely accuse him. The set up and obvious conspiracy!

The Jewish court originated the charges against Jesus and they did not have the authority to charge him AND hold him accountable for any crime. Even though in the historical records of Roman courts record that no crime was ever stated. The Holy Bible is not the only record of the trial and crucifixion of Jesus. Roman and Jewish records both agree.

According to Holy Scripture found in John 18:28, the trial of world history began a day before the annual Sabbath. Jewish law did not permit the trial of a capital offense to begin on Friday or the day before Sabbath. A capital offense was one where death was the sentence.

Jesus was tried, convicted and sentenced to death in a matter of a few hours. This was settled by a few and before the sun rose so no witnesses would be permitted to rebuke the unlawful accusations, trial, conviction and ultimate sentence of Jesus.

Jesus was charged for His own testimony, which is allowed by Jewish law. The charges of blasphemy were His own words and the charge that He would destroy the temple with His own hands was thought to be laughable. So they laughed . . . Mind you, in the courtroom were Romans and Priests. It was the church that condemned Christ and provoked the crowd. Rome simply carried out the order to Calvary.

Deuteronomy 13:12-14 should have been the judge's ruling guide but was ignored. In less than 9 hours this act included an arrest, charge, trial, conviction and sentence. There was no investigation and this passage by Jewish law would have required it. The priests present in the courtroom knew this law by heart.

The crime was changed from blasphemy to treason so the law would be administers by Roman law instead of Jewish law. This would place the blood of Jesus on Roman hands instead of Jewish hands and would move the anger from the priests to the power of the Roman Empire.

It also shifted the anger and blame held by followers of Christ from the church to Rome.

Pilate never pronounced Jesus guilty of any crime whereby capital punishment would have been the sentence. He merely turned Jesus over to the soldiers after hearing the plea for crucifixion. I believe Pilate knew Jesus was innocent and could not look Him in the eyes with the mark of death. So this was a lynching and murder in the first degree.

The sentence was carried out and no formal criminal charges read. Crucifixion was a capital offense execution method, period. This was used for public display of the worst offenders of all crimes. No crime was or has ever been recorded so there was no foundation for any of the process followed.

The only word that gave the death of Christ purpose was God's word. John 3:15-16

Acts Chapter 23 Paul speaks of his so-called trial before the Counsel and Paul boldly said, "God is going to strike you, you whitewashed wall!" And after the trial as the soldiers lead him away, the Lord stood by Paul's side and said, "Take courage; for as you have solemnly witnessed to My cause at Jerusalem, so you must witness at Rome also." So, Paul faced many battles but the task of spreading the gospel had only just begun. There would be many battles to face.

Since the 1st Century many battles have been fought, many religious wars destroyed nations, many have died defending the right to worship God, and many have suffered because they believed in God's word and His will. These battles have been fought across the globe and even though the faces have changed, the mission has not. The crusades of then are still the crusades of today.

We are meant to be on the battle field until our King arrives or death takes us to Him first!

Christians are always on trial before the world counsels and the critics are more than one can count. In our own government, in our communities, on public television, on radio airwaves, on the Internet and other venues, Jesus Christ is still challenged. So now we know that being a Christian has been tested since the original twelve and will continue until Jesus returns. So what do Today's Christian Crusaders do?

Here are a few concepts that I have thought of and you may have some of your own:

1. We must have an administration that will bring God back into the center of the White House and on the floor of Congress. Your role is to vote and help elect those who are Godly. Those who vote against God must be voted out. A President that cannot find his/ Her knees cannot be trusted with a like-Christ decision.

2. We must have a legislative branch that will establish the foundational value of God in the laws that are written for our people across these United States. Again, vote for Godly legislators that understand Freedom **of** Religion, not freedom from it.

3. We need our legislators to remember that the separation of church and state was to prevent government from regulating church business not the church out of the government. This will take a stand of united Christian Crusaders in every voting booth.

4. We need to ensure we elect politicians that understand who is in charge and He (God) must be at the center of our future. Every Christian vote is part of discipleship. You are making a stand for God and making a statement of your witness. God is in control and He will call on you to do what is right for His people.

5. We must unite the church, one church under God and one nation under God. Rev. Martin Luther King Jr. led a mass of united people to the steps for "I Have A Dream". I have a dream was the call to freedom of free will and equality. Free will includes your firm understanding that God is in control. November 2010 and November 2012 will provide all Christian's with a renewal of the "I have a dream" that was started just a few years ago. "I have a Dream" was about the voice of God and we cannot allow this to be turned into I HAD a dream . . .

6. Move "I Have a Dream" to "We Have a Prayer". If God be for us who can stand against us?

We will not unite unless the power of the country unites in prayer. We will not survive the future because of the division among us. But know this; the global population of 6,790,500,000 could not agree on White House paint color much less what religion to believe in. This is also why Jesus must return and take His people from this soil so it may be burned of its filth.

"Beloved, while I was making every effort to write you about our common salvation, I felt the necessity to write to you appealing that you <u>continue earnestly for the faith</u> which was once for all handed down to the saints."

Jude 5

The Sword should be found in every soldier's field pack. His comfort in battle has been since the beginning and it is the Ark of the Covenant that provided strength in the face of many enemies. When the Israelites crossed the Jordan into the Promised Land, Joshua called upon twelve men, one from each tribe to pick up one stone. One stone, each from the dry bed of the Jordan River as they crossed. These stones would serve as a reminder that God had delivered them from their oppressors and enemies. The Ark of the Covenant was carried across the Jordan into the Promised Land. Joshua chapter 4 will gives you both comfort and confidence in the Holy Sword you carry.

If a movement in a one-world government and a one-world church was decided, just how many troops could be deployed to secure the measure?
Today there are over 500,000,000 uniformed soldiers in the world.
Sworn dedicated soldiers to defend its people from enemies, both foreign and domestic! Who are our domestic enemies?

At what cost does it take to carry the Sword and Shield across the USA and the globe? There have been great costs in people's lives and money to move God's word across the land and to every tribe. Who pays and who doesn't? Look back at the population then understand that less than 25% of the Christian's donate as well. Less than 25% is probably a stretch but

I don't want to upset the bean counters . . . I know, why start now, right? Here are some dollars wasted that just blows my mind. Just how many stupid people are there in this world? According to this event, 200!

In October 2009 an auction house held a private auction in Chicago, Illinois of some of Elvis Presley's personal items that were collected by Gary Pepper who was the President of the Tankers Fan Club. So these were items collected by a collector who collected some collector items collected from the alleged estate of Elvis. Okay, here are some of the items that were "believed" to have come from the Elvis collection:
$66,100 for one cream collared cotton shirt, $37,300 for one red ultra suede shirt, and $18,300 for a pile of hair "believed" to have been Elvis's when he got his haircut in the Army. It was "believed" to have been his hair. Other items sold that were "believed" to have been part of the famous Elvis collection was a bath robe, Pez dispenser, dolls, photo's, Christmas cards, records and another 190 or so items. The total included the $3,300 auctioneer fee, **per item**.

And you wonder why some people don't believe in biblical events but take complete faith in a collector's word? It just isn't logical, right? Are there other things that the globally challenged buys into? What do we waste our money on that could be invested in viable efforts that actually care for people? Here are a few "common family" type expenses that dig into the wisdom of why in the world we waste our blessings:

- ! Buying a car with a monthly payment over 30% of your take-home income! Then understanding what being "upside down" means. Or negotiating a fair car price then getting killed with interest and add-ons in the finance office because you either don't understand an interest loan or they bait you on a higher interest rate because of your questionable credit.
- ! Buying groceries on an empty stomach with a credit card. Always shop when you are full and with a list. This is a difficult thing to do but it will keep you from buying junk.
- ! Hair clubs for men. Less hair means less mess and a hat is around ten bucks!
- ! Breast implants. This is to feel better about you. If you plan to cover them up then what's the point? If it is to repair from

life's unfortunate disease or accident, then yes. But then again, it becomes more about confidence and less about your sexuality.

! Bowtox injections. Do you really want to look like the joker in the next batman movie?

! Cosmetic plastic survey. I'm not speaking of corrections made due to an injury or burns. Excessive cosmetic surgery changed Michael Jackson from a man into a weird looking mannequin. Teenager girls look at themselves and see the need for cosmetic enhancements.

! Home exercise equipment that turns into expensive clothes racks. How many $1,000 machines have sold for $100 in yard sales? I'm guilty as charged on this one!

! Name brand verses generic brand purchases. There are people who live to shop by name brand only and can't wear a t-shirt unless it has a famous logo on it. Harley Davidson people are fanatics about logo t-shirts. At the next sporting event you see, how many fans, who are not actually on the field playing, are wearing logo shirts? Logo shirt = $50 > plain white Hanes t-shirt = $4.98 at Wal-Mart!

! Just look in your kid's toy room. Just how much stuff do they need?

! Clothes that we hold on to, that we have grown out of and we hope to get back into one day. Go take a look at your closet. Pull out everything you haven't worn this year and donate it.

! $500 watch when a $10 watch tells the same time.

! Magazine subscriptions. Did you know that you could read the same articles and see the same pictures on the Internet for free? Duh!

! Lotto tickets! They can't give away 30 million dollars without collecting 120 million and we still pay school tax. Take how much you spent on lotto and subtract how much you have actually won, then realize what you have wasted. Satan wants you to think that the next ticket you buy could be the one . . .

! Diet gimmicks. Oh my, what an industry. You'll never be able try them all, cause when you lose weight; the trick will be to keep it off. Trust me, I know.

! Male enhancement pills? Lose weight and get enhanced. Take a bath and be more attractive. Do the things you did when you dated and your love life will enhance.

! Daily trips to Starbucks! Just how much should a cup of coffee cost?

! Garage/yard sales mean you are buying other peoples stuff that they didn't want either.

! Gourmet foods or organic produce. You really think it is organically maintained? To farm in volume you have got to control the soil and the things that flying the air to make a profit. Growers need to make a profit too.

! Snacks! Not nourishing or healthy and typically very expensive. If you eat at the local convenient store then you are being very foolish.

! Bottled water. Why not install a filter on your faucet; it's what the bottle water manufacture did. Get a thermos or quality bottle and fill it before leaving home. You say you just have to have flavored water? You will not miss what you have never had!

! Eating in any restaurant rather than eating at home. You are paying for food, prep and service as well as the building. Also the average glass of soda, tea or juice from a restaurant costs $1.99 to $2.99 and you may get a refill. Think of how many times you buy a beverage every day then total the day's beverage expense. Multiply this daily total times 260 days (5 work days a week x 52 weeks gives an average) to see how much you spend. Mine was $2,971.11 in one year and I don't drink Starbucks coffee. Sounds big doesn't it? If you are honest with your math your amount may surprise you . . . If you were REAL honest and included alcohol, beer-wine-mixed drinks . . . WOW! The reality is that all we need is clear clean water to hydrate. All the rest feeds self, "because I want it" . . .

! Bank late fees are ridicules. You bought it so pay the bill when it is due!

! Snail mail US stamps when you can pay on-line.

! When you buy it and don't use it, then return it for a refund. Even if it is store credit you still benefit with a credit, gift card or cash rather than holding stuff that you can't or won't use.

! That monthly gym membership when you never seem to have time to go. It is only a value if you do it right. Not unless you really use it as a social club then it really pegs the stupid needle.

! Buying a DVD when you can rent it for a couple of bucks or order it on-line.

! Upgraded fast food bonus meals that you really don't need but it sounds so good because it is only a few cents more. Yeah, biggie-size that heart attack meal! Does this really make *cents*?

! Replacing stuff that you can't find. Like TV cables, socks, winter gloves, suntan lotion, bug spray, chap stick, batteries, sunglasses, and so on.

! Buying cigarettes! An expensive habit with zero gain. On average it is a $5,700 a year habit and that is if you are a light smoker buying basics.

! Buying anything from your neighborhood Pharmacy is totally stupid. Save at your discount store. At Wal-Mart and Sam's Club I pay $4 per prescription on most scripts. If you are a veteran then the V.A. has more assistance. What are you paying?

! Pulling a lever or pushing a button on a casino slot machine. Sure, the very next pull or push will make you a millionaire. If the odds were on the players side, the owners would not live in mansions and live the life of kings-n-queens. You would!

! CD's, DVD's and self help books on how to play casino card games. 1st you waste the money on "how to play" then you give away your money when you play. Who do you think created this program?

! Palm readers, mediums, shrinks, mental therapists, dog whisperers and snake charmers. You might as well go to a witch doctor and have them shake a chicken foot at you. This is Satan's world with Satan's people doing the work of Satan.

! Store bought Halloween costumes. The kids are cute in simple costumes but when the kids become an adult then the costume leads to a party so you can be seen, that is probably not where you should be. For the kids, make it at home and be creative while saving money. For the adults that feel the need to dress up and party, what costume do you recommend for Christ? If you call yourself Christian, then this means you are taking Him with you. Right?

! CLEARANCE SALES are stuff that didn't sell so they mark it down and put it on sale. It is okay if you use it but generally it sits in a closet or saved to give away later.

! Parking tickets are the direct result of stupidity and laziness. They can cost you from $25 to $100 and they add interest when you forget to pay them.

! Credit Card late fees make credit card companies richer than rich and you poorer than poor. This is great if you are in the banking business but foolish if you are paying them. If everyone paid their monthly charges off each month then credit card companies would be out of business.

! ATM fees are the dumbest thing you can pay. You will get charged about $2 for every transaction just to have access to your own money? Be better prepared to avoid the dumb fees and keep a little cash handy OR just don't buy it.

! 35mm film? If you haven't moved to digital yet then you are still throwing money away with wasted film and printing costs. With a digital camera you can see the picture you took before you print it so you may delete what isn't wanted. Then pick your best printing value store and many Sam's Club Photo Centers have .13 to .17 cent prints. Catch a special and print for free! A little plug for Sam's Club . . .

! When you buy a new car you generally get a one time free visit to the dealers' service dept. This is to lure you into a lifetime of overspending for the same service that the corner's lube express or Wal-Mart charges for much, much less.

! Christmas ornaments, yard decorations and electricity to run them. This is not a Christian practice but a protestant pagan tradition. Bring the family together and make your ornaments and decorations rather than spending hundreds on store bought brands. It also seems to be a growing tradition to buy gifts until you are completely in debt. How many people get to November and still have last Christmas charges on their credit cards? Just in case you forgot, this time of year celebrates the birth of Jesus. The media and commercialization of Christmas has buried the true reason for the season in your family. And if you ever use the abbreviation, X-mas, **STOP**, you are placing an X on Christ.

Ouch, some of those hurt!!! I would love to have some of this wasted money to afford a boatload of Christmas shoebox gifts for the children who need the support. To support a small mission group overseas that is taking the message of Christ to the world. To support a shelter close to home where I can see their good works. I can't live in the past of wasted moments but I can sure change today before another blessing falls away.

But at what physical cost does it take to carry the voice of freedom to other parts of the world that is bondage and suffering? Two different programs have two very different costs. One is for missions and these are not cheap. Most church organizations have some sort of mission that they are doing or supporting. If you can't find one, go to www.olivebaptist.org or www. newhopemarianna.org/ and click the mission tab. These teams will assist you in supporting a worthy cause. Generally the help they need would be less than $25 a month. That's 3 or 4 beverages at Starbucks for the average cup of fancy loaded java . . . These teams would sincerely appreciate anything you might offer and I thank you on their behalf.

The other cost is your life given in service for another. We know their faces; their families and this cost cannot be placed on a calculator. In Afghanistan, Pakistan and Uzbekistan alone from 2001 to 2009 we have lost 614 military men and women due to hostile action. This number was as of October 16, 2009 by the Defense department. On November 5, 2009 a lone gunman entered an administration building at Fort Hood, Texas and opened fire on soldiers and civilians because he did not want to be shipped off to the fight in Aphganstan. This was not a common terrorist. This shooter was an officer in the Army and he was heard yelling Allah! Thirteen died that day and many were wounded because this coward could not fire on the enemy but felt compelled to fire on his own uniform brothers and sisters. How does a born again believer in Christ understand the taking of a life from an individual that uses their god as a reason for murder? How can Today's Christian Crusader understand the words from a religion that directs them to kill anyone who desires information outside of their own religion? How could we ever understand why a man could kill his fellow soldiers but could not kill a stranger on foreign soil who is killing innocent women and children? Praise be to the female officer who rang a shot out that dropped this coward to the ground and stopped the hate within him from being forced on those in his path. To protect and defend. This was his oath of service and it was hers also. She understood the difference!

And the fight continues. Our men and women of the united forces are paving the way for this country to have the opportunity to worship in peace, walk the streets safely and move terrorists out of their neighborhoods. They are on foreign soil extending that right to other nations as they pursue Christ as well. I salute our men and women of the armed forces for you are the reason why I take a breath of freedom every day. For those lives, both friendly and non taken on foreign soil, we must remember that we all belong to God. We were born with His blessing, if saved, we are given His grace and we will all be taken one day to His Holy Place. Close your eyes, bow your head and say a prayer with me for our troops today . . .

A Soldier's Prayer

The soldier stood and faced his God, which must always come to pass. He hoped his boots were shined just as bright as his brass. The single voice of his authority will call his name and say, "Step forward young soldier have you turned the other cheek and to my church have you been true?" The soldiers will snap the heals of their boots and sound a voice of plea, "no Lord, I have served my country and my duty on seven days of thunder; I have carried and fired my weapon for the freedom that our flag flies under. The streets and terrain are evil and I am protecting your sheep well. I have seen way to many of my brothers and sisters fall and I have many friends in them all. I have embraced the weak and poor as well as those who could take no more. God forgive me for I have wept many tears. I am in the center of struggle and the protector of many fears. I serve my country far from those I love and have left behind. I answer the call of duty even when I do not understand. I ask to forgive those lives I've taken and bless the lives I've saved. Come to me now oh Lord in my hour of need to be saved. For only you know my hands are dirty but my heart is forever so pure." There was a silence around the throne of God as the twelve who saddled chairs beside Him knelt in silent prayer. God looked the soldier in the eyes with a loving stare. He said, "Step forward young soldier for you have done well. Your reward is heaven because you have spent enough time in hell. Step forward young soldier into the gate that I have prepared for you. My lamb has traveled far to come in my Holy hand. You have honored your brothers and sisters and fought a crusaders fight. You my child will remain with me in peace and in eternal Light"

〜〜〜〜〜〜〜〜〜〜〜〜〜〜〜〜〜〜〜〜

I assure you, you have never lived a day in the light of honor, until you have folded a United States flag to the sound of a military trumpet playing taps, then to the serenity of a bagpipe playing Amazing Grace. The respect of a twenty-one-gun salute and hearing the pop of a battalion snapping they're heals from parade rest to attention. There is not stronger brotherly love and kindness that is shown when one gives their life for another. I pray for our men and women of the armed forces and also for our men and women who serve on American soil in Law Enforcement, Fire protection and medical responders. We pray each day that families hold their loved ones once again. To those who have laid their life on the line both on foreign or domestic soil for the freedom that we fly our flag over, I salute you my brother and sister for in God's eye's we are one . . .

Today's Christian Crusader risks life and limb for God, country and the freedom our forefathers wrote of so long ago.

Today's Christian Crusader leaves family and friends to fight side by side with the only brothers and sisters that they truly know.

Today's Christian Crusader understands the risks they take and are more prepared today than ever as well as more aware of their role because their leadership sees the bondage that terror holds.

Today's Christian Crusader stands in prayer when our administration will not and stands together when our administration chooses not.

Today's Christian Crusader is affirmed of a loyalty to God and one another in a knowing that Christian Crusader's of yesterday will stand beside those deployed today in honor of those who have fallen before us

Today's Christian Crusaders are in the trenches, in the hospitals and in the mission field for freedom. Freedom from those who battle against the freedom of worshiping our Redeemer, our Lord and eternal King. He is the reason why we Crusade.

May God protect my brothers and sisters in safe keeping today for you are in the hands of Christ our King, in nail scarred hands where you are eternally secured.

1st John 1:1-4

Living by the Sword

"If we say that we have fellowship with Him and yet walk in darkness, we lie and do not practice the truth; but if we walk in the Light as He Himself is in the Light, we have fellowship with one, another, and the blood of Jesus His Son cleanses us from all sin."

1st John 1:6-7

Today's civilization is not a single note different than the civilizations before Jesus, while Jesus taught, after Jesus rose, during the Crusades or whenever. It is the same complaining, the same greed, the same jealous pride, the same immoralities, the same lies, the same corruptions and the same deception in the tribe/nation's leadership. The differences we face are in modernization, technical advancements and an incredible amount of increasing distractions. The major difference in 1st century and 21st century is we know what is happening around the world just moments as after it happens or as it is happening. This is part of prophecy. We could see them as a disadvantage or an advantage but first; let's understand some facts that we face in every day life today. Here are some snapshots of reality:

But I don't, I can't, I won't. Some people have a favorite word for a part of the Bible that they either don't understand, don't agree with or can't live by and it is the word "*but*". Like: "Oh sure, *but* how did He part the Red Sea?" "Oh sure, *but* how did He make Lazarus walk out of a dead man's tomb?" "Oh sure, *but* my friend says . . ." For those *buts* you really need to Draw Your Sword and bring your *buts* to the alter where all things are revealed to those who seek to know. God will help you remove your *but* from blinded eyes to clear vision and help you see through all the *buts* that stand before you. You will replace the; I don't, I can't and I won't with **I will**.

But He hasn't answered any of my prayers. First, it is less about you and more about Him. Second, prayer is not a 24-hour request line for you to place an order and get it at the next window. Walk over to that favorite mirror and asks that person, "does Christ live in my life and does He have all my heart, my soul, my mind and my body?" If that is an uncomfortable question then you are walking around half empty or bone dry of His Holy Spirit.

But I go to church sometimes, isn't that enough? Have you ever heard of anyone who was almost pregnant? No, you are either all in or you are all out. If you love Him you will follow Him. Can you be almost dead?

But do I really have to be baptized? Jesus traveled about 30 miles to have John the Baptist submerge Him completely under water. When He came up from the water God spoke to all who witnessed that this was His Son of whom He is proud. This began His ministry, as it will be yours. Your ministry is to disciple (learn), speak His name (tell) and give your testimony (live in Christ). The real question is, "if you love Him why then would you not willingly obey His word?"

But my friends are not Christian. If your life is not respectful of God's direction, others will have a difficult time seeing the benefit of faith. If you were drowning would you want to be tossed a life jacket or a boat anchor? Your life jacket is your Bible and instructions how to use it. Your friends will need to make the same decision you do. Follow your friends and die. Follow Christ and live.

But my family and friends are likely to walk away from me. The quickest way to know who around you walks in the Light of Christ is to ask your friends, "Do you know Jesus." Peer pressure has got to be near the top of obstructions in people's lives. It is a barrier between you and God. Are your peers giving you better advice than God? You are not pressured or forced to be a born again believer in Christ. You are called. Then witness to your lost family and friends or find new ones that follow Christ. If they walk away, they walk away in darkness. Your role as God's disciple is to tell them.

If your peer group is stronger than your prayer group then by whose authority do you live by? A peer or God?

But I have a really bad past and I don't know if my sins are entirely forgivable. Others see what you do and what you say. God sees who you are and knows your heart. Who you are tends to impact what you do. There is an old saying, "If you always do what you've always done, you'll always get what you've always got!" If you continue to walk in darkness then you are guaranteed to always find darkness. If you turn away from darkness and walk in His Light, then your life will find an abundance of life in His Light. Is it and will it always be a bouquet of flowers? Nope, welcome to a sinful world where you'll find many thorns in a bed of roses. Know this for sure; Jesus died that you might live with Him in eternity and He made no stipulation to the baggage you bring to the cross. He wore the thorns in a crown so you could have the roses . . .

But God wants us to be happy, right? Recently I attended a service and Rick Burgess, half of the team from the Rick and Bubba radio show, was the key note speaker. I mentioned this radio program in my first book, "2012 Global Warning" and this dynamic team is founded on Christ and just happens to include others stuff that is entertaining as well as informative. Rick's message was of saving grace from one who understands that being saved is combined with telling your testimony. His message was clear in the true understanding between being happy with your life and being holy in your life's walk in Christ. It is a life that Christ has given us, a life that Christ suffered for us and it is a life that He expects us to testify on His behalf. As the world felt the loss with the Burgess family's loss of young life, God's message through this family is that they cannot live strong enough through the testimony of the loss of a child but that Christ can. With Christ in our life then anything is possible. Rick's testimony today is from Matthew 28, the final command that Jesus gave all His children and it is the commitment to testify unto the world, to make disciples and baptize in the name of the Father, and the Son and His Holy Spirit. His message parallels mine through the book of John in a clear understanding of the great commission of living a holy life. If you are living just to live a happy life then you are living to be satisfied with the pleasures of this world. If you are living to live a holy life then your life is larger than this world and your destiny is living testimony of the love of Jesus Christ. The gift of eternal life through the sacrifice of our Lord and Savior is a portal through the same expectation that a grape vine is to be fruitful in bearing grapes in abundance. It's about going home . . .

But people will say I am acting holier than thou! You see, our life is separated at the point of knowing the life's message of Christ and each one of us makes a decision to believe or not to believe. That moment is called a time of decision. It is a choice from worldly happiness and heavenly holiness. Rick and Sherry Burgess focus in on this point because it is the point of separation from a born again believer in Christ and the rest of the world. It is the difference between the saved and the unsaved, the blessed and the lost, the gifted and the gift-less. Rick is dead on when he quotes the words through John inspired by God's Holy Spirit in 1st John 2:4-6. Jesus Christ is holy and He fills your life with holiness so if you are holier than those who are categorizing you then they are sadly correct. Live it, embrace it and love Him for it. If Christ lives in you then my friend, you are holy . . .

~ ~ ~

If you are influenced or led by a peer or media/popular personality rather than Jesus, then know your idol well because it is leading you straight to Hell!

~ ~ ~ ~ ~ ~ ~

"The one who says, "I have come to know Him" and does not keep His commandments, is a liar, and the truth is not in him; but whoever keeps His word, in him the love of God has truly been perfected. By this we know that we are in Him; the one who says he abides in Him ought himself to walk in the same manner as He walked."

1st John 2:4-6

But just how narrow is the gate to heaven? Your lifestyle is a reflection of your testimony and your testimony is a testament to your character and your character comes from what is imbedded in your heart. If you say you are saved yet you live a life in sinful behavior then you are not saved. If you are still drinking, still cussing, still looking at porn on the Internet, still going to strip clubs, still unwilling to forgive someone, still downgrading a different race, still in conflict over church denomination, still laying out of church, still intentionally acting in sinful thoughts then you have not accepted Christ in full sanctification. God does not seek all His people to be pastors, preachers, bishops and traveling evangelists. He calls you to testify of your faith and conduct yourself according to Christ's' teaching. This dark seeded sinful world breeds pride in personal belongings and personal feelings that form us into feeling that we need to be happy to exist. Rick Burgess said firmly that it ain't about whether we are happy here or not, it is about being holy as well as being about God's business. Many are confused about this and it has got Satan and his band of demons extremely happy that you are happy about being here. Please do not allow this world's happiness to steal your heavenly joy.

Why can't a rich man enter heaven? Greed breeds from a physical desire for wealth and people want it bad enough to take it from you. The wealthy want to be wealthier and the rich wanting to become richer and the desire far exceed the basic necessities of a life's need to exist. You do not have to be wealthy to be greedy. You can be poor and just as greedy. A greedy man will die poor just as a greedy wealthy man will die wealthy and both will drown in their greediness. The difference in wanting and giving is in the heart. God loves a cheerful giver. 2 Corinthians 9:7. Have money, be prosperous, and place the money behind you. Always have God in front, help where you can and walk in Godliness. This means to walk as Christ taught us to walk. The Sermon on the Mount will refresh your memory of what it takes, what it means and what His plan is for us. Is it tough? It is very tough for those who have given only a part of themselves to have it. It is tough for those who just barely meet Christ half way. It is extremely tough for those who want Christ but want all of what the world has to offer as well. If you still feel that you deserve a happy life here and are willing to sacrifice your holiness in heaven then you have been told and I have done what Christ has asked of me to do. Testify . . .

~ ~ ~ ~ ~ ~ ~

In today's physical world we are judged by what we look like, where we stay, what we drive, how we live, what we wear, the color of our skin, the size of our body, the style of our hair, the condition of our shoes, the level of our career and the amount of money we have. In the Olympics it means to go for the gold. In the NFL it means to go for the championship ring. In the NBL it means to win the pennant. In the NHL it means to win the cup. In the NBA it means everything to be champions. Having an MBA seems to bring respect. Joel Osteen is looking for a champion inside. American idol fans vote for an idol. In dancing with the stars it represents skimpy outfits and a disco ball trophy. The actors and actresses go for the Emmy. The movie industry seeks gold in an Oscar. Michael Jordan is known for flying in clean air to the hoop. Michael Jackson is remembered as the king of pop. James Brown is best known as the king of soul. Elvis Presley will be forever known as the king of rock and roll. But in the end, God will judge us for our decision of faith and then hand out rewards for service in a faithful life. It is the difference between the outer man and the inner man. Paul spoke of this in Ephesians 3, so draw your Sword.

In the end all will know, without any doubt or reservation that Jesus Christ is King of Kings, Lord of Lords, Master Teacher, Savior, Redeemer of all that have been born again to Him.
It is beyond a moment of celebration as it is completeness of salvation.

Being Pentecostal is an "experience or emotion". Your call to Jesus Christ is solely based on an accepting faith and beyond emotion into a **real change** in your lifestyle to glorify Him. Be emotional, passionate, and make sure this is not just while you are in church or a Christian concert. You don't need to turn the volume up and bust a decimal for God to hear you. Just tell Him you love Him and you are ready to follow Him. Then do it!

Some disciples teach, some screech, some act like creatures of the wild. A quacking disciple walks around saying the same thing over and over with little growth. A strutting peacock disciple may look pretty but makes no sense when he opens his mouth. An ostrich disciple sticks his head in the ground when there is the first sign of trouble. A buzzard disciple hangs around looking for left-overs. A lion disciple growls really loud and eats a lot of groceries then disappears on the couch. A giraffe disciple always sticks his neck out and is very awkward in the community. A weasel disciple is always into mischief, into trouble and winds up in a hole. An otter disciple can be foolish, eats and plays. An eagle disciple always looks for prey and is proud on himself. A pig disciple, well, eats like a pig and only shows up to feast . . .

But the Dove is quiet when they need to be, elegant in flight, speaks in spiritual tone, brings life to those who search for it, hope for the needy and is blessed by the Holy Spirit. It was a white dove that carried the olive leaf, a sign of life for Noah and the new land of opportunity. Be a dove and rise above the beasts of the lands.

If you want to see more of God, He needs to see more of you. Christianity is not used like a passport, only for occasional use when it benefits you. Be a full time life time career Christian and give it all to Christ!

A born again believer in Christ is not a secret agent and as a follower of Christ you can't be a double 0 secret agent in His service. A bondservant is <u>seen</u> doing for the service of Christ. God calls it deeds and He sees it all . . .

Every individual born in this world is given an empty well. The moment you receive Christ, He will fill your well so you will never thirst again. There is never a day that you need to walk around empty. Make sure your well stays full, fresh and clean with daily devotion and prayer. John 4:7-15

As a Christian you are guaranteed that your faith will be challenged. As a Christian you will suffer. Sometimes we need to be broken in order for our soul to understand true healing. He will absolutely mend and heal every broken man/woman.

Pray—Stay—Obey—Always
And you will be okay . . .

Accept all people for who and what they are. You will not make a white person black or a black person white, or a red person yellow or a yellow person red but you can help any person live the Christian way. Who is saved by the grace of God through the Holy Spirit will never ever stray . . . Bring them in close and tell them about Jesus. Their shell will remain the same while the contents will be cleansed. God welcomes all people to His Kingdom who ask.

I have a challenge for you and I believe with all my heart that it will help anyone understand God's creation and His love for us better than any other exercise. Go out to a busy public park or busy mall food court or a busy public area and sit on a bench. Find or borrow a walking stick then take a pair of dark shades/glasses, place them over your eyes. Close and seal your eyes while you sit in this place just for one hour and listen carefully to the sounds of everyday life. With your eyes closed you to tune out what you see and tune in to what you hear. The conversations people have will be beyond your imagination. People think because you are blind that you cannot hear. You will be able to testify that the common language among people is mixed with profanity, lies, gossip and some beyond belief. You will also be able to testify on how many people that you observed walking in the Light of Christ and how many were not. Remember, we have discussed deeply that your Christian acceptance comes also with Christian behavior that is your character in how you act, how you dress, how you talk and how you walk. Do people make mistakes? Yes, because we are born in sin. However, a Christian is reborn into a new life with a daily holy walk in Christ therefore you will not willingly or purposely commit sin. To know Him is to follow Him . . .

You will fail at some things. You will win at some things. You will learn more from your failures than your wins. Let's face it, if you make a mistake you will remember the mistake longer than they will. That thought process is of this world. Your challenge is to get out there and at least try. Go ahead, make a mistake witnessing. God is all about forgiveness therefore, so should we? If God can forgive you, then you must be able to forgive yourself. Living in the past is an obstacle to moving in the righteous direction that is promised for you future.

Around every corner is someone suffering, in pain, experiencing life's misfortune, death, relationship problems, health problems and so on. These are all problems of this world and our challenge from Christ is to comfort these people in His name. He is the eternal answer.

Darkness is in all you do when all you see is you. In Him all things are possible but you must give it all to him. Drop your own agenda and walk in His Light. His path has no obstacles that can't be resolved with His redeeming grace.

Every crushing moment you experienced, so did He. Every challenging moment you face, so did He. Every obstacle you run up against so did He. That moment when you received horrible news, He received it with you. When you were in difficult times, He was with you. When you were in the greatest of times, He was with you. How far do you think you have to look for Him? He is with you right at this very moment. Remember, close your eyes, call His name and find Him with you always. When you commit to a daily devotional walk and a daily devotional prayer, then you will find that your fellowship with Christ is filled with daily devotional conversations. If you are confused about your way, then you are missing your devotion each day.

Before any marriage can begin, the man must be firm in where he is, what he wants and where he is going. If the man does not know this then he is in no position to take on a wife much less a family. You cannot think of changing a man's character after you are married. A man's character is not a change of clothes and a haircut. It is his DNA and is the condition of his heart. If man's heart is dark then so will his actions be. If man's heart is filled with Christ then his Christian love will shine through. Before you say, "I do", make sure you know his heart and make sure your heart is filled with Christ so there is little room for deception. If you really want the truth; if your pastor doesn't know you and doesn't know your partner then there is a chance that Christ may not know you either.

While no one knows what is in your heart they can only see what is in your actions. You can witness a person's testimony by what they do, what they say, and how they live. Life begins when you are willing to take the risks included with the trust in your decisions. Here is an example of one man's desire for freedom of religion.

Henry "Box" Brown

On March 29, 1849, Henry Brown, a slave who watched his wife and children sold in North Carolina came up with an idea to place himself in a wooden box and ship himself to freedom. This box was about 2 foot wide, 2 ½ foot deep and 3 foot long. Brown was 5 foot 8 inch and weight about 200 pounds. He stuffed himself in this box along with a bladder of water and made 3 breathing holes in the box.

He began his journey from the Richmond express office in Virginia and traveled for 27 hours by wagon, then by railroad then by ferry then by railroad again and finally by wagon in Philadelphia. The owners of the box heard a voice from within and opened the box. Henry Brown tried to stand and immediately fell then passed out. Brown mailed himself to freedom but endured suffering, hardship and had to be broken before he was free. Through Brown's suffering God graced him with freedom, a new life and a new family. He published his autobiography in 1875 and is a worthy read to understand his story.

> *"In debt, ashamed with no where to turn*
> *Beaten abused lost with nowhere to go*
> *Turn to the cross and Christ you will learn*
> *Where your strength ends His will grow*
> *Believe in His promise, trust in His will*
> *Forever know you have His seed to sow."*
>
> *John W Edwards III*

Freedom has been fought and sought since the beginning of time. Freedom is only a consideration or is required when someone gains power and authority over you. The Romans held Israel in slavery and bondage. Germany held Israel in slavery and bondage. America held Africans in slavery and bondage. This is historical reality and these next two people understood it all too well.

Two Tickets to Freedom

In December of 1848 in Macon, Georgia, William and Ellen Craft were slaves who escaped bondage and journeyed from Macon, Georgia to Savannah then by steamship to Charleston, South Carolina. From there they traveled by steamboat to Wilmington, North Carolina then by train to Fredericksburg, Virginia. They boarded another steamboat headed for Washington, D.C. and on to Baltimore, Maryland and by land to Philadelphia to freedom. So they thought. The Fugitive Slave Act had just been written and signed whereby making the Crafts felons fleeing from the law or worse, bounty hunters.

Ellen Craft was half white and William was dark skinned. Ellen traveled as a southern slave owner while William traveled as her slave valet. So it wasn't enough to travel through all the connections they were required to do but also they were in costume waiting any moment to be detected as imposters. Two bounty hunters named Hughes and Knight traveled from Macon to Philadelphia to either return the two fugitives by fare or force, and they didn't care either way. The Crafts had local help from both black and white Bostonians where they were able to board a ship and set sail to England. And again, they were on their way to freedom.

The Crafts settled, had five children, lectured in England, and in June 1851 they lead a demonstration in London that was an influential time in the 19th century. In 1870 the Crafts returned to the U.S. and settled in Savannah, Georgia where they organized friends to purchase 1,800 acres of land and began a co-op farm school for teaching newly released slaves how to survive, live without fear and be free.

~~~~~~~

Fear . . .

Today is no different from yesterday when it comes to people's fear. This is reality of living in these times. If you asked most people what they fear the most in this world they would probably list these fears at the top of their list:

- o   Child missing, abduction and/or abuse
- o   Their child sick with a major illness
- o   Sudden death of a close family member
- o   Diagnosis of Cancer
- o   Terrorist attack again
- o   Plane crash, not the crash but the trip to the ground
- o   Being burned to death
- o   Drowning
- o   Being the victim of a violent crime or sex offense
- o   Being kidnapped, then abused
- o   Losing a job, source of income

Those were grown up fears and are very real. You may have a few more but these were from my research. Now let's look at a few youthful fears. These are the fears that a child or young teen would have. Pay attention parents.

- o   Peer pressure
- o   Being humiliated
- o   Have an operation
- o   Getting caught stealing or smoking
- o   Being rejected by their parent(s)
- o   Mom and Dad separate in divorce
- o   Being called to speak in front of the class
- o   Being dumped by boyfriend / girlfriend
- o   Having sex for the first time
- o   Failure, not passing an exam
- o   Getting a job / money

Sometimes a parent may think they are respecting their child's privacy by not asking when they are actually ignoring a path to disaster. Fear is resolved with trust and faith. A child trusts that their parents will protect them and faith that they will do this when they are asleep or unaware of danger. Jesus Christ is that comfort and confidence you seek. He is the solution to all fears. If you cannot see in your child's heart then this means you are human like all the rest of us. If you want your child to feel safe then place them in the only hands that know their fears, their heart and their needs. His name is Jesus . . .

Draw your Sword
2nd Corinthians 1:3-11

~ ~ ~ ~ ~ ~ ~

Living by the Sword has two sides: One for you and the other to share.

1. One side is **your** ownership in your own fears and ability to stay centered on God. Trusting in your faith, your family, your Sword Skills, your fellowship with other Christians, relying on your Pastor, your Sunday school teacher and the wisdom you have developed.
2. The other side is for you to **share** with someone who has fear, or burdens, or problems or is lost, confused or troubled. Your Sword is your support and Christ is your center for life. Sometimes just reading scriptures opens doors, provides comfort and invites Light in the darkest of times. Keeping it to yourself is selfish, worthless and you will die by yourself.

There are about 2.1 billion Christian's in the world according to WikiAnswers.com. Christ is the first part of Christianity, faith is the second and trust is in the belief. When your faith is tested, always lean back on your trust. Your faith may waiver but your trust in Christ will forever be your rock to stand on. Once you are in His hands, no one or nothing can remove you. It is our Fathers promise, so who can challenge His mighty hands? Isaiah 40:11-14

There are many stories in the Bible and they have many meanings. One of my favorite stories lets me know that not only did Jesus enjoy a good feast but He also had a very good sense of humor. In Luke chapter 24 beginning verse 13 there are two men walking to Emmaus, which is about seven miles outside of Jerusalem. They were talking about the days and events that had occurred. Jesus had been crucified and they knew of His promise to rise on the third day. Out of nowhere, Jesus appears on the road and begins walking with them and plays the "distant traveler" who was oblivious to the local current events. He initiates conversations with the two. The two were unable to recognize Jesus and they were dumbfounded that He had no idea of what had happened. Jesus walked with them and they talked Him into stopping in their home. Jesus kicked back at their table broke bread and blessed it. At that very blessed moment, the two instantly recognized Him and in that moment He vanished. The two ran to where the disciples had gathered to tell their story. No doubt Jesus got a good chuckle out of playing with these two men while gaining two valid witnesses of His resurrection. And no doubt they remembered the day that Jesus sat at their table and blessed their home. The message of the story for today's living is clear. Always stay in the faith, be ready each day and simply speak of what you know to be true. Tell what you have seen then witness to the story of Jesus, especially to strangers. Your discipleship counts on the delivery of your testimony to anyone who will listen.

Today's need for your testimony is not simply by you reading the word of God or talking about Jesus. It will be in the reflection of your character. Would Jesus be proud of what you do? Would He be proud of the way you speak? Would He be proud to call you His child? It begins with your looking in the mirror and knowing who lives within the reflection you see.

~ ~ ~ ~ ~ ~

Thank you Jesus

On May 25, 1979, a team of salesmen traveling from Chicago to a regional sales convention rushed to O'Hare International Airport. They arrived at the airport, walked up to the ticket counter and purchased their tickets for their flight. Their plane was scheduled to depart gate 37 which just happened to be at the other end of the terminal so they knew they would have to move quicker than a sprint.

The men hurried through the terminal and in their haste one of the men's suitcases caught the corner of an apple display stand sending apples everywhere. Without hesitation all continued their dash and made it to their plane on time. All but one! One man paused, took a deep breath, looked across the floor at the apples and had a conscious thought of grace and kindness. He looked at the young girl attending the snack stand and watched his team run through the terminal ahead of him.

The young clerk said, "oh no", and knelt to pick up the apples close to her. The salesman knelt on the floor and began retrieving the apples scattered across the floor. As travelers passed by they weaved around the two as they crawled across the floor picking up all they could find. He helps the clerk return the baskets on the display and straighten the stand as she quietly wipes her tears. But then he noticed that several of the apples had become bruised and slightly scared from their fall. He pulled out $40 and said, "I want to buy these apples and compensate you for what was clearly our mistake". He handed the bills to her and her saw her move the bills through a portable scanner. The scanner gave an audible announcement, "Forty dollars". He stopped dead in his tracks and could only stare for a moment. In his rush to pick up the apples he had not noticed her feeling around on the floor to located the scattered apples. As she receive the bills she said; "thank you sir" and felt for the brail keys on the register. He had no idea the young girl was blind.

As he collected his bags and walked away he heard her gentle voice say, "thank you Jesus". A tear filled his eye as he made his back to the travel counter to update his ticket for the next flight out. He handed his ticket to the airline attendant. As she looked at the ticket she paused and looked up at him then said these few words that will forever live in his heart. She said; "sir this ticket was on Flight 191". He nodded his head to agree and said, "Yes, I was delayed a bit and need to catch another flight." She continued saying, "well sir this flight, I mean your flight just crashed at the end of the runway. All flights are on hold until they say it is clear and okay." The salesman's felt his heart stop and for a moment he ha d to catch his breath. He had a flash of memory replay in his mind of his friends running ahead of him to catch that flight. As he slowly walked across the terminal gate to the glass windows he noticed a small blaze of fire and smoke billowing in the distance. That should have could have been him . . .

On this day American Airlines DC-10 Flight 191 crashed at the end of runway 32R. All 271 passengers lost their lives. There are 271 messages in this single incident of life. One such message is never allow an opportunity pass by to show someone an act of kindness. With blind eyes you have the same vision every day. Close your eyes and you will see no fault in anyone; you will see no color, no hate and no evil around you. It will only be reflected in the actions you create. These 271 people lost their lives in an instant. They had mere seconds of fear and in the blink of an eye they were gone. Before Flight 191 moved away from the gate, how many passengers were immediately ready for heavens gate? How many of these had an opportunity to say "thank you Jesus"? The correct answer would be, all of them! It may be sad but it is the realty of life. Our time here is limited and any moment might be your last.

When driving around the highways, interstates and roadways have you noticed the crosses, flowers, signs and/or wreaths placed on the sides of the road? They are in memory of one whose life ended in that very location? These are markers for the many souls whose life stopped in one single sudden impact. You may know someone who has a marker placed in their name. You may have placed a marker yourself at one of these locations for a loved one. Do you think that they planned their ending this way? Did they know their destination was going to be in that very location, on that day and in that way? I think not. What if tomorrow was your day? What would your destination be and can you say now, without hesitation and know you would immediately see paradise? Would your family and friends know without a doubt where your spirit went? Would Jesus choose you based on your decision? Would He be proud of your character, your work in His name and the lives you have touched on His behalf? If you saw Him today and He looked at you and said; "Lay down your world and follow Me." What would you do? Today's Christian Crusader is always ready to answer God's call.

When Jesus decided and selected His disciples He first stopped by the sea shore of Galilee and saw Peter and Andrew. In Matthew 4:19 He simply said, "Follow Me, and I will make you fishers of men." These two immediately dropped their nets and answered His call. Zero hesitation, they looked into His eyes and moved. "Fishers of Men" . . . What does this mean? When you go fishing with a net, you go to an area where there are fish, drop your nets and collect as many fish as possible. If you were fishing for people you would use the same concept. You would go to a place where people gather, tell them of Jesus and collect as many as you can. There will be those that do not want to be saved, or do not want to go now or are afraid of the net. Jesus said many times, "Those who have an ear, let them listen." Those that do not want to hear His word or listen to the documented evidence then move on to someone that does. I will not waste my time arguing with people who choose to be lost. The Net is similar to the web of scriptures collected in God's Holy Word. Today's Christian Crusader takes their Net, wields their Sword and uses the gospel of good news.

On October 12, 2009 a fierce fire broke out in a suburban home in Pittsburgh. The fire department was called at 2:40am to respond to the blaze. The fire engines roared up, the men and women of this team rushed to connect the hoses as flames broke through the roof. They put water to the fire for two hours before firefighters could enter the home due to extreme heat, flames and a collapsed roof.

The towns Fire Marshall, John Reubi sent his team into the house and they were shocked to find the owner of the home still sleeping in his bed. Not a hair harmed, not a place singed on his body and was rather taken by all the attention he received around his bed. Firefighters and neighbors as well as a team of reporters witnessed this incident. It made the print of the local paper and headline news. An unbeliever would say, "Awe he was just lucky". A born again believer in Christ would tell him he lived by the mercy of God and he now has a purpose to speak of grace. This is called a testimony.

There is another story that was witnessed and well documented very similar to this story. It is the story of three young men that Martin Luther King Jr. referenced in his letter while he was in the Birmingham Jail. Meshach, Shadrach and Abednigo refused to bow before King Nebuchadnezzar and had an experience with the city's fiery furnace. The law was that all the kingdom people were to worship the king during music and festive idol worship. When the king was informed that these three men were not abiding by the law, the king had them tied with ropes and tossed into the city furnace. The soldiers that threw them into the furnace were burnt to death because they had cranked the heat so severe it melted the entrance to the furnace. But all who looked upon the sight were witness to a fourth figure standing beside the three men in the furnace. King Neuchadnezzar stood in astonishment not knowing where the fourth figure came from much less all four figures where still in the blaze standing. Then the three men walked out of the furnace no longer bound and not a hair harmed. Martin Luther King Jr. referred to the three men as examples of a higher calling to obey God, not man. So could there have been another figure in the bedroom of the man who slept through the fiery blaze in his home? I am a born again believer in Jesus Christ and I say He was there.

The challenges we face today are foundationally the same as people have faced for centuries but the trends and faces of the challenges change almost daily. Satan is a created being and I believe he adapts before we do and he is always on top of his game. Our culture today is driven off of a fast paced, want it now, got to have it quick and it's got to be a perfect lifestyle. God's word serves us as a living voice of yesterday, today and tomorrow. This is why our Holy Bible serves as His living word because He is our Living God.

The teens of today's society face some of these lifestyles that will test their belief, faith and way of thinking. Think of the reality series called "American Idol" and how much this title means to the contestant, their family, their friends and America. They have placed their entire heart, mind, body and soul on the line for the title, "Idol". How's that grab ya? You say it is just a show like; XFactor, Americas Got Talent, So You Think You Can Dance, The Bachelor, The Bachelorette, Big Brothers, The Housewife's of wherever, and so on. How many millions of people would sell their soul to be in that light, with that fame, feeling that adrenalin rush and in that big money with record deals, magazine deals, talk show appearances and then there is the life of luxury that comes with the "Idol" title. Teens will buy into this first but many adults are glued to these reality dramas. When people try to live their life through a mad-for-TV reality show, they fall short of reality itself. When many live their life through the advice given in one of a dozen talk shows, they fall short of reality itself. When many fall short, they are crushed and will lean on the physical world for support and lose sense of their spiritual value. It is a hopeless walk into utter darkness.

Again, peer pressure and "going along to get along" seems to be the top of everyone's list. Teens do not want to be outside of the "in crowd" and it is cool to be popular or at least close to the popular crowd. This test of faith occurs when this crowd begins to step over the boundary line of faithful following of Christ and into a world of fleshly pleasures. It is most difficult for a teen to say no to this world because it is attractive to the eye and pleasing to the flesh. The issue is that Satan deals on the front side of this pleasure and never warns of the consequences of their actions. Several examples could be premarital sex, teasing-sexting, drug dependency, alcohol addiction, pregnancy, criminal records, DUI's and so on. Some have ended in death. There are many instances where kids drove away from a party where alcohol was served, crashed and ended in deaths. Satan never tells a soul that there is danger in what lies ahead. It just ends that way and the realty is no lost spirit is prepared for what is just beyond death. It is endless hopeless and irreversible.

This is not a threat, it is an ultimatum.

Perfection and the great need for acceptance is most important in our youth. Our teens want to be perfect in sports, perfect in academics, perfect in friendship and perfect in looks. It is this perfection that is shown to them on TV and in magazines. Some will be prone to cheat so they will be seen as perfect. Some will use steroids to improve their chances at sports and stardom. Some will become depressed because they are not accepted as perfect in looks or dress. If they can't afford that nice shirt or blouse then they steal it or sell themselves to buy it. Some may end in suicide because an email or a sexting image was sent to all their friends at school. These are the realities you will face and if you are not living by the Sword then you may end up as a lost statistic. Today's Christian Crusader lives by the Sword.

Loneliness! No teen wants to go it alone. They are closer to their friends than they are their parents. They listen more to their friends than their parents. They didn't receive it from their parents so they look to their best friends for advice. That's great! A child is giving another child advice? What about that big dance coming soon and no one has asked her to the dance? What about the teen that has asked several to go with him and they have shot him down? What about the teen that thought one boy was going to ask her but he asked her best friend? This is a society within a society that models their future in the big society. If you are in this age group you need to show them how to live by the example you set. A lifestyle that reflects your Christian faith removes the hypocrisy that is so famously labeled on born again believers in Christ. Walk the talk!

Sexual activity, pornography and dealing with homosexuality are big! Get real! Back seat petting is bigger now than it was in years past because back in the day not all teens could afford a car. Now all of them are driving. Among teens most boys want to experience sex, most girls don't want to be the only virgin in school, most teens become sexually active at thirteen and they are learning it from Internet porn as well as their teachers. Many schools now teach sex education and provide condoms for "safety". This is not safety; it is an excuse for them to practice. It is the younger generation that is experimenting. Sexting, u-tube, twitter, facebook and other instruments of communication are rapidly showing teens experimenting with real life sex games once only imagined by porn film directors and actors. Young girls are performing fellatio on boys but not just in the back seat of a car, they are performing in group sex acts and feel it is a part of "growing up." Dr. Phil and Oprah regularly speak on the subject because this lends to other issues that are not for the teen to endure but are very real for adults. These realities are sex diseases that are typical of unprotected sex, pregnancy that generally leads to abortions, drugs to enhance the "experience" and no doubt that alcohol is the key ingredient that gets the party going. The Internet is full of sex tips for teens, recommended sex games for teens and the power of teen peer pressure extends far beyond the advice of any adult. Dr Phil and Oprah's advice, although morally and spiritually correct, is not accepted by the teen world because just one or two teens confessing their sin to the world on TV doesn't give the majority of teens a majority teen view. If you want to make an impact on teens then the parents must be educated first how not to blame but how to teach, inform and recognize the symptoms of a child in trouble. If you continue to promote entertainment then the quality of the message will be diluted in the entertainment, not in the quality of the statement. If the message is not partnered with God then it will fail! We must move the statistics of poor decisions from the majority to the minority.

Schools are now teaching homosexuality in some states and this pressure to approve boy on boy and girl on girl as normal and immoral relationships are accelerating at an alarming rate. Watch a gay lesbian rally and look at the crowds. The crowd is not made up of a bunch of middle-aged fruit bars any longer. Gays and lesbians are now accepted in many Catholic Churches as clergy. This makes the statement that God's church accepts these relationships as holy and acceptable by the standards set by God. Gay/lesbian curriculums now taught in schools are directed toward a history lesson of who made an impact in our nation's history that was gay/

lesbian. These many, many people who believe and buy into this fallacy have either not read the Bible or they pick and choose what scriptures to omit or they make up what they need to fit their desired lifestyle into today's ever changing society. For all those who are gay and lesbian in their choice of sexual partner and sexual lifestyle, I am not your judge and no one in this world will or can convince you of your physical or spiritual choices. No one can compare this world's standard to man because God's word is very clear on His divine creation and direction for Man, then of Woman to be man's companion. If you ignore His word and create your own then you are no different than those over 2,000 years ago that screamed, "Crucify Him!" Now you may argue, shout, scoff and murmur but here are a few words spoken by God for God's people:

"For this reason a man shall leave his father and his mother, and be joined to his wife and they shall be one flesh. And the man and his wife, were both naked and were not ashamed."

Genesis 2:24-25

"Marriage is to be held in honor among all, and the marriage bed undefiled: for fornicators and adulterers God will judge."

Hebrew 13:4

"And they called to Lot and said to him; "Where are the men who came to you tonight? Bring them out to us that we may have relations with them." But Lot went out to them at the doorway, and shut the door behind him, and said, "Please, my brothers, do not act wickedly."

Genesis 19:5-7

"You shall not lie with a male as one lies with a female; it is an abomination."

Leviticus 18:22

"If there is a man who lies with a male as those who lay with a woman, both of them have committed a detestable act; they shall be put to death. Their blood-guiltiness is upon them."

Leviticus 20:13

"Or do you not know that the unrighteous will not inherit the kingdom of God? Do not be deceived; neither fornicators, nor idolaters, nor adulterers, nor effeminate, nor homosexuals, nor thieves, nor the covetous, nor drunkards, nor revilers, nor swindlers, will inherit the kingdom of God."

1 Corinthians 6:9-10

Mans word OR God's word. It is a decision of faith and there is no standard in between.

According to Adherents.com, they estimate the total number of gay, lesbian and bi-sexual population to be about 4.3 million just in the United States alone. In almost every language that you can imagine, homosexuality is defined as sexual attraction or behavior among members of the same sex. The Catholic and some independent religions are accepting homosexuals, gays and lesbians in the church and even in leadership positions within the church. This provides a whole new definition of "church" and who they might think is the head of this church. The church, founded by Jesus Christ, places Him at the head of the church by His blood and His body. But if you are not following the teachings of Jesus Christ, all of them, then someone or something else must head the church of homosexuality, gays and lesbians. If homosexuality, gay, lesbianism is equal in the eyes of God then we all serve an imperfect God who is a liar. Just how bold does one individual much less groups of people have to be to question God's authority over His own creation? These generations of homosexual, gay and lesbian people are not the first. This has been going on for centuries and Sodom & Gomorrah was an example of a people who questioned God's patience for immorality and disobedience. It seems that sometimes the world thinks that Jerry Springer show stretches beyond the boundaries of the trailer park and has drifted into all the areas of the globe. When Abraham and Sarah traveled, they saw things that would place San Francisco in the minor league of immorality.

If you are homosexual, gay or lesbian you are not Christian and you obviously hold no value in God's Holy Word. There is hope for homosexuals, gays, lesbians and even the homophobic as well. In the same boat are porn stars, porn producers, porn actors and porn participants. In the same boat are deniers of God as the sole galactic authority and not some UFO club that has placed all their faith in the return of the mother ship. In the front of that boat is all the leaders who blaze the path of corruptness, adulteress, deceitfulness and coveting that a trusting leader should abstain from. God hates sin but loves mankind even though we sin because we were born of sin. He waits to hear us call His name, ask for forgiveness and walk the path provided for eternal salvation. Or, do your own thing and let the justifications roll, but understand that these behaviors are not Biblical or a reflection of obedience to God's word. He will have His final say about it with you personally. Remember, only the Father will be your judge, my role is to simply tell. And as a Christian Crusader of today's world you must be willing to tell the truth because you extend your brotherly love to everyone. As a born again believer in Jesus Christ, you cannot accept, condone or give passage to immoral behavior. You must say NO.

Christianity begins at home and there are a bazillion times more broken and unsaved homes today as there used to be. Because both the mom and dad work we leave it up to the schools, TV and video games to educate inform and raise our children. The majority of our educators are stuck in a science book or chemistry lab and teaching children of philosophy not Christianity or even morality. To them, there was no creation but evolution and seismic activity that caused the earth's formation and not our Creator and His work according to Genesis. Teachers and professors create doubt in Bible theology and view the books in the Bible as unreliable. They base their theories on distrust in the eyewitness's accounts, the word of our Creator and present a counter offer of personal textbook options. These are man-made textbooks that they offer up as scientific evidence and man-made theory. Scientist places their belief in a test tube, a rock and man-made charts and graphs of man-made theories. The formation is probably correct, however, the path of formation and timelines are wrong. Scientists continue to change their original calculations and evolve their opinions. The Bible contains God's Holy Word and it has not wavered or moved an inch. This book doesn't replace the Bible, it supports it.

The last teen fear that I believe is apparent is when they become an unexpected parent. Some teens truly believe that parenthood will come natural to them no matter their age or development. Those parents reading this know that parenthood comes with major responsibility but for their growing years a teen has not experienced any sort of real responsibility and this is truer today than ever before. Many teens make this life decision while still living at home with mommy and daddy. As an adult parent today both mom and dad work and they have but a small window of time between diner and bedtime to impact their child's little lives. Think of this as about 2 hours every day because many families seldom speak to each other. We now text each other rather than dial the phone because it is easier. For a teen it is a whirlwind adventure that can turn dark very quickly. Here are some examples of demonic moments that got to dark to shed.

- ☹ On October 9, 2009 a guilty verdict was returned for Nancy Ortiz, a young mother of three children when one child was found dead of heat exhaustion in a pickup truck, one found wandering around the streets in a diaper and the other hanging on to life. The verdict was second-degree murder and 22 years prison.

- ☹ On February 3, 2009 a jury handed a verdict of murder to the judge with less than two hours of deliberation. Two-year-old Riley was found in October 2007. She was beaten with leather belts, flung across a tiled floor like a rag doll; her head was dunked in cold bath water, stuffed in a plastic box and dumped in the Galveston Bay. The mother at the time was eighteen and the significant other was twenty-five. She said she was controlled by him and couldn't stop the abuse.

- ☹ Another extreme case comes from a recent incident where a young mom goes out for an evening of fun that turns into a weekend of lust with her newfound love of her life. She and her new boyfriend enjoyed Friday evening dinner and return to his place to continue their enjoyment of each other. Petting leads to the bedroom and they stayed there until Sunday afternoon. Sounds like a weekend of sex, alcohol and intimacy? Probably, but the catch is that she had three children locked in her home with no access to food, drink or supervision from Friday morning until she returned Sunday evening. The children included twin 18-month-old girls and a 2-year-old son. The children had no electricity, no running water and could not reach the food in the cabinets. Upon her return from a good time with her "friend", the mom found one of her baby girls dead. Starved and dehydrated. The mom placed her baby girl in a garbage can outside the home.

☹ A young girl at seventeen became pregnant in 2007 and does her best to hide the pregnancy until the child's birth. The infant is born alive but Truitt decides to place her in a garbage shoot where her tiny baby dropped seven stories into a metal bin. The child died instantly from severe blunt force trauma.

☹ In 2006 a sixteen-year-old teen gave birth to a child in a Las Vegas, Nevada strip hotel room. She wrapped the infant in hotel towels and left her to die in the hotels trash bin. In August of 2009 she went through the same ordeal in Henderson, Nevada where she delivered the baby herself then suffocated it. She called the hospital to report a stillborn baby but investigators revealed a much different story later that day.

☹ In 1996 a New Jersey teenager gave birth at a Delaware hotel to a newborn son. She stuffed him in a plastic bag then placed him in the dumpster outside the hotel which was close to the University of Delaware.

☹ In 2011 the trial of Casey Marie Anthony ended in a not guilty verdict to the death of her daughter. In 2008 Cindy, Casey's mother, reported Casey's child missing after she had been missing for 31 days. Casey had not reported her daughter missing for 31 days and in those 31 days she partied, got a tattoo, entered a babe contest and found zero remorse for her daughter's absence. Later, her daughter, Caylee Marie Anthony's little skeletal remains were found. She had been bound and gagged with gray duct tape and shoved in a black plastic garbage bag then tossed like waste into a swamp just minutes from her grand-parents home. While the cause of death is questionable, her partying while her child decomposed in a garbage bag is inexcusable.

"People were bringing little children to Jesus to have Him touch them, but the disciples rebuked them. When Jesus saw this, He was indignant.

He said, "Let the little children come to Me, and do not hinder them, for the kingdom of God belongs to such as these."

Mark 10:13

There are many more stories of children who have lost their youth. These are a few of the extreme cases that a young teenager, young mother goes through but this is not the root cause of the issue. These are simply the results. Satan does not deal in the results but only the pleasures of the flesh. The more you hear this the more you will understand his temptation. The root cause comes from a child either afraid to speak to her parents or parents that do not give a rip about their child. As a parent you are not always going to see danger in your child's eyes. "In God we Trust" is more than a cliché, it is our DNA. If we do not know our Sword and how to use our Shield as children, then we are not prepared to face the trials of a youth then become an adult. If we do not know our Sword and how to use our Shield as a parent then we cannot properly prepare our children for what they will encounter. This is the reality of life and Today's Christian Crusader should prepare themselves for worst!

I heard a popular actor/comedian once say, "If your momma raised you right, you will never worry or wonder what your answer should be to this world's evil. There is some nasty stuff happening around here. I miss my momma every day and thank God for her teaching me right from wrong." This is certainly not word for word but the tears of Mr. Steve Harvey will always ring close to my heart. My momma and his momma would have had a lot in common to talk about . . .

Congregational reverence . . . We have reviewed individual faith, individual worship, family values and how we should disciple. How we act, learn and perform in God's house is honor and reverence to Him. Our respect for His works, for His love, for His grace upon us and His ability to love us even when we do not love ourselves is important to understand. But I truly don't understand why some people go to church. I am speaking of the few that can't sit still for an hour and the few that pop up three to four times during a service to go do whatever they do. They can't sit still in church for an hour but can go watch a movie at the theater for two hours and fifteen minutes, never utter a sound and never have to get up. They may be afraid they will miss something. The forgetful few that have their cell-phone ring in worship service then get mad at whoever called them. It couldn't be your fault for not turning your phone off for an hour. The few that just cannot take their children to the nursery and would rather have them sit and rustle paper, thump their little toe on the wood pew, ask for candy, walk around between the pew and may let out a scream when you tell them "NO". To those few with children; it is called a NURSERY . . . We do not give our fine folks enough credit for attending our children in the church nursery and I know deep in my heart that God has a special gift in heaven for these wonderful people and I am sure it will not include a tissue, wet wipe or a diaper. People attend church to honor our Father in Heaven who came as flesh so we might learn His will upon us and be obedient to His word. Irreverence and inability to listen and learn may very well be the cause of some not receiving His word. Next Sunday act as if Jesus was sitting in a chair behind the Pastor and if you do not see Him then He may be sitting behind you. If you cannot hear Him, then learn to remove the sounds that do not sound like Him. I assure you, He sees you and hears you . . .

We must all be reminded, every day that we must seek the face of God and that Satan will seek us every minute of the day. He looks for a weak moment like a germ does in a weakened immune system. He looks for that weak moment when you are down, when you have lost a loved one, when you have lost your job, when you have lost a best friend, when temptation is pulling you to do what you know is not right, when your loan wasn't approved, when everyone is going to that party and you know drugs and alcohol will be there, when that injury prevents you from an athletic scholarship, when the boy or girl of your dreams says no, when that message comes that you'll be confined to a chair, when a moment of passion turns into a panic of pregnancy, when they can't save the leg and it must be removed, OR when you are married and that sweet little innocent tempting moment passes your way. Or, in a moment of loneliness when you stared into thin air. In that very moment when you think no one cares and when you least expect it, he will be there! Then, **Draw your Sword and wield your Shield** then know that God is always here. He gives the gift of eternal life. Come and drink from His cup and never thirst again. Know this and know this today that every day that you delay is one more day away from the gift of love like you have never known. Jesus Christ hung on a cross for hours and suffered so that you would not suffer the consequence of your sins. He suffered then so you would not suffer now . . .

If you are still unsaved today then you are simply procrastinating and avoiding what you know to be true today. If you are saved and not engaged today then you are simply procrastinating and prolonging what you know to be true today. If you are being called from discipleship into the ministry then stop today and meet with your pastor. He will help guide you in God's plans for you beyond today. Your pastor will not only guide you in the correct direction but support your development. If you are hesitant in any direction then understand this commission very clearly:

"But the eleven disciples proceeded to Galilee, to the mountain which Jesus has designated. When they saw Him, they worshiped Him; but some were doubtful. And Jesus came up to them and spoke to them, saying, "All authority has been given to Me in heaven and on earth. Go therefore and make disciples of all nations, baptizing them in the name of the Father, and the Son and Holy Spirit. Teaching them to observe all that I have commanded you; and lo, I am with you always, even to the end of the age."
Matthew 28:16-20

ALL authority . . .

   On **H**eaven and **E**arth . . . **Go** make disciples . . .

     Baptize them . . .

       In the name of the **F**ather, **S**on & **H**oly **S**pirit

       Teach them **ALL** I have commanded

       And Lo, I am with you **always**

        <u>Even to the end of the age . . .</u>

Let His words speak to you and place His plan in motion . . .

Life & Death

In life a saved man never stops working for God.
In life a saved man will never fear death.
In life a saved man walks in trust and faith.
In life a saved man leaves godly footprints for others.
At death a saved man loses his shell or body.
At death a saved man will be raised.
At death a saved man is immediately with Christ.
At death a saved man is rewarded for his deeds.
At death a saved man will walk with God through eternity.

"Who is the liar but the one who denies that Jesus is the Christ? This is the antichrist, the one who denies the Father and the Son. Whoever denies the Son does not have the Father; the one who confesses the Son has the Father also."

1st John 2:22-23

In life an unsaved man walks in denial of God, His authority, and does not accept His gift of eternal life. At death an unsaved man immediately enters darkness. This darkness is not prejudice to race, age, creed, color, religion, sex, or degree of sinfulness. It receives no argument of guilt or innocence. It hears no plea of a life's achievements. It sees no value in worldly awards. It has no cheers for championship seasons. It does not see a star movie performance. It does not acknowledge Olympic gold medals. It offers only eternal spiritual misery.

The older you become the outer shell you wear gradually becomes worn, weary and frail. Your life is spent creating habits created by your inner spirit. These habits either include a strong guardian angel or you do not believe so you have no angels to watch over you. When your body and your mind become worn down to a thread, it is your spiritual strength that calls the angels to tend to your spirit. Non-believers wither away and become consumed by their own worth with no way up. It is the inner man that will navigate your vessel correctly and Christ is not only your only compass, His Holy Spirit is the wind within your sails.

Do you remember when you were a child and you heard the sweet sound of the ice-cream man coming down your street? You may even be able to remember the time frame that he ran through your neighborhood and could sense the sound of the music coming out of that sick single speaker on his truck. I remember it vividly and I remember screaming, ICE CREAM, ICE-CREAM MAN!!! And I would run to find my mom to get some change for a grape pop-cycle, or a nutty buddy bar or a solid fudge-cycle on a stick . . . I could never make up my mind. What a great time of my youth and it was the music that created the excitement. This excitement was addictive and it was an expectation that I grew to want daily. What brings your excitement to a point of daily need or craving? What sound makes your world stop still in its tracts? What sound gives your heart, soul and mind a rush of excitement? For a born again believer in Christ, one day it will be the trumpet that blows . . .

Well on a cloudy day, one day, every saved spirit will hear the sweetest sound of trumpets playing in the clouds. Sad as it may be, not everyone will hear this sound or feel this experience. The saved will rise upon his call: first the dead in Christ will rise (1 Thessalonians 4:16), then those who are alive and remain will be caught up together with them in the clouds (1 Thessalonians 4:17). Before this day, for every birth there is an end in death and it is a natural process when every spirit loses his or her physical body. As the saved ascend, Jesus will open the clouds and we will meet Him in the heavens to receive our new body and see the New Jerusalem. And this day <u>will</u> come to pass. It may not be today, it may not be tomorrow but it is an inevitable truth where in a mere moment we will be called home. That call could very well come tonight soon after you close your eyes to sleep. It could happen on your way home, from school, from a sporting event or from the store. The common statement from a victims family member is; 'we never thought it would happen to our family." Well, the family of God expects it and waits in anticipation.

~ ~ ~ ~ ~ ~ ~

The national vital statistics compiles data of deaths and causes of deaths. Here is the data collected for 2009:

  #1 killer—accidental automobile crash/death
  #2 killer—falling
  #3 killer—poisoning
  #4 killer—drowning
  #5 killer—fire or smoke inhalation

<u>**#1 GUARANTEE**</u>—you are closer to death with every breath. And some are dieing quicker than others. Some live like they are dieing and some live like they are dead. Some live with no cares of this world and some live with no cares of the next world. No matter how you live, ultimately everyone exits life the same spiritual way. The only thing that may differ is the method of your death and then if you see His Light when you pass, Or if all you know is complete darkness . . .

I ended my book "2012 Global Warning" with a piece of the apocalypse and pieces of signs when the end is near or here. My discipleship is based off a readiness always and your decision <u>today</u> rather than visions of tomorrow. There are many who are fascinated about rapture and return, let's look at our world. When people should be living and focusing on life, many are consumed with destroying the foundation of Christianity. Remember, Jesus only sees two distinct diverse groups: the saved and the unsaved or those who follow Him and those who do not. When the rapture occurs, millions will vanish and the unsaved will have no warning or awareness of the instant until it is over. Many across the globe will simply be missing. There will be two in the field and one will be taken. There will be two in the mill and one will be taken. There will be two on the assembly line and one will be taken. There will be two on registers and one will be taken. There will be one at the fast food window and one taking the order when one will be taken. There will be some on the golf course and a few may not make the 18th green. The many who remain will have heard His word in their past but ignored His call. Many today make light of the rapture and say it isn't possible. There were many who stood on the sidelines and said Lazarus would not walk out of his grave after four days of death. There were thousands that did not buy into Jesus rising from a sealed tomb. There were hundreds that witnessed both. If you have not committed your life to Christ and you die, you will not rise from your grave.

Upon His return, Jesus will call to the seven churches and call for a report of their condition and their faithful bounty. What will Jesus find in these churches? I have walked the land of the seven churches and at the time was unaware of the magnitude that they had in the 1st Century and how relative that the conditions of these locations are on the rest of the world today. As you walk through the location of the seven churches, think of the bigger picture and the condition of the churches spiritually, not physically. The major population of the world fits into the design of these churches because they have been taught the path of Christ, have the same Bible access and have made a conscious decision not to follow His word exactly as He has written it. Many choose to make the Bible fit their lives rather than living a life according to God's word. This is not being judgmental. God knows your heart, but others see your character. You may fool your spouse, your family and/or your friends but I assure you, you will not put one over on God because He knows beyond what you do or what you say. He knows your thoughts and what moves in your heart. Is your faith genuine? You know the truth and so does He. If you love them, you will take this truth to your family and friends.

~ ~ ~ ~ ~ ~ ~

Before continuing any further, you should really stop and read the book of Revelation in its entirety. I will not review all the words recorded by Jesus Christ through John because I cannot write it better than He already has. What I will do is identify the current conditions of the state of our world as it relates to the seven original churches. The key role in the world's church will be in the governing by the Catholic Church. The Catholic Church will bring other church denominations under its wing to form an alliance in thought, in vision and in strategy when the antichrist is revealed. Remember, the path is narrow and if you have not lived a covenant with God, you will not meet the standards that God spoke very clearly of. Many church leaders today would fall outside of this narrow path and they will scramble to solidify their belief to meet His commandments. There are several key reasons that will bring the Vatican, Catholic leadership, Islam,

Protestant and world church leaders to this understanding. I believe the world will form an alliance of one god for all religions. All paths lead to the same god. Draw your Sword Crusader; this will be the battle of all battles!

➢   Revelation opened to the Seven Churches as Jesus revealed in Revelation 2-3:

1. **Ephesus** was a trail from Athens to Turkey that charted the western part of Asia Minor church founded by Paul and supported by John. The main cities and population that support this area today are located in Izmir, West Turkey. This area has moved from Christian to Moslem and people have lost sight of Christ. Would Jesus be pleased with the current condition of His church?

2. **Smyrna** is the ancient city now named Izmir, runs along the Aegean Coast of Anatolia and to Malatya where I spent a year and is located about three hundred miles northeast of Antioch. This is where followers of Christ were first called Christian and today worships Allah rather than Christ. Would Jesus be pleased with the current condition of His church?

3. **Pergamos** is recognized as the largest of all Christian churches and is, of course, Roman Catholic. The Catholic church is the "power and authority" of all churches and has a clear definition of at least a sixth of the worlds population with more than twenty Eastern Catholic churches divided into about 2,782 jurisdictions around the world and all look to the Pope for divine guidance. If the Vatican says it, then they move with it, and then the Vatican becomes the "soul" authority of the Catholic Church. The Catholic Church has stepped away from the teachings of Jesus and has hidden child abuse as well as immorality within its leadership. Would Jesus be please with the current condition of His church? The Vatican also happens to be built upon Roman soil.

4. **Thyatira** was located about forty-two miles from the Aegean Sea in the valley of the Lycus River. Three main roads lead from Thyatira that led thirty-seven miles one way to Pergamum, the road southeast was forty-seven miles to Smyrna and Sardis was thirty-seven miles to the southeast. Today's version of Thyatira is the Turkish town of Ashisar with a population little over 80,000

people. This location once thrived in manufacturing and trade now is poor and little sign of any importance to anyone. Would Jesus be pleased with the current condition of His church?

5. **Sardis** was the ancient capital of the kingdom of Lydia, which was about forty-six miles east of Smyrna and twenty-eight miles west of Philadelphia. The wealth of this little city was legendary and was said that they took wet sheepskins and dipped them in the Pactolus to collect gold partials. Earthquakes and severe weather have destroyed much of this area but large dirt mounds may still be seen where the wealthy and royalty were buried, much like the Egyptian pyramid tombs. Sardis still lies in ruins after being destroyed by Arabs and Ottoman Turks. Would Jesus be pleased with the current condition of His church?

6. **Philadelphia** stands at the base of Mount Tmotus or Bozdag of today's language. It was supported by the Gediz River about seventy-three miles east of Smyrna and was named by King Attalus II. The name means "brother love" and Pennsylvania named its city Philadelphia, the city of brotherly love. This city is now called, Alasehir a Christian presence has been maintained from the days of Christ through medieval times and still today. The Philadelphia Church of St. John is holding firm and is most likely to hear these words: "Because you have kept the word of My perseverance, I also will keep you from the hour of testing, that hour which is about to come, to test those who dwell upon the earth." Revelation 3:10

7. **Laodicea** was named after the wife of Antiochus II Theos, ruler of Syria and this little city was the main financial junction of Roman banking. The location was about forty-five miles southeast of Philadelphia and a hundred miles from Ephesus. Paul's witness to these people in Colossians is a warning for their ill behavior and resistance to disciple. They certainly were built to hear God's word as they sported two theaters: one holding about 8,000 people and the other around 15,000. As a matter of fact, many of the stones bear the owners name so this may have been the very beginning of season ticket holders . . . The people of this land run hot and cold in their beliefs and Jesus will call to them in this manner. Today they have an opportunity to change but continue to struggle with

any consistency. When He returns, will Jesus be pleased in the condition of His church.

If Jesus returned today would He be pleased with the condition of His church? If Jesus returned today would He be pleased with the efforts you have made in carrying His name to all who will listen? Are you a partner of His church and are you hearing His word regularly? Are you seeking and studying His word regularly? Are you speaking His word regularly? This is your life, you have one shot at it and He will ask these very questions. I would expect that He will look for a firm response of YES to each of His questions because if you believe then the second part of belief is in your actions.

Remember, frozen fruit does not multiply . . .

1) Where will God's people be during the seven-year tribulation and during the wrath of God upon those who ignored His word? All who have faithfully followed Christ will be with Him in the rapture and several key scriptures validate the Christian faithful. Sometimes it is what He says and sometimes it is in the exclusion of His people from wrath, pain, suffering and condemnation.
   - ✰ 1 Corinthians 15: 20-22
   - ✰ 1 Thessalonians 4:13-18
   - ✰ 1 Thessalonians 5:1-11

2) When people should be living and focusing on life, many are consumed with death, how they will die, when they will die and the apocalypse. John wrote the Revelation of Jesus Christ when he was on the Island of Patmos as illustrated in Revelation 1:1, which God gave him to reveal the things that will soon take place. The Book of Redemption brings closure of life and the Lambs Book of Life of the ages. Christ will deliver all seven ages that are sealed into Christ by the Holy Spirit and when the seventh seal is broken, prophesy of God will be finished and the fullness of His word will reveal the truth. The scroll of the seven seals comes from The Throne of God as He returns again to reveal earth's wrath for its sin. The return of Jesus Christ is in His prophecies as well as Daniels and Paul's. Revelation 5:5 speaks to the world

that Jesus Christ is the only one worthy of opening the seals and He returns as King. And then the world will feel seven years of trials, terror and tribulation. (Luke 21:36 and Revelation 3:10) I will not know this time for I will be with my Father in heaven so if you are still in question of your salvation let me explain the seven years that you will endure with the seven seals of wrath. Tighten your bootstraps!

The first four are known as the four horseman of the apocalypse:

1. The First Seal is **religious deception** and persecution
2. The Second Seal is **war**
3. The Third Seal is **famine**
4. The Fourth Seal is **pestilence**
5. The Fifth Seal is tribulation and martyrdom
6. The Sixth Seal is signs in the heavens
7. The **Seventh** Seal will cause silence for about 30 minutes then **seven** angels will stand before God with **seven** trumpets.

1. The First Trumpet will be hail and blood and a third of the earth will burn. This will begin the rain of terror across the globe.
2. The Second Trumpet will bring something like a mountain thrown into the sea and a third of the sea will turn to blood, a third of the living creatures of the sea will die and a third of the ships will be destroyed. This rain of terror will be thrown from the galaxy.
3. The Third Trumpet sets a blazing star falling from the sky and it will fall on a third of the rivers and the water will turn bitter and many people will die from the bitter water. The name of this star is "Wormwood." Did you see the movie "Armageddon" with the meteor? That was a movie, this is reality!
4. The Fourth Trumpet will be sounded and a third of the sun will be struck, a third of the moon and a third of the stars so that a third of them will turn dark. A third of the day will be night and also a third of the night. Darkness will consume day as well as night and what happens to people when the lights go out? There will be panic and pestilence mixed with violence.
5. The Fifth Trumpet set a star falling from the sky into the abyss; smoke filled the sky from the impact and out of the smoke came

locusts with powers of scorpions on the earth. Their command was not to harm the grass or the trees but to the people who did not bear the mark of God on their forehead. Their command was not to kill but to torture for five months and in those days men will seek death and will not find it. This torment will be set upon the antichrist and his faithful followers. These times will feel the burn of nuclear holocaust and extreme droughts. Water will be more valuable than oil ever thought about being.

6. The Sixth Trumpet releases the four angels who have been bound at the river Euphrates and released on God's command to kill a third of mankind and still many will not stop their worship of idols, demons and their physical sin. >And then God shows mercy again, Revelation 7 when He will call upon those who have accepted His gift of eternal salvation during the first six seals of wrath. The wrath will be halted for those to rise so they may praise His Holy name and call Him Lord of Lords, King of Kings and our God forever. They will adorn white robes and kneel to the one they once ignored. This will be only a brief intermission of sort until then wrath is again unleashed on those who still refuse to believe. These are truly the idiots of the world that are consumed in demonic pleasures where they just cannot let go of this world. But this will also include those who are in survival mode and clinging to man's promises rather than God's.

7. The Seventh Trumpet announces the reign of the Lord Jesus Christ, King who will reign forever and ever. The twenty-four elders, who sit on their thrones before God, fall upon their faces and worship God.

And then a loud voice from the temple says to the **seven** angels; "Go and pour out on the earth the **seven** bowls of the wrath of God." This is the vision through John's eyes.

1. The first angel pours out his bowl on the land and ugly, painful sores broke out on the people who had the mark of the beast. These are Satan's followers or better explained as those who have still ignored God's word and His gift of life. Moses commanded release of the first disease agents and this will be the final. All they

must do is **A**ccept, **B**elieve and **C**ommit to follow Him. It is not popular but it is the only way.

2. <u>The second angel</u> poured out his bowl on the sea and it turned to blood and every living thing in the sea died. This is plain and clear. When God says enough is enough then you can count on His word as the final authority on the subject. Red-tide is a mass amount of blooming microorganism algae that release toxins that impact water flow that release toxins that become airborne and affect the respiratory system of every living-breathing creature. We have already seen toxin warnings of times to come.

3. <u>The third angel</u> poured out his bowl on the rivers and springs of water and they became blood. This could be a combination of blood from animals and humans killed along with the toxins from red-tide in our water systems. Without fresh drinking water all living creatures do what? _____

4. <u>The fourth angel</u> poured out his bowl on the sun and was given power to scorch people with fire. The elimination or dissolving of our magnetic field and ozone layer simply magnifies the sun. This is not nuclear or atomic but is heavenly upon all the earth. Buildings to trees will have been leveled thus far so there will be little shade or cover to hide from the unbridled heat.

5. <u>The fifth angel</u> poured out his bowl on the throne of the beast and his kingdom plunged into darkness. The beast is the anti-christ, the palace he has built and the land he calls his. If you are close to him then look forward to a good plunging as well.

6. <u>The sixth angel</u> poured out his bowl on the great river Euphrates and the water dried up. The Euphrates runs from the Persian Gulf up through Turkey into Asian Minor of old. This was the river that I provided images of earlier. The river runs along Iraq, Syria and was the life water supply for Babylon. This is the area that is considered to be a focal point for those nations set against Israel. Will they be able to drink their oil to survive?

7. <u>The seventh angel</u> poured out his bowl into the air and out of the temple came a loud voice saying it is done. Lightening, thunder, rumblings, peals of thunder and a severe earthquake like no other with huge hailstones of about a hundred pounds fell upon men. If you want a comparison then look at the early earthquake in southern California in the 90's to a more recent 8.8 earthquake

in Chili, South America that rippled shockwaves to California, Hawaii then all the way to Alaska in February 2010. The 2010 Haiti earthquake then the ground shaker in China then Japan. The Weather Channel has its very own "wave expert", Dr. Lyons that was the "hurricane expert" that was the "storm expert" and now includes earth movement on his resume. I am not sure if he will develop into the channels "dry earth" or "burnt soil" expert but I don't plan to be here to watch him forecast Hell on earth.

These seven bowls remove mankind's lifeline: **water**. Egypt experienced this from God through the hands of Moses and Aaron. Here is just a moment of clarification: Moses was a prophet, not a god and had zero authority to move water much less part the seas. Moses did what he did only because God is who He is. Pharaoh's heart hardened because he truly believed that his power on earth was stronger than anything and that his gods could match play by play with The Almighty God of heaven. The Scientologist of today feel the same way and they rely on "mother nature" to be miraculous. Blood, contaminated water supplies, contaminated food supplies and a human disease is not God's wishes but is man's choice to endure. It is truly about choices and taking a side on heavenly authority OR man's foolish way of allowing history to repeat itself. Chapter 1 in "2012 Global Warning" goes into greater detail about choices. Every day that mankind takes a breath and wakes in the morning and is able to stand upright has an opportunity to choose an eternal life. It is a choice!

Draw your Sword: Matthew 24:1-51 Jesus in His glory will return and all those who have an ear listen.

Revelation 11 speaks of a future moment in time that God will send two witnesses who will prophesy for twelve hundred and sixty days. The number of 1,260 days is pretty specific and a little over 2 ½ years that they will not be allowed to die, even though the antichrist will attempt to kill them just to shut them up. Ultimately the two witnesses will lay dead in the square for three days, for all to see and no one will be allowed to touch them. Then a loud voice will call them to heaven and they will ascend. Many will witness their ascension into the heavens and the anti-Christ will explain the incident as probable trick cinema photography, or such . . . In the same time frame a great earthquake will occur and <u>seven</u> thousand will lose their lives. Then, for the galactically challenged that are here and still have a desire to suffer rather than live eternally with God, will continue to suffer starvation, dehydration, war, the daily fight for food and global warming like no one could imagine. Al Gore and Michael Moore are correct in their predictions but they are just a little early in their statements. Their timing is a little off and their motives were fed by greed not in Christian prophetic warnings.

Then we'll skip over to Revelation Chapter 19 through 22 where the Christians, who have been persecuted for centuries, become valiant and the New Heaven or New Jerusalem is revealed. In the end, we win!

As you have read through these pages with me, has your heart and soul strengthened for your walk with Christ? As a born again believing Christian Crusader in today's world our body is home to the security and safety of our faith. The only one that can see our soul is Christ. What fills your soul is what fuels your character. Others see what you do, what you say, how you act and how you respond to different stresses of today's temptations. If you tell others you are Christian and your soul is not filled with Christ then your character will reveal it. If you tell others you are Christian and your heart is not full of Christ then the only one that you are truly deceiving is yourself. If there is one worldly thing that one can place a higher value on than God, then your cup is in trouble. Your cup is your sins. When you worship Him it is not a part time, occasional, when you have time sort of commitment. When you tell Him you love Him it is not a passing thought of when it is convenient for you. When you ask Him to forgive you but you still cling on to a past anger or trouble that you have not found it in your heart to forgive someone of. When you tell Him that you surrender all it is not just the part that you can afford to give Him at that moment. No, it is a faithful partnership, a faithful walk in His Light, a daily worship with prayer, a love that is unconditional and a surrender of all your heart, all your body, all your spirit, all your mind, all your faith and all your love. This is the faith that Jesus spoke of when He said you could move a mountain. When you can find peace in Christ to forgive all those in your past who have crossed you and find brotherly love for all those around you then you are ready to humble yourself before Him. Who are those who ask when the earth will end and will Christ return again? Who are those who ask about the Revelation of Jesus and the revealing of the end of times? Who are those who are ready to stand before our Almighty Living God and hear their judgment? Are you ready today? Is your family ready? Are your friends ready? Like a thief in the night could be your destiny tonight. Like a thief in the night is certain for someone tonight. As a Christian Crusader, follower of Jesus Christ it is your destiny to listen to others and tell the story of how Christ loves them as He does you. When Christ comes in, then let your new life begin. A Christian Crusader is a disciple of Jesus Christ, bondservant, in a covenant with God, filled with His Holy Spirit and speaks His name each and every day.

Millions of people are consumed with WHEN. A question of WHEN can be seen in two different lights. One Light is when you die. The other Light is if Jesus decides to part the skies before you die. Either Light could be shined today and the unsaved gamble on one happening before the other. The sin is that millions do not think of it at all. His return will be some time, some day, therefore giving the unsaved some "grace" before the final trumpets begin to sound is love like no other. Death can find you at any time. Billions have died an untimely death and the graveyards are filled with names of lost souls. Those who thought they had another day to deal with God found that the final date on their grave marker was their destiny to stand before Him.

I was once one of those who lived like I had the world in my hands and took advantage of people, lied, made many mistakes and did not honor God with the way I was living my life. What a waste of good time that I was given. I am so incredibly thankful for a Heavenly Father who loves me enough to forgive my sins then to forget them. I now have a clear understanding of my role and I want so for you to know it as well. In God's word His message is so very clear and has not wavered for over 2,000 years. In the very moment that you call out to Christ to enter your life and you truly surrender your life to Him, the stars seem a little brighter, the skies a little clearer, the days a little calmer, emotions of the heart a little warmer, recognition of evil much clearer, the presence of God felt closer and the hope of eternal peace is sought after with greater importance. He is my King, Lord of Lords and Prince of eternal Peace. I am His and all that I have is His. I am humbled in Jesus name and for the unconditional love He so freely gives. My protector, my Redeemer, I give my all to serve

Him. In my testimony I will offer you the only sign that you will ever need to recognize as the sign of a love like you have never known before. In my testimony I will offer you all the signs of Christ who's a merciful God that forgives all sin and goes to prepare an eternal life for us that is beyond the imagination of peace paid for life. In my testimony I will offer you my humble service as a bondservant in a faithful covenant with God the only sign where eternal life begins. In my testimony I will offer you all I have because it was laid at the cross where my Savior shed every drop of blood that He had even though I am not worthy of the pain He suffered. In my testimony all I have to offer you is the only sign you will ever need again.

He will return like a thief in the night and here's your sign. On that glorious day, everyone will know that His name is Jesus, His city is in the New Jerusalem, His promise will be revealed and every eye shall see Him on His rightful Throne. All will bow before His presence and all will call His name for mercy. And we can talk about all the multiples of seven, Armageddon, the apocalypse, the thousand year millennium, the judgment and earths purification but today you should just call His name, find a peaceful place to pray, ask Christ to fill your life with His Holy Spirit and thank Him with the full knowing of His unconditional love.

Jesus ascension was the Father calling His Spirit through the clouds as a sign of His presence . . . Acts 1:1-9 What a wonderful day it will be to experience His return . . .

285

Deadly Deceptions

"The wicked earns deceptive wages, but he who sows righteousness gets a true reward. He who is steadfast in righteousness will attain to life, and he who pursues evil will bring about his own death."

Proverbs 11:18-19

As Today's Christian Crusader you will be faced with daily deception, daily false prophecy and daily temptation like you have never seen before. In a world where everyone is incredibly opinionated and people have more stuff to play with than ever before, it is very difficult to avoid the subtle temptations that can turn deadly. If you think of the Ozzie and Harriet show from years gone by, they had the model marriage, the model respect for one another, the model home, the model children, the model family communication, the model neighbors, and it was the ideal models model . . . It was ideal everywhere except in the homes where Christ did not live. In these homes it was not reality, therefore, Hollywood had to move the viewer more toward what the home of reality looked like, so they could actually relate. Since then, in most cases, Hollywood has painted the world darker and has led many into darker worlds. "All in the Family" with Carroll O'Conner, Rob Reiner and Sally Struthers painted reality gray but not quite dark enough. Because to Hollywood, darker is their common ground and common ground is physical entertainment. Hollywood gave them a look at what a family would look like with no God at all: The Osborn's!

Look at the deadly delirious reality series of The Osborn's. Here you had a drugged out rocker that barely has one thread keeping his brain from falling through his neck. The wife's job was holding on to her husband's last thread as she continues to thrive on his coat tails. This zombie has survived from show to show, despite the drug and alcohol issues that stemmed from a life of obvious satanic influence. As the dark side typically does, this one had children. They extended their habits through their children and it has all but destroyed them. The deceptions of Hollywood move through the movie industry and the music industry. People, especially the younger more influenced, are moved by the behavior of those who walk in "so called" stardom. The foundational motivation for MTV used to be music and now has entered into dorm cams, sex, reality *disfunctionality* and layers upon layers of stupid people doing stupid things. Then barely unedited TV has found a way to show a series of sports magazine swimsuit photo shoots of girls wearing barely threads, girls in their underwear in pro-cheerleading tryouts, runway models illustrating just how malnourished they can get and these begin to push the envelope of public nudity on TV. It is a rarity today to turn on the TV and not be exposed to profanity, nudity, vulgarity, violence, stupidity, weird behaviors and encouraged immorality. All these reflect acts of deadly deceptions. If you call it anything else then you have been deceived and your path is clouded with a deadly pulse. From "The Osborn's" to "Jackass", Satan was waiting on his Emmy!

The laws and discipline of Christ are from the cradle to the grave. You were born in sin and you will die in sin but you have an insurance policy in forgiveness and it has been pre-approved as well as pre-paid. From a *teenager* to an *oldager* it comes down to a conscious choice. But it doesn't matter what your age is as much as it is in your understanding. If you sing "Yes Jesus loves me" and know who Jesus is then your path has a starting or reference point. There are specifics of understanding that were written and specifics of obedience that are non-negotiable. So before we close the book and run out into the mission field to witness for Christ, there are some final thoughts of your destiny that you need to know. Let us review some very important keys to not only opening doors to the promised land but to secure any risk of temptation getting through an open windows, crack in the wall, faulty door or loose hinges that may offer an opening for demonic temptation. Don't take this lightly or laugh! No, never laugh because Satan is dead serious, so then we shall be.

☆ Your weakest moment is your open access for Satan's attempt on your life. When you least expect it he will slide your favorite temptation in your way. Know what worldly desire would temp you and know very well what you must do when it steps in your way. If you recognize the symptom then you will be better equipped to defend against it and put a solution in place. A long term solution is recommended.

☆ Know what your weak points are and know how to detect a weak moment. The worst time you can have is idle time, boredom or loneness. Fill these moments with Christ, His word and in prayer so opportunity for evil will fade away.

☆ Know what the prevention measures are for curing these weak moments. I keep my Bible handy and make sure that I keep God's word close to me. Jesus made a solemn promise that Satan can never take you from His hands. Know it and keep your shield filled with His word and His promise.

☆ Never argue or attempt to defend God. He will do a fine job in defending Himself. Your call as a Christian Crusader is to speak His name, testify what He has done for you and know that His name is Jesus. We tell and He rescues.

☆ Understand the wisdom of Jesus and the direction He gave. There will be many who will come in His name. There will be many who will say they carry His word. There will be many who say angels are directing them to move you. Jesus has already warned us that these false people and false days will come to pass. When you see it or hear it, open your Bible and read His words from the only Apostles authorized to record His word.

☆ Let no man move you away from God's word in the Holy Bible. Let no man move you to an additional book and say that it is part of or equal to the Holy Bible. Let no man move you away from Mark 16:16.

All that I own outside of my Christian faith is a liability. A different way of saying this is that anything I can take with me to Heaven is fact and anything that I cannot was fiction. It is my responsibility to know the difference.

Relationships: 1st Corinthians 13:4-8

"Love is patient, love is kind and is not jealous; love does not brag and is not arrogant, does not act unbecomingly; it does not seek its own, is not provoked, does not take into account a wrong suffered, does not rejoice in unrighteousness, but rejoices with the

truth; bears all things, believes all things, hopes all things, endures all things. Love never fails; but if there are gifts of prophecy, they will be done away; if there are tongues, they will cease; if there is knowledge, it will be done away."

This scripture was never intended for you to open and point it at someone. It was written for you to measure YOU to His word and His way . . .

~ ~ ~ ~ ~ ~ ~

Everyone is born with an internal rubber band mentality. Some take this mental theory and use it in different methods or fashions to suit their personality or temptations. Some stretch it as pushing the limits of its ability, some twirl it to be different, some play with it like a comedian, some thump it to make music, some pop it to be evil, some shoot it to become more evil but here is the original truth. The creator of the rubber band intended it to hold things together. Our Creator made us to act united, perform united, speak united and follow His direction united. It is a simple thought and an easy concept, or so you would think.

When we want something and we want it our way, mankind has the uncanny ability to twist it and bend it to fit the life we want. We deceive ourselves in saying it is okay or it is not really that bad? What do we really ask God to bless in our lives each day? In your "personal" relationship with God, in your walk with Christ and in your claim to Christianity, what do you ask God to bless? We learn to say "please" when we want stuff to make us happy. What if we asked God for happy stuff? Are we asking God for happiness or holiness? Let's see . . .

* God please bless all my excuses for not worshiping you daily?
* God please bless my job even though I sometimes place it between you and me?
* God please bless my car even though I'm driving it somewhere other than to your house of worship?
* God please bless this "light" porn site that I occasionally look at?
* God please bless this weed I am smoking cause all my friends do it?

* ✻ God please bless this strip bar that I only go into cause my friends are going?
* ✻ God please bless my marriage even though I place it second behind me?
* ✻ God please bless my profanity even though I only use it every now and then?
* ✻ God please bless this night in hopes she might give her body to me just once?
* ✻ God please bless this one time affair cause you know I won't do it again?
* ✻ God please bless this lotto ticket that I might hit it big this time?
* ✻ God please bless this alcohol that it might nourish my body?
* ✻ God please bless this casino and the money that I donate to its goodness?
* ✻ God please bless this beer cause you know it is not like drinking real alcohol?
* ✻ God please bless this little lie and you know I won't tell another one?
* ✻ God please bless my flirting with this person even though I am married?
* ✻ God please bless my anger and when I raised my voice in hate?
* ✻ God please bless my need for money even though I often place its value before you?
* ✻ God please forgive me even though I am unwilling to forgive him/her?
* ✻ God please get me out of this mess I'm in and I will never do it again?

God please forgive me if I place anything between us and forgive my foolish behavior because I know I have failed to walk in the Light of Your holiness. Father you are my Creator, the Almighty God, Lord and precious Savior who loves me no matter what I have done and you know my heart that I could never hide behind. Forgive me Father; cleanse my heart, my mind and my soul so that I might go forward and sin no more . . . Amen.

Money and the deception of greed:
"For the love of money is a root of all sorts of evil, and some by longing for it have wandered away from the faith and pierced

themselves with many griefs. But flee from these things, you man of God, and pursue righteousness, godliness, faith, love, perseverance and gentleness."

1st Timothy 6:10-11

Jesus was a carpenter by trade and built things with His hands. How original is it that God in flesh would build things with His hands. Do you think Jesus ever took a shortcut on a building project? Do you think He ever cheated a friend on a business deal? Do you think He ever used a business associate for personal gain? Do you think Jesus ever cheated on a building code? Do you think He ever chose a less quality material but represented it for the finest available? Do you think He ever judged an employee or customer by the way he or she looked? Do you think He ever embezzled or gambled the business profits away? Do you think Jesus ever lied on an exam to gain a promotion or license? Do you think He ever cheated on His taxes and didn't pay His money due? Do you think He ever called out sick just to play a round of golf? Do you think He ever called out sick just to go to the beach? Do you think He ever played games on the weekend and let Sunday's worship service go with no value? Do you think He ever skipped school because the fish were biting that day? Do you think He was lazy and wanted to lie in bed all day? Do you believe Jesus would tell a joke that His Father would be ashamed to hear Him say? Do you think that Jesus ever said; "I hope you go to Hell"? Do these thoughts bring reality a little closer to home? Jesus is God who took flesh by His Holy Spirit to save us of our sinful nature. Honor Him by staying faithful in His way. Follow Him!

Business / trade:

An education is an awesome thing to have and to be informed, have knowledge, grow wisdom and develop a sense of common reality are genuine values to this world as well as learning of the next. Reading, writing and arithmetic are key values to studying God's word. Here are some additional degrees that I believe you should achieve during this lifetime in order to prepare you for life after death:

- ➢ **A.A.**—**A**ccept **A**lways in the word of God
- ➢ **A.B.C.**—**A**ccept **B**elieve **C**ommit then go and sin no more
- ➢ **B.S.**—**B**een **S**aved and filled with the Holy Spirit

- **B.A.**—**B**orn **A**gain and baptized according to the Father, Son & Holy Spirit
- **PHD**—**P**rophetical **H**umble **D**iscipleship according to 2nd Peter 1
- **DDS**—**D**edicated **D**aily **S**tudy in the gospel of Jesus Christ.

When I think of a business philosophy combined with Today's Christian Crusader, I think:

- Jesus began as a businessman then was baptized into His missions work.
- Jesus was Master Teacher and expects us to listen, learn and tell.
- Jesus set the example of daily prayer and the need for divine guidance.
- Jesus knew we could not survive life without His Holy Spirit.
- Jesus established His work on truth and forgiveness of debt.
- Jesus didn't come as a wealthy King; He came as a humbled servant.
- Jesus chose His words carefully and wasted none.
- Jesus treated others, as an example as He would expect us to treat others.
- Jesus knows the heart and if the heart is pure then so shall be your actions.
- Jesus knew the value of money as a need to give before expecting to receive.
- Jesus set an example of recognizing demonic behavior and how to admonish it.
- Jesus sacrificed Himself in death so we would speak His name and have life.
- Jesus respected His Fathers creations and always spoke more of His world to come.
- Jesus spoke often that in Him all things are possible.
- Jesus had authority over death so you would have a choice in your eternal life.
- Jesus inspired love with an eternal promise and this promise is just behind the small gate and down the narrow path that only those who follow Him will find.

Marketing / Media of deception: Matthew 7:15-21

> "Beware of the false prophets, who come to you in sheep's clothing, but inwardly are ravenous wolves. You will know them by their fruits. Grapes are not gathered from thorn bushes nor figs from thistles, are they? So every good tree bears good fruit, but the bad tree bears bad fruit. A good tree cannot produce bad fruit, nor can a bad tree produce good fruit. Every tree that does not bear good fruit is cut down and thrown into the fire. So then, you will know them by their fruits. Not everyone who says to Me, 'Lord, Lord,' will enter the kingdom of heaven, but he who does the will of My Father who is in heaven will enter. Many will say to Me on that day, 'Lord, Lord, did we not prophesy in Your name, and in Your name cast out demons, and in Your name perform many miracles? And then I will declare to them, 'I never knew you; DEPART FROM ME, YOU WHO PRACTICE LAWLESSNESS. Therefore everyone who hears these words of Mine and acts on them, may be compared to a wise man who built his house on the rock. And the rain fell, and the floods came, and the winds blew and slammed against that house; and yet it did not fall, for it had been founded on the rock. Everyone who hears these words of Mine and does not act on them, will be like a foolish man who built his house on the sand."

There are three groups or categories of unsaved souls:

1. **The Doubter**—this is the person that knows there is a God, knows that Jesus was called the Christ, knows He was crucified and knows right from wrong but never received Him and just can't make himself or herself walk in the righteousness of Christ. These many, many people do not believe that you can walk in holiness.
2. **The Denier**—this is the person who says Jesus lived and He died but He didn't rise. That God exists in some form but could be an evolutionist, tree hugger or worshiping a false idol as their god. Like Buddha, Allah, Earth, Mother Mary or Kermit the frog as a few examples. They too do not believe that a Christian can walk in holiness.

3. **The Dead**—this is a person who states firmly that God does not exist. There are very few of these people and if they claim true atheism then they have faith that there is no God. This faith then becomes their religion.

One and two still have an open line for a reservation to heaven, all the way up until their last breath. The second that last breath is taken; they will fall into darkness to await judgment. The third unsaved spirit has denied God's Holy Spirit and is spiritually doomed, dead and eternally damned.

Yes, it is sad but it is a choice and it is what it is. I know a few people in the third category and all the marketing strategies in the world could not change their mind. Many believe there is a God, they attend church but still partake of Satan's worldly pleasures. Many call themselves "Christian" but still need the pleasures of this world to maintain the lifestyle with their "friends". Many will discover that using the label will become a liability. These folks confuse "label" with "lifestyle" and Jesus was very specific and deliberate in His word. This is a deadly risk and playing both sides of the fence is outside the will of everything Jesus taught. The gates are small and the path is very narrow. Just in case someone forgot . . .

"He who is not with Me is against Me; and he who does not gather with Me scatters."

Matthew 12:30

<u>Trusting Your Conscience:</u>

Many struggle with knowing who to listen to and who the authority on any given topic is. If Jim Cantore of the Weather Channel was seen in your neighborhood carrying a microphone with a film crew trailing behind him would you be alarmed? If he had "Breaking News" of earthquake conditions that would cause impending devastating then what would your next move be? Then you catch his interview on TV and he gives detailed illustrations of earth seismic movements around the world on the NOAA satellite link that has dots of every color on the rainbow and there are dots on every continent. Based on his word, would you move into action or would you sit idle in non-belief? If Obama came on TV, again, and said that NASA had an image on their galactic planetary radar that reflected an image, which had the appearance of a terrestrial starship and it was headed to earth, what would you do? If he continued to say that it could be a meteor moving but he just wanted to give his "expert" opinion.

In either or any scenario you will be listening to a "man or woman" give their "expert opinion" but they will have no factual evidence to provide you with confidence of what they are speaking about but they can give you a few "opinions" of what they feel will occur. There are many who can provide you with the results from their studies but unless they have discussed the data with the Creator then they will be giving you their personal opinion based on their personal faith in the topic as well as the results. Your faith and your belief system will calculate a conscious decision of what to believe. It will fall under one of two categories: FACT or FICTION . . .

How do you learn to trust your conscience and how do you learn the paths to follow? This means to simply trust your inner thoughts and those little voices in your head that you know are right but they cause friction against earthly pleasures.

- ➢ Make a conscious choice to believe in Christ or not.
- ➢ Make a conscious habit to study His word and His direction or not.
- ➢ Make a conscious habit to humble yourself in prayer or not.
- ➢ Make a conscious choice to push away what you know is true or not.
- ➢ Make a conscious awareness of who is the authority and who is not.
- ➢ Make a conscious daily effort to silence the world and meditate in thought or not.
- ➢ Make a conscious daily effort to walk in His Light and do what is right or not.
- ➢ Make a conscious effort to listen to God and know His voice or not.
- ➢ Make a conscious effort to love Him, worship Him and be obedient to Him or not.

To believe or not to believe, to trust or not to trust, to have faith or not to have faith; these are certainties that must be settled in your heart. A Christian's life is not walking to the front of a church, saying a prayer with the pastor, or eating a wafer, or having a pastor thump you on the forehead then returning back to the same life and same lifestyle you had before. If you did this and thought you had received Christ's precious gift of eternal life then you need to revisit this day in your life. If you don't remember anything else remember this: there is only you and Jesus Christ that truly knows your heart. You may fool others and you may fool yourself but you are a fool to hide your eternal life behind a foolish statement of faith. A Christian's path is filled with unpopular days and it is impossible to walk between the boundaries without Christ. You cannot be holy if Christ's' Holy Spirit is not in your heart, mind, body and spirit then filled to the brim. It is unquestionably the only path to follow and only a dead man would consciously walk in the ditch . . .

Trusting your conscience becomes stronger as your maturity as a Christian grows. An immature Christian is a child in Christ that has developed the understanding and knowledge of Jesus but has not grown into full submission. A mature Christian has fully **A**ccepted Christ as their personal Savior, has fully **B**elieved that Christ is the only path to salvation as well as eternal life and has fully **C**ommitted to Christ, which means you have a covenant with God. The term "saved" means filled with the Holy Spirit and moved from an old life of sinful living into a committed life of worship, testimony and living an example of Christ. The symbol that Jesus established is in a fully-submerged baptism. Draw your Sword and read Mark 16:16. Your character will reflect Christianity when no one is looking. And you will know His voice because you know Him, you know His word and you know His divine path.

Religious denominations / traditions: 1st John 4:1-4
"Beloved, do not believe every spirit, but test the spirits to see whether they are from God, because many false prophets have gone out into the world. By this you know the Spirit of God: every spirit that confesses that Jesus Christ has come in the flesh is from God; and every spirit that does not confess Jesus is not from God; this is the spirit of the antichrist, of which you have heard that it is coming, and now it is already in the world. You are from

God, little children, and have overcome them; because greater is He who is in you than he who is in the world."

The Bible is not a denomination, it is a living record of God's word, God's will, a book of seeds to sow, a compass for a life in His Light and the map that He has written for His people to follow. Your free will is a conscious choice of whether you will follow His word or you will not. Being religious without a <u>daily</u> commitment to Christ is like wearing a pilot's uniform and not knowing to fly! Attending church and saying this makes you saved is like attending a concert and saying you are with the band. Going to a priest and confessing your sin to a mortal man is like going to your neighbor's boss and asking him for a promotion. Kneeling before a statue of the mother of Jesus Christ and lighting a candle for blessings is like walking into Barnes-n-Nobles shopping for a new car. Comparing a book or composition and saying it is equal to the Holy Bible is like walking into a library and saying all books have the same ending. Praying for any dead soul thinking that enough prayers will elevate him or her from an unsaved eternity into a saved eternal life is like walking into a store and purchasing a lotto ticket for last weeks drawing. Saying you are Christian but drinking it up at the local night club is like the pope greeting his cardinals with as-salamu alaykum! You are either a born again believer in Christ or you are not. There is no maybe I will, or I will do part of this, or I'll meet Him half way. No, it is all or none! Satan's deception illustrates a much easier path but with deadly results. It is a deception of having both lives and "feeling" okay with your worldly walk. It is that little notion of false hope that God will love you even though you just cannot pull yourself away from a worldly pleasure that you know is wrong. The path of Christ is narrow and the gatekeeper will not be negotiable.

Religions practice rituals and traditions. Jesus is not a religion and He is not a tradition and He never quoted a ritual. Many ceremonies of today still follow traditions and rituals of the Old Testament. Jesus is the New Testament, He is THE Christ and a follower of Christ is like Christ. Jesus was very specific in His direction and deliberate in His words. There will be those who say they are Jesus, the Christ, and the Messiah. There will be those who will say they come on His behalf or that an angel has delivered holy words to them. There will be those who claim to have received divine word and offer different direction other than His Holy word. And these will hold the same characteristics of deception, as did the serpent in the Garden of Eden. Yes the very one who spoke to Eve and encouraged her to take the fruit and enjoy the visions it provides. These practices are not new and it is your conscious decision that will ultimately reveal and seal your eternal direction.

Deadly deceptions will reveal themselves in the justification of sin. They will not seem deadly to the eyes, to the taste, to the smell or to the touch. Your conscious thoughts will softly urge you to enjoy the pleasures, you deserve these impurities and you have the right to take what you want of this world. To enjoy God and all of His creation is our gift but to place His creations between you and your Creator is sinful and most deadly.

To prepare yourself as a Crusader for Christ in today's world it will take these final thoughts before you walk away:

- ➤ Love the Lord your God with all your heart and with all your might.
- ➤ Know today that you own nothing in this world that was not provided by God.
- ➤ Jesus Christ is the Truth, the Light and the only Way.
- ➤ You must profess His name on earth in order for Him to call your name in Heaven.
- ➤ You must be faithful in obedience to His every word.
- ➤ The three simple words will always set you free: **A**ccept—**B**elieve—**C**ommit
- ➤ If you are temptation free then you are living in false hope.
- ➤ If you are walking in and out of Christian partnership then you are lost with no compass.
- ➤ Being afraid to die is natural. Being afraid of death is an unsaved man's fear.
- ➤ Your faith is your shield and your Bible is your sword. It is a humbled lifestyle.
- ➤ The center of all choices is the cross . . .

  This is where Jesus paid the price that you might have a choice.
  Choose wisely and walk in Christ as a proud Christian . . .

Teaching He taught me
Living He loved me
Dieing He saved me
Rising He promised me
Returning He will claim me

And all He ever asked of me is to love Him and follow Him . . .

Walk the Walk, Talk the Talk!

We begin to fail when we compare ourselves to the world instead of to God's Holy Word. It is the only point of measurement that really matters.

Today's Christian Crusader is measured with the same instrument of measurement used long ago.

The Gospel!

There is one common statement that every person in the world can admit is that on at least one occasion a person who has claimed the Christian title has acted in hypocrisy or mediocrity as compared to the gospel of Jesus Christ. Both hypocrisy and meritocracy are derivatives of SIN. Both of these are deadly to your witness and hell has a party every time a Christian trips or stumbles. A hypocrite says they are but their character reflects they are not. A witness with mediocrity is one that said the prayer, attends church and puts on their religious jacket when it suits the moment. The other half of the time they find worldly reasoning for the "feel good" happiness they seek. It is comfortable to be in Christian meritocracy mode and if you are quiet everyone will leave you alone. Yes, the "go along to get along" so everyone will love you. Hypocrite! Here are just a few examples of what I have witnessed and some of what I have experienced in good ole church folk. We'll put an X beside them.

If one or more of these apply to you then you might be *ivveleth*!

X   Attending church worship services then leaving your seat during the alter call is not only disrespectful; it means you do not celebrate new life in Christ. What's the hurry? A born again believer in Christ is respectful.

X   Talking during prayer is not only rude; it means you are not interested in speaking with God. What could be more interesting? A born again believer in Christ is not rude.

X   Using any excuse other than illness to not be in church somewhere is a sign. It is a sign that you hold something more important than your united fellowship with God. What could be standing between you and God? A born again believer in Christ desires devotion, worship and always in thanksgiving to God.

X   Some women or girls attend church showing more breast, thighs and legs than a grocery store meat counter. Dressing inappropriately for worship is not cute, fashionable or in style. It just means that you attend for you and not for Him. A born again believer in Christ is conservative and dresses with respect to Christ.

X   Drinking a beer with the guys or having a margarita with the girls is not against Bible teachings. Would you be proud to invite Jesus where you consume it and give Him what you consume? If you just hesitated then we are sure that He wouldn't appreciate the example you set . . . A born again believer in Christ would not serve alcohol or drugs in his/her temple.

X   They say that 98% of Christians never speak of Jesus Christ outside of church. So this means most folks are only "Christian" while in church? A born again believer in Christ speaks of Christ because he/she loves Him.

X   Using profanity when you are angered and gossiping about others. The hypocrisy of a Christian is measured by what comes from the heart. If it is in your heart it will surely come off of your lips. If you were filled with the Holy Spirit then where would the immorality come from? A born again believer in Christ corrects immorality, not condones it.

X   You still question the reality of angels, the voice of Christ and the majesty in His mercy and grace. These questions come from doubt and doubt comes from a lack of fulfillment. A born again believer in Christ walks in confidence that their sins are forgiven.

X   I have learned that divorce today is more of a convenience than a covenant. We will dump one and move on to another Lillie-pad because it is convenient. A born again believer in Christ understand their commitment to God and loves God first then leaves the relationship mending to Him.

X   Arguing with a fool makes for a foolish conversation. This is a stubborn act of who knows more, you or them? Christianity is not a contest; it is a lifestyle with a foundation of Christ. Listen to them, be concerned of their eternal security and testify of what He has done for you. Send an email of forgiveness. Call a friend and tell them how your life has changed. Ask someone that is down on their luck if you can pray for them. A born again believer in Christ will support and assist with the truth then leave the consequences to God.

X   Defending God is not only futile it is foolish. A statement of faith is simply telling someone how good God is and how good He has been to you. We are not worthy of <u>arguing</u> His deity. As I have done all through this literature; state the facts, give the references and answer questions as best you can. A born again believer in Christ will understand that their will be those who refuse to listen.

It is so common for Christians to be held accountable to some higher level of accountability than the world. The world will point their finger and announce all the mistakes, errors and short comings along our way. Here is your defining moment; did you willfully go out of your way to seek sinful behavior or did sin cross your path and you get sucked into it?

Example: You are flipping the channels on TV and stop upon a station with pure nudity and yes, they are butt naked. Did you move past or did you sit on the channel for a few extra seconds. One was sin and was not.

Example: You are with a bunch of real close friends and they invite you to a party Friday night. ALL the influential people will be there. There will also be alcohol, party drugs and these parties have been known to get a little out of control. But your friends really want you to go. To want to go and go is physical sin. To want to go and not go is spiritual sin. To not want to be in that environment and take a moment to witness to others that are going is a born again believer in Christ.

If Paul had been reminded daily of all the things he did as Saul, then Paul would have battled every day in ministering the gospel. Paul held himself accountable to Christ and moved forward knowing his sins had been forgiven. If Peter had been held to the line for his three moments of denial then Christ would have hesitated in building His church on the rock of Peter. Those who walk daily in the light of Christ will not intentionally fold to Satan's temptation. This is why we struggle when we are alone and find strength united with the body of Christ. Like a flock of sheep we are safer in numbers.

How murderers, rapists, child molesters, thieves and such find forgiveness is a puzzle to unbelievers? Forgiveness period is something that an unsaved person struggles with. A sin is when someone tells you a lie and hurts your feels. A sin is when someone slaps you and hurts your skin. A sin is when someone shoots you in the foot and places you in severe pain. Think of someone in your past that REALLY made you mad, dumped on you, started a vicious rumor about you, or worst. Did you ever forgive them? To forgive and be forgiven is a clean spirit to serve Christ in completeness. If you are hanging on to excess baggage, you will struggle in your faithful witness.

"Forgive us our trespasses <u>as</u> we forgive those who trespass against us."

"As" means at the same time and at the same time is a partnership. If we expect God to forgive us for ALL our sins, then shouldn't we be willing to forgive ALL those who have wronged us? Even today, all those who call Christian names, slander our King, create web sites that deny His name and call for others to see the same. It is our role as bondservants to tell our story, speak His name and let the Holy Spirit work from there. Remember, we cannot forgive sin and we cannot will/lure someone into heaven. Only Jesus Christ can.

- ☆ Sin was in you before you were born.
- ☆ Sin was paid for through the blood of Jesus.
- ☆ Sin was corruptive before you accepted Christ as your Savior.
- ☆ Sin is corrosive and spreads without the forgiveness of Jesus Christ.
- ☆ Sin cannot corrupt you unless your mind sees it and your heart accepts it.
- ☆ Sin will be in front of you the rest of your life.
- ☆ Sin cannot enter heaven and your name must be recorded in The Book of Life.

<u>S</u>in is <u>S</u>atan's way of saying thank you for giving <u>in</u>!

The one single thing that the world forgets is that no matter who you are, you are born a sinner, you have a sinful nature and you are tempted in sin every day. As a born again believer in Christ you need to be able to identify a fool consumed of sin.

1.   A simple or naïve fool is one who just doesn't think before doing or is gullible as well as easily persuaded. These fools are uneducated about God's word and too lazy to engage in basic study. If you do not like to read then go to Sunday school and someone will read to you. If you know someone who struggles with scripture, hold a small study group and invite them in.
2.   A self confident or cocky fool is one who takes pieces of scripture and either plays them out of context or twists them into their own favor. This person is also unwilling to listen to reason or consider ancient prophets as people of integrity or nobility. Some will discard a scripture because it doesn't fit their lifestyle.
3.   A committed fool is one who has owned an oath of defiant actions, marches in protests and may even join a web site of unbelievers. They may join because of peer influence but you can be assured that somewhere in the back of their mind there is that burning voice; "What if I'm wrong?" But the foolish demon inside will not be willing to let go of such a prize without a fight!
4.   The mocking fool is the down right satanic fool in defiance and organizes leadership or mentorship of hell bound acts and/ or actions. This demonic fool creates billboards that denounces God, form hate groups and leads others to a dry well.

A fool is a fool and our role is not to respect them for their opinion but we are to love them in brotherly love then move on. Offer Christ as an answer to their eternal damnation and then move on. Once they know Christ's name and they choose a life without Him, then they are not worthy of an argument, a litigated session or a battle of wits. The Holy Spirit is more qualified at this than we are so allow the Holy Spirit to convict them. Just so you know Jesus knows this is not easy and He knows you cannot walk this walk alone. So don't try, just move on . . .

Ivveleth is Hebrew for a fool or being foolish at any level. Be strong in your faith, carry your Sword proudly and work for the pride of Christ. There will be many crowns in heaven for those who simply speak His name aloud. Every time you say His name an angel spreads their wings in pride. Every time you sing His praise an angel sets off in flight. Every time you speak to Him in prayer an angel lights a star at night. Every time you need His strength a proud angel fly's at night. Your testimony is in how you live, it is how you speak and it is even how you are remembered when you die. Your covenant with God is in security of knowing Him, seeking Him daily, planning your day beginning with Him and never allowing a day to pass by without thanking Him. It should be your desire to maintain devotion - fellowship with Christ.

Walk in His Light and you will know His Light. Walk in His word and you will know His voice. Seek Him daily and He will embrace you always. Enter the small gate, walk the narrow path in faith and every day know that He will move the sky to welcome you in His home . . .

Know What You Know

"And the wolf will dwell with the lamb, and the leopard will lie down with the young goat, and the calf and the young lion and the fatling together, and the little boy will lead them."

Isaiah 11:6

You will never know it all but know what you know really well . . .

About the Sword—we learned of the library that the Bible contains and that it is the word of God and every word combined with all His words shows the Christian path.

Divine Swordsmanship—we learned of good and evil, angels and demons as well as those who think they speak to the other side. We learned what to believe in and what is deception.

Sword Training—we learned good study habits, planting God's "P's", some key study resources and how to listen to the experts while following Jesus.

Continued Sword Training—we learned the most difficult habits to create are to be consistent in the word, plan quality study habits, and look at several civilizations that perished because they had no foundation in the Living God.

Skilled Swordsmanship—we learned of the importance for mission work, fielding the questions from those who struggle to believe, the realties of those who do not believe and what challenges we face in the mission field.

The History of the Sword—we learned who created the practices we use today, what challenges they faced and heard from the very best that God selected to carry His Sword forward.

The Sword of Discipleship—we learned how to be an effective Disciple for Christ and how to prioritize our lives so we may clear our mind of "me" and move forward for Him.

History of the Crusades—we learned of past human struggles and the ones who took the fight to foreign lands so that people would be free to worship God. We studied the history of Islam, jihad, religions, denominations and popular beliefs of yesterday to today. Our history is much like our future.

Today's Crusades & Sword of Freedom—The early Crusades are very similar to the worlds fight today in areas where it is against the law to study Christianity and announce your faith in Jesus Christ.

Living by the Sword—we learned what it takes to stay centered in Christ and a real understanding in the sacrifice for freedom. Knowing the physical chains that you can see and spiritual chains you cannot see.

Life & Death—we learned in death there is life in what you believe, what faith you had and what deeds have you earned for that faith.

How important is your word? How important is God's word? How important is it for you to speak God's word? Here is a little outline I put together to bring it all together.

The Sword is my Bible and I need to understand it well. The Shield is my faith and I should know Him well. The handle of my Sword is my strength and trust in His promise. The tip is my compass point of following Him, needing Him, loving Him and being loyal to His Holy name. I understand that there are demons around me daily and they want my soul. They need me to slip and they are very crafty in their design. The things of this world are easy on the eyes and delicious to the taste. They also stand in my way of redemption and everlasting grace. When I am thirsty, tired, sick and feel alone, my Redeemer, Lord and Savior will be my Light in the field of the seeds I have sown. My sins have been great and my sins have been small. In the deepest hour of need Jesus saves and forgets them all. I shall no longer wonder or wander in this world for I know my God my Father, God His Son and God His Holy Spirit and He are one within me.

As Today's Christian Crusader for Christ I am faithful, fruitful and seek the crowns that Jesus wants to bless me with:

1. **Crown of Righteousness**—It is His gift for you living and walking daily in His Light.

2. **Crown of Imperishability**—It is for those who were called, heard the call and answered the call with faithful intention.

3. **Crown of Life**—Is the martyr's crown and Jesus will hand this crown Himself to those who have suffered greatly in hardship, testing, tribulation, torture and/or a physical death.

4. **Crown of Rejoicing**—Is the soul winning crown for those who have testified and because of their testimony have won souls to His kingdom. Evangelicals, pastors, bishops, Bible teachers and those who walk and talk the message of Christ will no doubt have crowns rained upon them. Remember, faith without works is unfruitful and an unfruitful tree is not recognized to the orchard owner as being worthy of continued life.

5. **Crown of Glory**—Is the crown given to the shepherds of the church, from preacher to teacher who glorified God's name to the masses.

Once you have collected your crowns, we will gather and cast our rewards at the feet of our Lord, King and Savior, Jesus Christ. This is the day every believer lives to know . . .

Many have died protecting and speaking upon the Sword that you carry so put on the armor of God and walk proudly knowing that when you die speaking the name of Jesus then your rewards will be great upon your arrival in heaven. Be confident of your walk and you talk while knowing His promise;

> **"Therefore everyone who confesses Me before men, I will also confess him before My Father who is in heaven."**
> Matthew 10:32

My Bible is my Sword my faith is my shield
God gives my direction and I shall not yield,
Through Jesus Christ are my words and my salvation
In Him all things are made possible without hesitation,
In Christ united we stand separated we drift away
Believe, follow, pray and stay in His Light today . . .

May God rain His love on you this day
So that you find His peace in your path along the way.

John W Edwards III

In 1945 at the close of the Nazi Empire and rule over the German people, many Jewish concentration camps were revealed and the gates of freedom were opened. There was one man who made the journey home to Luxembourg and the closest that the railroad train tracks could get them there was 7 miles away. The many war worn and damaged tracks were impossible to travel. The Jewish man stepped off the boxcar train step and began his walk home. His walk gave him so much time to remember better days gone by. He was married with three children all of whom had now passed. The scars of a cruel war had separated many families and six million Jews paid the ultimate price in the entire calamity. He pondered over those times as he walked and he noticed a young German solder was walking in the same direction on the opposite side of the dirt road alone. The soldier had no hat, wore only an undershirt, uniform pants, worn boots and a canteen of water slung over his shoulder. The man walked over to the youngster and asked him if he was okay. Imagine that, this elderly Jewish man just released from the most horrific of times in a prison camp asking a young, strong German soldier if he was okay. The boy looked at him and said, "It's over and I have nothing to go home to." The man looked him in the eyes and said, "I understand, I too struggle to walk to an empty home." The man asked the boy, "How old are you son?" The boy answered, "I am 17, and I just look young for my age." The man got a chuckle out of the boy's response and said, "Yes, I remember being 17." The boy began to cry and said, "I have done so many horrible things and I am not sure where to go from here." The man watched the boy crumble as he struggled to take his steps. The man asked the boy, "What is your name?" He answered, "Dominik." The man said, "Dominik, I am Simon and if you will help me walk home I will tell you of a man who knows what you are going through and I have something in my home that I want to show you. It is the most cherished possession that I have left in this world." Dominik shook his head in agreement. As they walked the boy placed his arm around Simon and gave him the support he needed to walk. Over the remaining few miles Simon told Dominik of a man whose name was Jesus. The life He lived and the death He suffered by the hands of the Roman Empire, very similar to the German Empire. Simon told Dominik how similar the German leaders were to the Roman leaders, and the similarity to their country's Hitler and Romans Caesars. Dominik said he had never heard of this Jesus. They entered the city and Simon said, "It's just down this street, my home, it is still here." They walked up the steps and opened the door. It appeared to have been kicked open some time ago and the dusted footprint of a soldiers boot was still on the solid wood door. As Simon struggled to walk in the room, he turned to the right where the living room was and his knees buckled in sorrow. The room had be vandalized, furniture broken and nothing was the same. Dominik was angered and said to Simon, "I curse the men who did this. I am so sorry for their stupidity. For their anger and hate I will never understand. Sir, please forgive them. They were probably young like me and didn't know what they were doing." Simon looked up at Dominik and said, "Yes, I once had that fire in my belly as well. Jesus once said the same thing to His Father. Now help me to my feet, it is right over there". Dominik placed his hands under Simon's arms and lifted him to his feet. Then Simon walked over to the fireplace and scratched at the wood boards in the wall. A board fell and Simon reached his hand inside the wall and pulled a black leather Bible from the space in the wall. Simon looked at the Bible and said, "This is my most cherished possession in this world. I read it to my wife and children each night by the light of that broken oil lamp. Jesus spoke those very words and He is the only Light that you seek in your heart. You see the good in people and you help. You see the bad in people and you ask to forgive them? The man in this book is the King and holds the same love for all man. Yes, even the Romans who were killing Him that very day. I want you to have this book, read it and feel the love from this man. The story of Jesus and the life He gave for all people. Go now, read His word, understand your gift and tell others what you have learned this day. I will see you in heaven, my new friend and I ask God to love you each and every step of your way." Dominik turned and walked through the front doors then looked to thank Simon for the book. When he looked both ways, Simon was not there and he didn't hear a sound, just the whisper of the wind. He stood quietly then opened the Bible cover to read a hand written inscription on the inside covers. It said:

"My Lord, I have tended your sheep and he is well.
Simon Peter"

Knowing our historical walk from the Garden of Eden to today is important. Knowing who God chose to record His word is important. Knowing His divine message within His word is important. Knowing your skills and staying sharp in His word is important. Knowing these things develops a path of right learning which leads to a confident walk-talk for others. Knowing why the Crusades were important will make knowing the crusade of today important. Knowing how to live by the Sword today will offer blessed assurance of dieing by the Sword eternally important. Knowing the deceptions that lay in ones way will offer wisdom on a wicked and war torn way.

How important is "knowing that you know"? Simon Peter was a hand selected follower of Jesus Christ who became an eternal man of God by knowing what was truly, truly important. He believed in Jesus and followed Christ. Peter was not a perfect man. He made mistakes, he had moments of doubt, he questioned even the miracles that happened before his eyes and in every step he made, he continued to walk in the Light of One God, for one purpose and for one Word. Jesus gave Peter one last instruction and the same words Jesus gave to Peter, He gives to us today;

Do you trust that He is Jesus, the Christ and Savior of your eternal Spirit?

Will you believe in Him enough to follow Him?

If you choose to follow Him, will you tend to His sheep?

So simply asked, Do you love Him?

If you love Him;

"Go therefore and make disciples of all the nations, baptizing them in the name of the Father and the Son and the Holy Spirit, teaching them to observe all that I commanded you; and lo, I am with you always, even to the end of the age."
Matthew 28:19-20

"Now when they heard this, they were pierced to the heart, and said to Peter and the rest of the apostles, "Brethren, what shall we do?" Peter said to them, "Repent, and each of you be baptized in the name of Jesus Christ for the forgiveness of your sins; and you will receive the gift of the Holy Spirit. For the promise is for you and your children and for all who are far off, as many as the Lord our God will call to Himself. And with many other words he solemnly testified and kept on exhorting them, saying, "Be saved from this perverse generation!"

Acts 3:37-40

My Lord, I have tended to your sheep and they now know You . . .
Your faithful servant, John

Acknowledgements

I have mentioned several individuals that have been inspirational in my life, my studies and my research so I wanted to separate them in this section. I so appreciate them for their life's work, their inspiration and their dedication to the truth. Each one has their own testimony and they are listed in no particular order. No doubt God is very proud of what they do.

Dr David Jeremiah is Senior Pastor of Shadow Mountain Community Church and founder of Turning Point Ministries. He is without a doubt the most broadcasted pastor and is a Bible teacher.

Dr Charles Stanley is Senior Pastor of the 1st Baptist Church of Atlanta Georgia and In Touch Ministry. Dr. Stanley is my resolve, my truth in life's everyday paths and is a Bible teacher.

Paul E. Shepard founded Enduring Truth and has been the Senior Pastor at Abundant Life Fellowship in Mountain View California. His messages will move reality directly in front of you and you will have no doubt about the right solution. He has a down to earth message with heavenly passages and he is Bible teacher.

James McDonald is a pastor, author and founder of "walk in the word". He is a Bible teacher and friend of God's word, ALL of it.

Dr. Ed Young Sr. is the Senior Pastor of the 2nd Baptist Church of Houston Texas. What a delight he is to the word of God, to his discipline to the God's word and the fearless demeanor of his pulpit. I always say, Houston has a choice of the gospel truth or an ear tickled smiling preacher with no backbone to ALL of God's word. Pastor Young has plenty of backbone!

Chuck Missler holds Bible study at the Calvary Chapel Costa Mesa in Southern California and can be found on www.khouse.org. He is a Bible teacher.

Chuck Swindoll is Senior Pastor of Stonebriar Community Church and founder of Insight for Living. He the Senior and Founding Pastor of Stonebriar and is Chancellor of Dallas Theological Seminary. He is a Bible teacher.

Dr Tony Evans is Senior Pastor of Oak Cliff Bible Fellowship and founder of The Urban Alternative. He has an ability to make you not turn the channel and stay in his focus. Dr Evans is a Bible teacher and I listen to him every day.

Chip Ingram is the Senior Pastor of Living on the Edge, an author of several books and is President of Walk Thru the Bible. Yes, he is very much a Bible teacher.

Dr Jack Graham is the Senior Pastor of Prestonwood Baptist Church and founder of Power Point ministries. He is an author and awesome Bible teacher.

The late Dr Adrian Rogers was the Senior Pastor at Bellevue Baptist Church and dedicated his life to Love Worth Finding Ministries. Many have walked in his shadow and many have followed his footprints. His work and messages can be found on the net and the radio. I miss his lessons but listen to his archived messages. He is a model Bible teacher. I never met him here but I look forward to meeting him and thanking him in paradise.

Dr. John Piper is a Bible teacher, pastor and 1st Century preacher. He works tirelessly in administering the gospel . . . All of it! He is unique in delivery and is very animated in style while punctuating God's point. Luke and John would have been good friends.

Ravi Zacharias, International Ministries is what I have named as the modern day Solomon and it is because of his international wisdom and focuses on the apologetics for today's issues and today's solutions. He needs to be at the front of every Congressional hearing to ensure God is heard where the unbelievers could hear Him.

Paul Washer has become my new found friend in Christ because of his unwavering truth in God's word, his ability to push his passion for Christ through scripture and will fuse together a disciple, faith in surrender and the truth in a disciples walk. I believe John the Baptist would say to Paul; "right on brother, claim it like you own it!"

Joseph Prince is a Bible pastor and has captured my interest in Bible study, gospel confirmation, and true deep sincere knowledge of God's word. His fact based messages are straight out of God's word and to follow Pastor Prince you need your Bible opened. He is the one I would most want to sit down in a quiet room and study with.
JosephPrince.org P.O. Box 2115 Fort Mill SC 29716

"I waited patiently for the Lord; and He inclined to me and heard my cry. He brought me up out of the pit of destruction, out of the miry clay, and He set my feet upon a rock making my footsteps firm. He put a new song in my mouth, a song of praise to our God; many will see and fear and will trust in the Lord. How blessed is the man who has made the Lord his trust."

Psalm 40:1-4

May peace be with you, my beloved . . .